Port Wine Quintas of the Douro

Port Wine Quintas
of the Douro

Alex Liddell

Photography by Janet Price

Sotheby's Publications
IN ASSOCIATION WITH
The Wine Appreciation Guild

For Joaquim Manuel Cálem

Text © Alex Liddell 1992
Photographs © Janet Price 1992

First published 1992 for Sotheby's Publications
by Philip Wilson Publishers Ltd
26 Litchfield Street, London WC2H 9NJ

Available to the USA book trade from
Rizzoli International Publications, Inc.
300 Park Avenue South, New York, NY 10010

Exclusive distribution to the USA Wine Trade from
The Wine Appreciation Guild
155 Connecticut Street, San Francisco
California 94107 (415 864-1202)

ISBN 0 85667 410 9

LC 91-067538

Designed by Roy Cole
Typeset by Lasertext Ltd., Manchester
Printed and bound by Printer Portuguesa,
Portugal

Contents

Colour photographs

Maps

Acknowledgements

The publication of this book has been made possible by the very kind sponsorship of Dr Joaquim Manuel Cálem and generous support from members of the Association of Port Wine Shippers and others. We should like to express our special thanks to them, and to Bruce Guimaraens, who gave us the idea of this book, and who started the whole thing off.

During the preparation of the book we have both received hospitality, help and kindnesses quite out of the ordinary. For the hospitality of their quintas we wish to thank A A Cálem & Filho, Lda; Cockburn, Smithes & Ca, Lda; the Companhia Geral da Agricultura das Vinhas do Alto Douro, SA; Croft & Ca, Lda; A A Ferreira, SA; W & J Graham & Co; Montez Champalimaud, Lda; Messrs Peter and Richard Newman; Adriano Ramos-Pinto – Vinhos, SA; Sandeman & Ca; Silva & Cosens, Ltd, SA; the Sociedade Agrícola e Comercial dos Vinhos Messias, SA; the Sociedade Agrícola da Romaneira, SA; Taylor, Fladgate and Yeatman – Vinhos, SA.

We should also like to thank, jointly and individually, the following people who in various ways, and always with great cheerfulness and courtesy, answered our questions, facilitated our work, gave us their time, their advice and, in many cases, their hospitality: António Agrellos, José Carlos Agrellos, Dr Aires de Matos, Carlos Almeida, Engº João Nicolau de Almeida, Ricardo Nicolau de Almeida, Sra Maria Luzia M C Alves, Carlos M Pinto de Azevedo, Engº Manuel Ángelo Barros, Tim Bergqvist, Sophia Bergqvist, Paolo Borges, António de Borges e Sousa, José Bras, Ruy de Brito e Cunha, Dr José A M Bulas Cruz, Dr John Burnett, Engº Gonçalo de A de V Cabral, Joaquim M Cálem, Sra María Assunção S Cálem, Alfredo E Cálem e Hoelzer, Jaime A Q Cardoso, Dr Falcão Carneiro, José dos Anjos Carvalho, Miguel Champalimaud, Stephen A F Christie, Joanna M Delaforce, J Alberto Domingues, Dr Rogério B Felix, Engº Fernando Ferreira, Jorge M C Ferreira, Manuel M de Magalhães Ferreira, Mário Flores, Arnold Burmester Gilbert, António Graça, the late Colin Graham, John Graham, J A da Fonseca A Guedes, Dr Roberto Guedes, Dr Jorge Guimarães, J Gordon Guimaraens, Sra Magdalena G Guimaraens, Sra Rosário Heath, Ben Howkins, Gwynn Jennings, Sra Amélia Lorenz, Pedro Messias, Drª M Lúcia Moreira, Peter Newman, Rolf van der Niepoort, Dirk van der Niepoort, Engº Artur G Nogueira, Francisco J de Olazabal, Sra Zinha de Olazabal, Eduardo Serpa Pimentel, Dr Mário S Pinto, Manuel J P Pintão, Robin A Reid, OBE, Manuel da Silva Reis, Pedro da Silva Reis, Alastair Robertson, Jorge Roquette, José António R-P Rosas, João Roseira, Eduardo F de B P da Costa Seixas, Professor Dr César A C Sequeira, José Teles D da Silva, Albino J da Silva e Sousa, José Manuel and Maria Antónia Soares da Costa, James Suckling, Amyas Symington, Ian Symington, Michael Symington, OBE, Paul D Symington, Júlio

Valente, Dr António Barbosa Vinagre, Mme P Vranken, Fernando Xavier, Cristiano van Zeller, Dr Pedro van Zeller.

To the staff of the shippers and other organisations concerned with port; the managers, *caseiros* and other quinta staff; and to all the other many people who unstintingly gave of their help but who are, alas, too numerous to mention here, we should also like to extend our warmest thanks.

The author has some specific acknowledgements to make on his own behalf. First he would like to thank the owners of the copyright of the manuscript sources quoted in the text for permission to make use of them, and the owners of the copyright of the following books for their kind permission to use extracts from them in the text: Gerald Cobb, *Oporto Older and Newer* (privately printed); Wyndham Fletcher, *Port* (Sotheby's Publications); John Gibbons, *I Gathered No Moss* (Robert Hale, Ltd.).

Secondly, he wishes to thank Europäische Wein Investment Corp for varying the terms of his contract with them to enable him to have time to undertake the research for the book.

Thirdly, the author wishes to thank Dr John Burnett for so kindly reading a draft of the text and for giving him helpful advice and corrections which have saved him from many stupid errors. For those that remain he alone must take the blame.

Finally, the author wishes to express a particular and personal debt of gratitude to the van der Niepoort family: to Rolf and Ingrid, and to Dirk and Birgitte. During the course of researching the book they provided friendship and hospitality beyond the bounds of ordinary generosity which he will never forget, and which he is glad to have this opportunity of acknowledging.

Foreword

It is not often that one reads a book and says: 'I wish I had written that.' Writing is so peculiarly personal that it is normally difficult to visualize oneself as author of anything other than one's own words. However, the spell woven by Alex Liddell must incur envy in all writers. He has the ability to pick the reader up and put him down in a quinta as remote as Soalheira, leaving him standing in the hot dust among the guinea-fowl.

We need this book on the quintas, or farms, of the Douro. We have had books on the port houses, the names of the bottles, but nothing to describe life and work on the quintas. We know about Bordeaux châteaux, and Burgundian domains, but even the wine trade rarely finds time to visit the port quintas. This book is the result of more than a fleeting visit. Alex Liddell, with the integrity of the academic, went to live in the Douro. He has got 'under the skin' of the place, the people and the language. He has looked at the history of the area and observed what is happening today. The quintas are the life-blood of port – without the vineyards and dedicated growers there would be no raw material for our Vintage, our Tawny and our Late Bottled, and there would certainly be no Ruby.

The learning in this book sits lightly, as it always should. It is as full of fascinating historical information as of amusing asides. British influence in the Douro is delightfully chronicled, but this book rightfully belongs to the Douro farmer. For me, it is full of nostalgia, but also so much in the present that I immediately made plans to go back to the Douro, book in hand. Some of the blame for these rash plans must also lie with Janet Price, whose photographs shimmer with heat and life, space and domesticity. She has especial sensitivity when photographing wine estates and wine-making.

Port Wine Quintas of the Douro has enabled me to understand port, the wine, better. The book is an open sesame to a highly individual wine area, perhaps the most unspoilt and inaccessible in Europe. Alex Liddell and Janet Price know it and love it, and they have had the skill and generosity of spirit to unveil it for us.

Serena Sutcliffe MW

Preface

There already exist a number of well-written books on the history and production of port, and it is not intended that this book should cover the same ground. The emphasis here will be on the individual quintas, or farms, where the grapes are grown and, in general, the wine is made. We hope that our book will give the reader a vivid impression, both visual and factual, of what these quintas are like, their history, their variety in size and character, and how they function.

It is surprising that in the literature about port in English there is so little detailed mention of the individual quintas, and even in Portuguese the sources are thin. The older works — Vila Maior's[1] *Preliminares na Ampelographia e Oenologia do Paiz Vinhateiro do Douro* and *O Douro Illustrado*, and Monteiro's *O Douro* (published respectively in 1865-69, 1876 and 1911) are out of date, but invaluable for historical data; Cordeiro's *Quintas do Douro* (1941, republished in 1960) is little more than a check-list, though again a source of information about previous owners; and the one recent book, Azevedo's *O Douro Maravilhoso* (published in 1976) breaks little new ground. Although Vila Maior's *O Douro Illustrado* also exists in a quaint, rather inaccurate English version (used here only when it is not misleading), the only previous English books to deal in any detail with the quintas are Vizetelly's *Facts about Port and Madeira* and Sellers's *Oporto, Old and New* (published respectively in 1880 and 1899), likewise invaluable sources of historical information.

One of the themes of this book is the recurring cycle of decline and regeneration which is so much a part of the history of the Douro and of the quintas, revealing the contrasts and parallels between the end of last century and this. The text, therefore, draws extensively on all these books. References to them and to other sources are shown in the notes at the end of the book by quoting the author's name (and a number, where more than one work is cited). The books can be identified by referring to the name, and where appropriate the number, in the select bibliography.

To prevent the text from becoming overburdened with technical detail, statistical information regarding the individual quintas has been assembled in Appendix IV, and such discussion of technical problems of viticulture and production as there is has been largely confined to the Introduction.

The selection of the quintas for detailed consideration out of the many which exist has not been easy. Out of more than a hundred quintas visited, many have had to be omitted because of lack of space, and for this we should like to express our regret and disappointment to their owners. Those which are included have been chosen to give a balanced and representative picture of the Douro as a whole, and they fall into the following three categories:

1.   The main quintas belonging to the port shipping firms registered at Vila Nova de Gaia,

2.   The privately owned quintas known to be presently producing and marketing their own single quinta labelled port.[2]

3.   A small number of the privately owned quintas which, although not marketing their own ports, have a claim to importance for historical reasons, or are intending to market their own port shortly.

There is more of interest to be said about some quintas than others, and the lack of a uniform format in the individual entries reflects this. The entries vary in size and character; in some the emphasis is historical; in others the emphasis is one of mood or atmosphere. Although it would be too much to expect that our selection will please everyone, we hope that the result reflects some of the diversity which is one of the fascinations of the Douro valley.

All the quintas dealt with produce port, though several also produce table wines (e.g. Côtto, Seixo, Vale do Meão and Sidrô). Quintas within the demarcated region which produce only table wines, however famous (e.g. Mateus), have not been included.

Although it is hoped that our book will be helpful to the increasing number of visitors to the area, it is not designed to be a guide book. The brief passages linking the individual quinta entries are intended, in conjunction with the maps, to give readers a general idea of their location rather than to serve as full route directions. Some information about touring the area and visiting quintas can be found in Appendix III.

It is significant of the pace of change within the Douro that, during the year in which this book was prepared, five large quintas changed hands. The interest of shippers in acquiring quintas, and the relatively recent alteration of the law to enable individual quintas to market and export their own port under their own label, which is now beginning to show significant results and to focus the attention of port drinkers on the Douro quintas, make this an appropriate moment to look more closely at them.

Alex Liddell
Janet Price

Introduction

The River Douro

The Setting of the Quintas

The Douro, like the Rhine and the Rhone, is one of the great, long rivers of Europe, and, as the Spanish Duero, is already substantial before it reaches Portugal. Of its 927 km, only 213 are exclusively Portuguese. But, unlike the Rhine and the Rhone, the Douro for much of its length is a shy river. In its upper Portuguese reaches it hides in deep, ravine-like valleys between precipitous mountains, affording tantalizing glimpses of itself from time to time, suddenly to disappear from view as the road crests another hill. Only occasionally does the road come down to water level, and then most frequently only to stop, or to cross and abandon the river once more.

The 112 km, north-south, stretch of the river from Miranda do Douro to Barca d'Alva is known as the International Douro. It forms the boundary between Portugal and Spain. At Barca d'Alva the river turns westwards towards the Atlantic, and it is here that the demarcated port producing region begins.

The demarcated port area was first established by the Marquês de Pombal in 1757 and has been extended in a number of revisions,

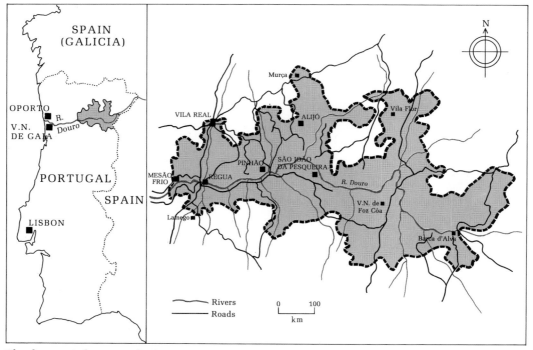

The demarcated port producing area

latterly of a very minor kind, of which the last was made as recently as 1986. It totals an immense 250,000 ha, divided into three sub-regions: the Douro Superior, the Cima Corgo and Baixo Corgo. These will be described in more detail in due course. Within the region there are two small Douro towns greatly concerned with port: Pinhão, standing where the river of the same name joins the Douro in the middle of the Cima Corgo, and, 24 km downstream, Peso da Régua, in the centre of the Baixo Corgo. Régua is larger and more imposing than Pinhão, which is a mean little place. Vila Maior describes Régua as 'showy and coquettish', but it is hardly more beautiful. Many port firms have offices and warehouses there, and the headquarters of the Casa do Douro (the Farmers' and Wine Growers' Association), the body which, in conjunction with the Instituto do Vinho do Porto (the Port Wine Institute) in Oporto, regulates the production of port, are in the centre of the town.

From Régua, roughly half-way between the Spanish border and Oporto, it is about 100 km downstream to the heart of the port trade, Vila Nova de Gaia, which faces Oporto across the Douro just where it loses itself in the Atlantic.

Both the river and its surrounding area have been changing rapidly within the last couple of decades. A large hydro-electric scheme, three of whose eight dams are within the demarcated area, has transformed the Douro into a series of ribbon lakes. This has had an impact on port production in a number of ways discussed later. The area itself is in rapid transition after having been very much a backwater for most of the century. The very look of the place is changing as the natives of a previous generation return from the countries to which they immigrated and build *nouveau-riche* villas at odds with the indigenous architectural styles. In addition television, better communications, and foreign travel in search of work have brought raised expectations of standards of living, and these have caused a considerable drain on the work force. As we shall see later, these phenomena are having an impact on the production of port.

I The quinta and its development: to the end of the eighteenth century

What is a quinta?

There are contrary accounts of the origin of the word *quinta*, the most plausible being that it derives from early mediaeval times when land was held in tenure from the crown in return for a rent or tribute of one fifth (*uma quinta parte*) of its produce. Whatever its derivation, the least misleading translation of *quinta* is 'farm' or 'estate'. Unfortunately, to the English imagination, accustomed to seigneurial mansions clustered on the Sintra and Colares hills south west of Lisbon, the word *quinta* is apt to conjure up a picture of a Portuguese country house.[1] In the context of the Douro such an idea could hardly be less appropriate, and anyone who expects a port quinta to be like a grand Bordeaux château will be surprised.

It is best, therefore, to think of a quinta not as a building at all, but as an area of land, ranging in size from a modest small-holding to a vast estate, which is used for farming or, in our case, for growing vines. This land may or may not have a quinta house, ranging likewise from the unpretentious to the extremely grand.

It is impossible to say exactly how many port producing quintas there are in the Douro, since there is no exact definition of what counts as a quinta. What can be said is that in 1989 there were 29,618 vineyard owners who were authorized to make at least part of their production into port. Each had an officially recognized port production allocation (known as the *benefício*), which varied from a tiny 10 litres to a colossal 290,000 litres. In terms of area, 66.4 per cent of their vineyards are less than 0.5 ha in area, and only 0.4 per cent are bigger than 10 ha.[2] It is immediately clear, therefore, that in the majority of cases we are dealing with *vinhas* (vineyards) rather than *quintas* (farms). As there is no hard and fast convention about what counts as a *vinha* and what as a *quinta,* and nothing, indeed, to stop anyone calling his vineyard a quinta if he wants to (the smallest dealt with in this book is only 3 ha), so there is no fixed number of quintas in the Douro. Cordeiro lists 1,427 named quintas in his check-list; my estimate would be nearer 2,000.[3]

This mosaic of vineyards is partly the result of laws based on the Code Napóleon, whereby all legitimate offspring have a right to inherit a proportion of landed property. There is therefore an inherent tendency towards the splintering of land ownership. This can result either in the physical division of land (including the splitting up of a quinta like Bom Retiro), or in property being owned collectively by a large number of the descendants of the original proprietor (like the Quinta de Monsul, or, until 1990, the Quinta do Vesúvio).

We are dealing, therefore, with a spectrum ranging from minute, almost negligible, plots of land, through tiny small-holdings (some with vines and other crops, others dedicated exclusively to the growing of grapes, but without a dwelling house), graduating to quintas through larger holdings, with dwellings of increasing size, to a relatively small number of big estates with correspondingly imposing mansions.

The emergence of the quinta

Wine has been made in the Douro region at least since Roman times. In the early Middle Ages many vineyards were established under the aegis of monastic foundations,[4] either for their own use or through leasing land to lay tenants. Thus, the Quinta do Monsul, although originally of royal origin, was leased to the forbears of its present owners by the Mosteirô de Santa Maria de Salzedas, which also owned the Quinta dos Frades.[5] The Quinta do Convento de São Pedro das Águias, the Quinta do Mosteirô (originally the property of the Mosteirô de São João de Tarouca), the Quinta da Igreja (originally, before 1543, the property of the Mosteirô da Madre Deus at Monchique, in the Algarve), and the Quinta de Valbom are all monastic foundations.

Opposite
1
A view looking down the Douro from Casal de Loivos. The road bridge at Pinhão is clearly visible, with Quinta das Carvalhas on the far side of the river on the left, and, beyond it, Quinta do Seixo. On the near side of the river, opposite Carvalhas, are Quinta da Foz, Quinta de la Rosa (the long range of white buildings by the river), and, beyond it, Quinta de Val da Figueira

Other quintas such as the Quinta de Vilarinho de São Romão (whose lease dates from 1462[6]), the Quinta de Ventozelo (on land leased in 1569 from the Convento de São Pedro das Águias),[7] the Quinta de Roriz, and the Quinta da Eira Velha were established on lands originally leased from monasteries.[8] On the other hand, a few quintas such as the Quinta do Côtto were manorial, or held independently by an important family, as in the case of Nápoles or Vesúvio.

Very few quintas can trace their histories back to such remote times, when, in any case, their primary crops would have been cereals rather than grapes. The region as it was at the end of the seventeenth century is described for us by Rebello da Fonseca, writing in 1791:

> In 1681 there were no large plantations of vineyards [such as exist today]: the English taste, inclining at this time towards sweet wines, led farmers, besides having vineyards sufficient for their own needs, to establish vineyards in choice sites on the slopes of river banks most exposed to the heat of the sun, comprising small plots of land scattered amidst the scrub.
>
> The big quintas we see today did not exist. The lagares at this period, of 3, 4 or 5 pipes at most, and the toneis of similar capacity, indicate how small the harvests of these farmers were . . . Such was this region in former times – one of the poorest in the kingdom, as is shown by the wretchedness of the buildings formerly put up, and the impossibility of finding the slightest vestiges of a single old structure of magnificence and style.[9]

We may suppose that this situation continued well into the eighteenth century, with only a few farmers starting to establish proper vineyards. For the majority it was a subsistence economy, with vines generally grown not on top of terraces, but planted horizontally in holes in the terrace walls, called *pilheiros*. This left the terraces free for growing other crops such as corn, thus maximizing the productivity of the available land. *Pilheiros*, so apparently contrary to nature, survived well into the nineteenth century – for example, at Roriz, and at Vesúvio, where vines were grown from the walls of terraces planted with olive trees.[10] Examples can still be seen in *mortórios*, as the Portuguese call the terraces which were not replanted after *phylloxera*, in quintas such as Romaneira, Manuela and Panascal.

Often, as in the case of the Quinta da Pacheca, a sizable property was painstakingly put together over the course of generations through the acquisition of small parcels of land. A few quintas existed in the Baixo Corgo before the middle of the eighteenth century, amongst them the Quinta do Rodo, the Quinta de Santa Ana, the Quinta das Massas, the Quinta do Casal da Moreira, the Quinta da Casa das Covas, and the Quinta de Vale de Abrahão, but in general, it was only after this date, when the increasing export of port brought prosperity to the region, that we find sizable properties being established on any scale. 'The majority of the Douro quintas are only a few years old', wrote Robert Jackson, the British consul in Oporto, in 1756.[11]

Opposite
2
Quinta do Bom Retiro, showing the old walled terraces on the steep bank of the aptly named, twisted Rio Torto

The Pombaline demarcations

This growing prosperity led to corruption, and the adulteration of wine led in turn to a serious slump in 1755. To restore order to the market, and partly to limit the English monopoly of the export trade, Dom José I's Prime Minister, Sebastião José de Carvalho e Melo, later the Marquês de Pombal, took action to control port production by setting up, in 1757, a Portuguese monopoly company. This was called the Companhia Geral da Agricultura das Vinhas do Alto Douro – the Old Company, as it became known – a company which survives today as the Real Companhia Velha, though in private hands and without monopoly powers.

As part of the measures to control production it was decided to demarcate the wine-producing area (the first such demarcated wine area anywhere in the world) by drawing up a register of all the vineyards on the banks of the Douro authorized to produce either wine of exportable quality or wine fit only for home consumption (including the colony of Brazil). The former category was called *vinho de feitoria* ('factory wine'), and the vineyards which produced it were referred to as being within the *feitoria*.[12] Wine of this category was divided into two classes: the finest, to be purchased at a guaranteed price of 25,000 réis a pipe, and 'wine of lesser quality, yet fit for lading' at 20,000 réis a pipe. In some cases *feitoria* wine was limited to white wine only. The second (non-exportable) category was called *vinho do ramo* ('branch wine', a name derived from the custom of indicating a tavern by hanging a branch outside it: hence 'good wine needs no bush'). These were table wines, graded into four (later six) classes by their guaranteed prices per pipe: 19,200 réis (usually ear-marked for Lisbon and Brazil), 15,500 réis, 10,500 réis and 6,400 réis (and, subsequently, also 4,200 and 3,200 réis).

It took three demarcations to put this scheme into effect. The first was in 1757.[13] It proved faulty because the commissioners exceeded both 'the sense and letter' of their instructions and included extraneous areas within the *feitoria*. It provoked a storm of criticism, not least from the owners of vineyards which had been excluded from it. In 1758 it was declared void, and a second demarcation took place to remedy its defects 'with justice and clarity' and 'all possible speed'. This was altogether a more detailed undertaking, and the written survey was supplemented by the erection of a series of granite markers to define rigorously the geographical limits of the *feitoria*. While the boundaries were now clearer than before, they were necessarily more restrictive and many owners who had been in the 1757 *feitoria* now found themselves excluded. This brought forth a deluge of petitions for re-inclusion, since farmers who now found themselves outside the *feitoria* had to sell their wine for lower prices. Predictably, fraudulent practices began to reappear, and as a result, in 1761, the commissioners carried out a third demarcation, redrawing the boundaries again and erecting more granite markers. This demarcation survived until 1788, after which, as a result of a huge increase in the overseas demand for port, the classified area was gradually extended until, by 1801, it was twice the size it had been forty years earlier.[14] Since then there have been various small revisions.[15]

While these demarcations can provide much interesting information about the quintas, their usefulness is limited by the way in which the surveys were made. To specify the boundaries of the demarcation the commissioners often referred simply to 'the vineyard belonging to X'; it is now virtually impossible after 230 years to identify either 'X' or his vineyard. Many of these little vineyards have in any case disappeared over time, having been absorbed into larger vineyards which, in turn, became amalgamated to form quintas. Moreover, names which are now particularly associated with a quinta were then used in a more general way to indicate a place or district.

II The quinta and its development: to the present day

Into the nineteenth century

Until the end of the eighteenth century the demarcated port region did not extend eastwards of the Cachão de Valeira, for the very practical reason that here the Douro was blocked by a huge rock cataract which made shipping, the sole means of moving port to Vila Nova de Gaia, impossible. As a result of engineering works lasting twelve years this obstacle was removed in 1792 (although the Cachão did not become fully navigable until 1807), thereby making the Douro Superior fully viable for port production. This explains why few of the quintas east of Valeira pre-date the nineteenth century, unless they were grain farms which were later adapted for wine growing.

The nineteenth century was one of variable fortunes for the port trade. After record exports of 64,402 pipes of port in 1798 the total had dipped to only 21,208 pipes by 1801, and it was not until nearly the end of the century that the previous figure was exceeded. To add to this woe came foreign invasion in the form of the Napoleonic Wars, followed by civil commotion in the War of the Two Brothers – a struggle for the throne between the liberal Pedro and the absolutist Miguel, the sons of the ineffectual Dom João VI, which lasted from 1820 until 1834 but which eventually established constitutional liberalism in Portugal. An important outcome of this was the expulsion of religious orders in 1834, resulting in the secularization of quintas belonging to monasteries or on lands leased from them. In the same year the Old Company's regulatory function was abolished, although the distinction between *feitoria* and *ramo* wines, which had latterly borne little relation to the quality of port produced in the various areas, had already lapsed in 1822. In reality, however, since 1788 many wines outside the *feitoria* had 'been listed and traded as genuine'[16] and were being freely exported by the beginning of the nineteenth century.

Throughout the nineteenth century single quinta wines were readily available in England: Boa Vista, Bom Retiro, Carvalhas, Noval, Roêda, Romaneira, Roncão, Roriz, Vargellas, Vesúvio, Zimbro and doubtless many, many others. Vizetelly remarks that Feuerheerd, for example, kept 'certain of its vintage wines from particular quintas intact'.[17] Single quinta wines also appeared at auction in the second half of the century, with Romaneira leading the way at Christie's in 1872.[18]

Such wines were normally shipped only in cask until the early 1840s, and until the 1860s were usually known by the name of the English wine merchants who sold them rather than by the shippers' names. Although the shipping of single quinta wines never quite died out, after about 1870 they began to be replaced by the so-called shippers' declared vintages. An incentive to this increasing quantity of blended vintages must surely have been the disastrous shortfalls of single quinta production which occurred for a number of reasons. The problems caused by war and civil commotion were succeeded in the second half of the century, just as foreign trade began to flourish again, by three natural disasters. First came the appearance in the vineyards of *Oïdium Tuckeri*, starting in 1851. No sooner had effective ways of combating this plague been discovered than an even deadlier one, *phylloxera*, made its appearance in 1868. More difficult to control, its devastation reached a peak around 1890, when 64 per cent of the port-growing area had been completely destroyed.[19] Only the discovery that the *americano* vine was resistant to *phylloxera*, and, more importantly, that traditional vine varieties could be grafted on to *americano* root stock, prevented the vineyards of the Douro from being completely wiped out. Lastly, as the final straw, just as the worst of *phylloxera* was over, mildew made its appearance in 1893.

The history of the quintas during the century reflects these vicissitudes. The pattern of consolidation of smaller parcels of land into new farms continued, and many large quintas were founded. In this Dona Antónia Ferreira[20] was pre-eminent, her crowning achievement being the creation of one of the largest Douro estates, Monte Meão (now called Vale do Meão). Such prosperity, however, was counterbalanced by the decay of other quintas. Many owners were bankrupted if not by *oïdium*, then by *phylloxera*, and Vila Maior, travelling through the area in the mid-1870s, is constantly remarking on the run-down state of many of the quintas – a decay which grew steadily worse until the last decade of the century.

It was this situation which brought about a widespread involvement by British shippers in quinta ownership. As owners went bankrupt quintas became available at knock-down prices, and the shippers moved in. This was partly because they sensed a bargain, but partly also because they were concerned to safeguard their supplies of good wines, and because they were in a financial position to support the costs of reconstruction and replanting.

It would not be true to say that shippers had not previously bothered about quinta ownership: Joseph Forrester's[21] Quinta da Boa Vista had always been associated with his firm, and John Fladgate[22] (of Taylor, Fladgate and Yeatman) had owned the Quinta da Roêda since 1844 until it was bought by Croft in 1875. Amongst the Portuguese shippers, Dona Antónia Ferreira had built up an empire of over thirty quintas by the time she died in 1896, and Cálem had bought the Quinta da Foz in 1885. But within a five year period at the end of the century, it became fashionable for the English to acquire quintas, amongst them Zimbro (pre-1888), Senhora da Ribeira (1889), Tua (1889), Bomfim (1890), Malvedos (1890), Val Coelho (c. 1890), and Vargellas (1893). At the same time, A J da Silva & Ca bought Quinta do Noval.

A notable consequence of this 'invasion' of the Douro by the British shippers was the introduction of a new type of quinta house modelled on an Indian tea-plantation bungalow. The vogue was apparently first started by George Warre at the Quinta do Bomfim in 1893, then copied at the Quinta de Vargellas and later at the Quinta da Roêda.

Before leaving the nineteenth century, mention should be made of Joseph Forrester's map of the Douro wine area published in 1852. On it are marked seventy-nine quintas: thirteen in the Baixo Corgo, fifty-four in the Cima Corgo, and twelve in the Douro Superior. One presumes that they were chosen for their celebrity, but the list makes curious reading today. Whilst many of the quintas are still famous, an equal number would now be considered unimportant. Such is the waywardness of fortune: but, more importantly, not only does it highlight the flux of development and decline which has characterized the progress of the quintas of the Douro, it also emphasizes the big difference between the quintas of the Douro and, let us say, the châteaux of the Medoc. Whereas it was possible by 1855 to produce a list of *crus classés* which has stood the test of time without significant alteration, such could not have been done for the Douro. Most Douro quintas (as will be seen) have swung between extremes of prosperity and decay. The Douro has always lacked the stability of Bordeaux, which is why it will take a very long time, if ever, for the hopes of supporters of the idea of an estate-dominated port trade to be realized.

The twentieth century

Perhaps the most dramatic change in the port trade during the present century has been the shrinkage of the number of independent shippers. From the eighty-one listed in the *Grémio* of exporters in 1954 the total has diminished, partly through the takeover of smaller companies by larger ones, to just twenty-seven in 1990. This reflects not only the strains caused by two major slumps in exports (in the 1930s, and the 50s and early 60s), but the increasing keenness of competition in selling in markets dominated by large international conglomerates. A smaller number of companies, however, has meant larger volumes for the survivors, and, despite the difficulties of the market, the decade up until 1989 showed a steady increase in port exports. The prevailing mood has therefore been one of cautious but expansionist optimism, as evidenced, for example, by PDRITM[23] and a new vogue in the purchase of quintas by shippers (both British and Portuguese).

While, on the whole, the British shippers remained out of the market until the 1970s, throughout the century there has been a steady acquisition of quintas by many of the Portuguese shippers, amongst them Barros Almeida, Ramos-Pinto, Messias, Poças, Real Companhia Velha, and C da Silva.

In terms of farm management there has been a slow but gradual improvement due to increased mechanization (discussed below). Domestic improvement, on the other hand, has been in the form of modernizing and extending existing houses, rather than the building of new ones. More belatedly some attempt is now being made to modernize the conditions in which the farm workers live, and this will also be discussed later on.

The quinta – its buildings and staff

The quinta buildings

Apart from its vineyards the quinta will normally (but not invariably) have a quinta house and a cluster of buildings to service it. We have already remarked that few quinta houses are really grand. Most of these (mainly in the Baixo Corgo) are *solars*, that is to say traditional manor houses, though there are a few exceptions like the Quinta de Vesúvio. More generally, however, one finds a farm-house, built according to a layout established about the middle of the eighteenth century, which remained current until the early nineteenth century. Its distinguishing feature is the inclusion within a single structure of facilities for both wine making (*adega*) and wine storage (*armazém*).

The traditional way of making port was (and still is for many farmers) by treading the grapes in a large, usually granite, tank known as a *lagar*. Before the eighteenth century many peasant farmers had had to pool their resources and use communal *lagares*.[24] Later, with the establishment of quintas, it became usual to incorporate independent wine-making capacity within the quinta house.

The cross-section of such a traditional farmhouse, combining accommodation, *lagares* and storage, is illustrated in the accompanying diagram. As dictated by the hilly terrain, the farmhouse was almost invariably built against a slope. Not only was this economic in relation to the site, but it had the advantage of harnessing gravity in the making of the wine, which could be run off from the *lagares* to the storage area below by means of pipes. The *adega*, containing the *lagares*, is at the rear of the top level of the building, whilst the *armazém*, in which the wine is stored, is at the bottom level. The living accommodation is in front of the *adega*, above the *armazém*.

The size and amenity of the original farm-house would have been commensurate with the wealth and standing of its owner. The grandest, though not necessarily the largest, would also (as was general throughout Portugal at this period) have had a chapel placed either at the side of the house or standing on its own. Good examples of traditional quinta houses of this type are the Quinta do Porto, which has a chapel, and the Quinta da Boa Vista, which does not.

The passage of time has wrought many changes. Some houses were abandoned after *phylloxera* and never re-inhabited. Others have

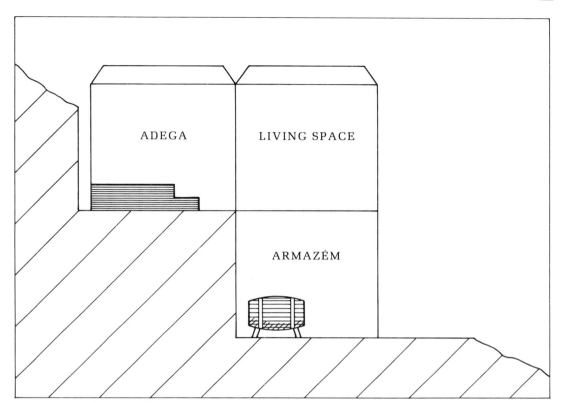

Cross-section of a quinta house

been allowed to become semi-derelict – their owners possibly interested only in the produce of the vineyards – while others, again, have been extended and modernised. If the quinta belongs to a shipper its house may well have been extensively renovated and extended to provide quite lavish facilities for the entertainment of trade guests.

Whereas quintas founded prior to the eighteenth century usually had *a solar* type of house without the arrangements we have just described, the pattern established here was closely followed in the principal buildings in quintas of the nineteenth century. Even when farmhouses did not contain *lagares*, they were still built with cellarage below the living accommodation.

The quinta house is sometimes called in Portuguese the *casa de patrão* – 'the master's house' – and was usually specifically designed for the owner and his family. In the smallest quintas, of course, the owner is his own farmer; but in the case of all of the quintas dealt with in detail in this book the owner, no matter how great the interest he takes in his vines, employs a farm foreman, normally called the *caseiro*, to deal on his behalf with the direction of the labourers and the day-to-day running of the quinta. In many cases the owner is an absentee landlord (earning his living at some less economically hazardous trade or profession) who will only visit the quinta occasionally.

In such cases the quinta house may remain empty for much of the time; but sometimes the whole or part of it has been given over to housing the *caseiro*. More usually there will be separate living accommodation for the *caseiro*, often part of an independent range of buildings housing, amongst other things, the large kitchen in which the meals for the quinta workers are cooked. This big and important room usually has a large traditional corner fireplace, covered with a square canopy supported at the corner which juts into the room. The fire is lit on the stone slabs which form a floor-level hearth, and almost invariably the fire has a large soup pot gently steaming away over it. This room is, in many ways, the heart of the quinta. In it the *caseiro*'s wife and her helpers will be chopping up vegetables and preparing food, children will often be playing on the floor or running about. Here a casual visitor will be offered a glass of port. The atmosphere is cheerful and relaxed, and in the winter, when it is bitingly cold outside, the quinta kitchen is invariably the warmest place to be. Depending on its situation in relation to his accommodation, it is often used by the *caseiro* as his living room.

Close to the kitchen will be the *refectório*, generally rather bleak and sparsely furnished, used by the workers for their evening meals or in inclement weather. (Normally, their meals are taken out to them in the vineyards.) Sometimes the same range of buildings will contain the *cardenhos*, the dormitory accommodation in which the resident quinta workers are housed (and the *roga*, or pickers, at the time of the harvest). In most quintas, however, the workers' accommodation forms a separate block, and this will sometimes also contain a small number of individual bedrooms for the *artistas*, the employees with special skills. In the largest quintas, such as those of the shippers, there may also be a separate dining room for the senior staff.

Apart from living accommodation there will, of course, be an *adega* and an *armazém*. Originally part of the house, as previously described, in the nineteenth century it became more usual to put them in a separate building which, nevertheless, retained the traditional two-tier structure. In the twentieth century, for the larger shippers these buildings can be very sizeable indeed, with either concrete or stainless steel vinifiers, and, very often, an office and a small laboratory.

Good examples of nineteenth century, separately constructed, two-level *adega* and *armazém* combinations can be found at the Quinta do Cachão, the Quinta da Romaneira and, most notably of all, at the Quinta do Vesúvio and the Quinta do Vale do Meão. Even in the second half of the twentieth century, in vinification centres in which modern equipment has replaced *lagares*, as in the new *adegas* at the Quinta da Roêda and at Quinta do Noval, this method of construction has persisted.

There will, of course, be a selection of additional buildings housing stores, a tractor shed, a stable for a horse or donkey (if such are still used), and, less commonly, an *alambique* (a distillery used for making *bagaceira* from the dried pips and skins remaining after the vintage) or an *azenha*, with a *lagar de azeite* for making olive oil. In traditional quintas one will also find enclosures for birds and animals – chickens, ducks, pigs – and, occasionally, dog kennels.

Quite often all these buildings are arranged round a farm yard which may have the shelter of a tree; but, if not, they may instead be interconnected by walk-ways through shady, vine-covered *ramadas* or pergolas. Somewhere there is almost bound to be a *tanque* (stone cistern) fed by a pipe whose gentle splash of water suggests a cool tranquillity which the summer heat belies. Invariably there will be a vegetable garden with cabbage for making soup, but while a flower garden is a less frequent luxury, plants in pots are found everywhere.

The quinta staff

To give a complete and detailed description of the working year of a quinta, or of the specialized functions of all the people who work there, would take up a disproportionate amount of space in a book which does not primarily seek to explain the processes by which port is produced.[25] Nevertheless, it is necessary to say something of the way in which a quinta is organized.

As has already been mentioned, its day-to-day running is in the hands of a *caseiro*. In privately owned quintas he will normally report directly to the owner, but in some cases the owner may have his quinta professionally managed for him. In such cases the *caseiro* will deal directly with the manager (perhaps the representative of a shipper) who will discuss the policy and management of the quinta with the owner. In the case of many shippers' quintas there is a complicated structure of technical management between the directors and the *caseiro*, and in such cases, although the directors of the firm will interest themselves closely in their quintas, a *comissário* or manager will coordinate the technical assistance of the firm's oenological and viticultural specialists in conjunction with the *caseiro*.

The *caseiro* will generally be responsible for hiring the labour needed on the quinta. He may, for example, have a contact in a village from which workmen come either to live in the quinta for two or three weeks at a time or, if situated sufficiently close at hand, from which a team of workmen comes on a daily basis. He will also be responsible for hiring the three teams of specialists which are periodically required at the quinta: the *podadores*, who prune the vines in November and December, and who may return to do the green pruning in June; the *enxertadores* who carry out grafting in February and March; and the *roga*, who pick the harvest and man the *lagares* (if in use) in September and early October. Often the *roga* comes from a very remote village year after year, and the contact between village and quinta is much valued.

Apart from this the *caseiro* will supervise the workmen in the routine tasks of maintaining the vineyards (repair of terraces, tilling of the soil, planting and grafting of new vines, application of chemical treatments, etc.), order and maintain stores, maintain tractors and other plant, pay staff, maintain accounts, and generally take care of unforeseen as well as routine happenings. At the vintage he may have, or at least share, the responsibility of supervising the actual making of the wine. The role of the *caseiro* is therefore a very responsible one.

It is common for the *caseiro*'s wife to be employed as the quinta cook. She may also act as housekeeper for the owner, ensuring that the *casa de patrão* is kept prepared to receive him, and running the house when he is in residence. In the case of the shippers who maintain their quinta houses as much to entertain trade guests as to put up their visiting technical staff, a professional cook-housekeeper and maids may be employed.

For the rest, the workmen on a quinta are generally employed on a casual basis. Some of them may have specialized jobs such as tractor-driver or donkey-man, but in general they are labourers who are expected to turn their hands to whatever job the moment requires.

Social life on a quinta

Then ...

> In the Upper Douro . . . owing to the absence of any kind of accommodation, the traveller is entirely dependent upon the courtesy of the owners or occupiers of the quintas along his line of route. When an invitation is given to you to take up your quarters in one of these quintas, it is invariably accompanied by the intimation that you must be prepared to 'rough it'. But it usually happens that the only roughing of it you have to undergo is over the villainous roads which lead to your destination.
>
> There is no lack of hospitality, and you are feasted on fowls, turkeys, and hams, and on beef and mutton . . . and the many preserves for which the Alto Douro is famous. These, moreover, will be frequently supplemented by delicacies bearing Crosse and Blackwell's well-known brand, while . . . the choicest of Tawny Port, which has lost all its fruitiness during a quarter of a century in the cask, is at your service . . . so that, on the whole, what is called 'roughing it' in an Upper Douro quinta is rather a sybaritical affair than otherwise.

Although Henry Vizetelly wrote these words[26] more than a hundred years ago, what he said then remains more or less true today. The quintas of the port shippers and larger farmers are invariably comfortable; the roads which lead to them are frequently dust tracks in summer and, in rainy weather, muddy tracks whose pot-holes test one's equanimity and car springs, and sometimes require four-wheel-drive vehicles; and there is still a desperate shortage of hotel accommodation in the Douro valley. But I must confess that I have never met with any products made by Crosse and Blackwell while staying in a quinta.

As explained above, quinta houses are primarily for occasional use and are seldom proper homes. Even after the British shippers came in force to the Douro at the turn of the century the situation did not much change. Quintas were seen essentially as masculine places, not made overly comfortable. It is said that John Smithes held out for years against putting a bathroom in the house at the Quinta de Val Coelho! Apart from routine business visits to inspect the vines or for the harvest itself, the most recreational use to which quintas were put was for shooting parties. Ladies were often actively discouraged from coming to the Douro, so weekends in the country were out — it was too time-consuming and difficult to get there in any case — and, as for summer holidays, the Douro was insufferably hot. Gerald Cobb quotes one lady as saying she thought it 'quite unbearable as regards climate, and conditions of living far too primitive for any of us' and, in 1966, himself encapsulated the prevailing view thus: 'Houses were indeed left as uncomfortable as possible, otherwise the ladies might insist on accompanying their husbands, and that would never do! Some firms retain this excellent custom; and it appears to me that wives and girl friends are about as much in place at a vintage as soldiers' womenfolk would be on annual military manoeuvres'.[27]

Nevertheless, to all generalizations there are exceptions. Colin Graham remembered schoolboy visits to the Quinta dos Malvedos before the war: 'The family went there often for holidays. It was used as a family home, and any partner could use it any time he wanted to . . . I mean, Malvedos was one of *the* things of my holidays. There were always friends of mine. We'd all have the most marvellous time, and we'd romp around the quinta and go and see the pigs.'[28] Moreover, the wives of shippers often did visit the quintas — even Val Coelho. John Gibbons,[29] an English writer who spent the 1938-39 winter at nearby Colejo, a primitive hamlet perched on a hillside, recalled visiting the quinta, which, after the privations of village life, he found to be an oasis where his hostess was 'perfectly charming'. Her return visit to Colejo was such an event that 'people have literally been brought into our kitchen to be shown the chair where she actually sat and ate her lunch'.[30]

Gibbons also left a vivid cameo of Senhora da Ribeira, though conscious that 'after a few weeks of a Portuguese cottage this seems extraspecially fine'. He wrote: 'This is a great Portuguese mansion, but with everything in it from England which can make for better comfort . . . It looks queer to find the London newspapers and magazines here, thrown down on an open-air terrace with orange trees round it and a fountain in the middle. There seems a sort of Arabian Night's touch about even their servants, Portuguese perfectly trained to English ways.'[31]

I am assured, however, that no matter how it appeared to Gibbons, pre-war life at Senhora da Ribeira was by modern standards very simple. 'Some of the luxuries we take for granted nowadays simply didn't exist. I imagine we had no fridge there at all. Bread had to be brought in from a long way off. Whereas at Bomfim today you can have Bell's whisky, or a gin and tonic, then — as far as I remember — it was table wine, port or water. If you didn't like that you had to have orange juice. There were no frills. The food was always simple but good. It would be chicken, or pork, or something from the property. One brought something up from Oporto. And the sugar was always that coarse Douro sugar: the coffee was local. We lived in a simple, straightforward way.'[32]

Again, rather exceptionally, Claire Bergqvist, in mid-century, made her home at the Quinta de la Rosa, though she was widely thought eccentric for having done so. In her father's time, she wrote, 'the Douro was not exactly comfortable . . . there were no bathrooms and not much sanitation, very little hot water and, of course, no ice to make life bearable in the summer. We used to keep the drinking-water in an earthenware jug wrapped in a wet cloth and leave it in a draught. All the same we changed for dinner in the evenings!'.[33] Under her aegis, however, the Quinta de la Rosa was, as it still is, exquisitely furnished and welcoming, and it became a byword for civilized comfort.

. . . and now

The visitors' books kept at English quintas testify that gradually, more particularly after the Second World War, both family visits and the entertainment of guests other than those from the shipping community became more common.[34] More recently, in the shippers' quintas, the entertainment of trade guests and wine writers has become an important public relations exercise and in some quintas groups are welcomed. Moreover, the vintage, which used to be such a sacrosanct activity, is now not just a party for the workers (which it always has been) but an excuse for the owner to invite his friends and to have his own fling. At some quintas the house-guests are even invited to get into the *lagares* and help with the treading.

    The days of dressing for dinner in the Douro, as elsewhere, have long since gone. Even ties and jackets for men are required only on special occasions and, as perhaps befits the working atmosphere of a quinta, sweaters in the winter and shirt sleeves in the summer are usual. Nevertheless, meals are plentiful and served with some ceremony. One is generally offered white port beforehand (the addition of ice and tonic water is not too much of a heresy in some quintas!) and almost invariably a fine tawny afterwards. If your host is a shipper it is likely to be one of his older blends or, less commonly, a vintage from the quinta: if you are being entertained in a private quinta you will probably have an old, cask-aged *colheita* with the 'baked' taste and smell, vaguely reminiscent of madeira, which characterizes port matured in the Douro. I have only met one British shipper who likes these old tawnies, but to my taste they are perfection. Wherever you are, you may rest assured that, as Vizetelly found, 'there is no lack of hospitality'.[35]

    If these reminiscences are all of British quintas, this is not deliberate chauvinism but simply a reflection of a regrettable lack of similar memoirs concerning Portuguese quintas. As it happens, British and Portuguese quintas hardly differ from each other at all. Even in the décor and furnishing of their houses there is little of difference to note. Although some of the British shippers have tried, with varying success, to reproduce an English country house atmosphere in their quintas – even a feminine, chintzy note as the ladies at last begin to make their presence felt – the use of old Portuguese furniture results only in a Portuguese ambiance with English overtones.

Life for the workers on a quinta

Then ...

Writing in 1966, Gerald Cobb succinctly epitomized his view of the relationship between the *patrão* and his workers by quoting the now rather unfashionable hymn 'All things bright and beautiful', which contains the lines

> *The rich man in his castle,*
> *The poor man at his gate;*
> *God made them, high and lowly,*
> *And order'd their estate.*

He went on: 'The poor man may still be very poor, and the rich man relatively rich, but the relations between the two . . . are conducted on the most amicable terms. In short, "paternalism" is the key.'[36]

It is perhaps unfair to saddle others with Cobb's viewpoint; and if, as he implies, this was the ethos of Douro life for many years, possibly it was already beginning to change in the 1960s. Nevertheless, it would be idle to pretend that, within living memory, some of the recipients of the paternalism he speaks of do not take a different view. When I asked one long-serving quinta manager what things had been like in the old days, I received a bitter, one word, reply: 'slavery!'

The vintage

Cobb quotes Claire Bergqvist: 'I have been accused of "grinding the faces of the poor". All I can say is that at the vintage they grind their own. I cannot believe that they would dance and sing with such obvious enjoyment if they were not happy. In fact they *are* happy.'[37] This picture of peasants merrily treading the grapes may, nevertheless, disguise the fact that, especially in the heady atmosphere of the *adega*, song and dance may have been an escape from misery.

There is plenty to suggest that life for the quinta workers in the remote past was far from jolly. Consider Vila Maior's account of the *lagareiros* hired specifically to work the *lagares* at Vesúvio last century:

> As soon as each lagar is full 70 men get into it – this in a space of barely more than 36 square metres. These men form close columns of 7 or 8 rows. In each row the men put their arms over the shoulders of those immediately next to them, and thus linked begin the work, marking time and shouting out left, right, left, right, like a platoon of recruits in a drill school. From time to time they utter loud, unruly shrieks of hideous savagery. This great uproar can only be explained by the necessity of their having to urge themselves on in work so monotonous and importunate that it verges on the barbarous, and in which the strongest set the pace for the weakest without giving them a moment's respite. Thus it happens that many fall ill in this laborious task . . . The

first stint lasts for 18 hours; there is then a respite of 6 hours, after which there is another stint of 18 hours.[38]

That, happily, was a thing of the past long before Claire Bergqvist's time, although, until machines for crushing the grapes before they go into the *lagar* became general in the 1960s, a first *corte* along the lines described above, but lasting only two hours, was required before *liberdade* (free individual movement) enabled the *lagareiros* to relax a bit. By comparison with accounts of the past, today's treading is, from what I have seen, positively languid.[39]

Vila Maior believed that, of all the arduous work done on a quinta, working the *lagares* was the most hazardous to health. 'I still hope,' he wrote, 'that the inventive genius of modern mechanics, which has performed so many services for the working class, might discover an economic and completely automated means of replacing the work of treading the grapes.'[40] How pleased, therefore, he would have been with *movi-mosto* pumps and autovinifiers!

Although modern vinifiers are somehow not quite as conducive to a festive atmosphere as *lagares*, the vintage represents the culmination of the quinta year, and there must be few workers who do not now enter wholeheartedly into its party spirit.

Accommodation

The brutishness of conditions in former times was not confined to the vintage. To quote Vila Maior once more:

> [The cardenhos *at Vesúvio] offer nothing if not a bleak shelter for the resident workers and are completely destitute of the most rudimentary comforts. It is true that the Gallegos,*[41] *for whom they are exclusively designed, are a rough lot used to the harshest treatment: however, they do not enjoy the privilege of unending good health, and should one of them fall ill he will not find here the slightest relief . . . For the Portuguese workers, a few years ago, a lodging of greater size than the others was put up, with the clear intention of providing better shelter . . . It is spacious and has wooden beds, which are completely lacking in the* cardenhos *of the Gallegos. It is, however, badly ventilated. Outside there are separate latrines for the workers. Here, certainly, the workers are tolerably lodged.*[42]

Miguel Torga's novel *Vindima* (Grape Harvest), which concerns the life of the *roga* on a fictional quinta at the beginning of the century, portrays conditions which are not significantly better. The accommodation in an outhouse of the quinta is primitive to a degree: the sexes are segregated only by a wooden screen; there are no beds, only slatted wooden trestles covered with hay, sacking and rough blankets, on which six or more people sleep; and there are no proper sanitary arrangements. A sentence from the Preface to the English translation draws the moral: 'Tyrannical land-owners, degrading *cardenhos* to house the workers and wages barely sufficient to appease hunger, no longer exist . . . Only the suffering and protests of many generations gave the workers today the relative dignity they possess.'[43]

Although strenuous efforts are being made by all proprietors to up-grade their *cardenhos*, they are still (with one or two notable exceptions) far from being luxurious. I have seen accommodation identical to that described by Torga which was in use until about fifteen years ago. Similar conditions may still survive in isolated cases – one or two quinta owners declined to show me their *cardenhos*. The norm now, however, is separate dormitories with hospital beds or two-tier bunks, and with toilets and showers – though not necessarily with hot water! 'Don't the workers protest?' I asked one *caseiro*. 'They protest,' he replied, 'but we don't do anything.'

Part of the problem lies in changing the long-established attitudes of some *caseiros* and managers. 'Dirty accommodation for dirty people' was one manager's crisp summary of his quinta's *cardenhos*. Another proprietor's enlightened policy was similarly sabotaged. Opening a storeroom door one day, his eye alighted on a stack of lavatory seats he had purchased for his workers' welfare. Summoning the *caseiro*, he enquired why they had not been fitted. 'They would only have got broken,' was the reply.

Wages

Any comparison of workers' wages last century and this would involve not just cash equivalents but complicated questions of exchange rates, the cost of living, etc., which are notoriously difficult to make and potentially misleading. It is perhaps more useful to look at present-day wages. Again, comparisons are treacherous, but by comparison with the minimum agricultural wage in Britain[44] or the wages of vineyard workers in France, Douro wages do not seem generous.

In 1989, according to figures supplied by a reputable shipper, male vineyard workers were paid on average 1,200 *escudos* a day (eight hours),[45] and women 850 *escudos* for the same period, plus food. Dormitory accommodation was valued at 500 *escudos* a day, and social security contributions (15 per cent employer, 8 per cent worker) were paid by the employer. Take home pay, translated into British equivalents at the rate of £1 : 243 *escudos*, gives £4.94 net a day for men, and £3.50 net for women.

Such figures may well surprise and shock non-Portuguese readers. To pursue the comparison suggested above, Portuguese vineyard workers receive about a fifth of the wages of their French equivalents. It is true, of course, that the cost of living in the two countries is different, but it is not five times different. As the Common Market of 1992 approaches, it is evident that wages will have to increase, both to keep pace as Portuguese prices gradually adjust to general European levels, and in order to keep the labour force in place.

Feeding

For a long time the food provided for workers has been inadequate and dull, though, as with living conditions, many proprietors are upgrading their standards. An insight into what it used to be like is provided by an entry in the Quinta da Boa Vista diary for 27 October 1897:

> *From 6th November (instant) every Gallego will receive the same rations as the Portuguese, which means that the daily food of each Gallego will be increased by 2 Sardines & 1 Measure of Rice (or potatoes). At a cost of 20 réis per man.*
>
> | | *Winter* | *Summer* |
> |---|---|---|
> | *Breakfast:* | *Caldo & Sardinha* | *Caldo & Sardinha* |
> | *Dinner:* | *Caldo & arroz* | *Caldo, arroz & Bacalhau* |
> | *Supper:* | *Caldo & Sardinha* | *Caldo & Sardinha* |
>
> *The women get the same quantity of food if they can eat it.*[46]

A telling note was added to this entry on 28 September, 1916:

> *This is not correct. The women for breakfast get only* A SINGLE SARDINE, *the idea being that they make up with* GRAPES!

Caldo verde, sardines and fish (though *bacalhau* has become rather expensive) still comprise the bulk of the rather unvaried fare offered to vineyard workers. Although most proprietors are advancing on the standards which have prevailed for a century, again there are others who still lag behind. A quinta manager of one well-known firm (best un-named) told me: 'For feeding the workers the amount is not great. I buy five chickens for twenty workers. A tin of tuna fish does two men – about 65 grams each. It's a meal. And the people work hard. If they go to France they will eat properly – three courses and wine. Here they get a lot to drink: that could be our problem!'

It is this recognition that the standard of living of the vineyard workers is not high enough, and that many more workers may seek better pay and conditions elsewhere, which has spurred on the improvements in accommodation and conditions which are now taking place. Whether they will prove to be sufficiently timely and extensive remains to be seen.

Port production

Brief mention must be made of four things which are important to understanding recent developments on the quintas.

Mechanization

As pointed out earlier, the Douro region is changing quickly after having remained relatively isolated for most of this century. The lure of work abroad, to say nothing of work in the construction industry as EEC money is pumped into improving Portugal's infrastructure, is tempting away the work force.[47] For such a labour-intensive industry as port, the results are beginning to look catastrophic: and with full

Opposite
3
A typical granite marker erected to signify the boundary of the demarcated area for the production of port authorized by the Marquês de Pombal in the mid-eighteenth century. With the passage of time, this specimen at Parada do Bispo has become marooned in the village street

Overleaf
4
Quinta do Seixo – empty containers used for harvesting grapes beside the disused gate into the quinta

labour mobility within the market after 1992, and competing and more congenial forms of employment (such as the development of leisure facilities within the region) certain to come about, things can only get worse. The great cry, therefore, is 'Mechanize or perish'.

This, then, is the big incentive to the creation of *patamares*, or 'contour terraces' as they are known to the British shippers. Ugly as they may be, and some would add wasteful of land, they can be worked by a tractor between their two rows of vines, while their sloping shoulders can be kept weed-free with herbicides. They have no walls to be kept in repair, and, although they still require manpower (notably for pruning and harvesting), they can be maintained by a relatively small work force.

An alternative system of mechanization – vertical planting – has many supporters. Its advantages are seen largely in its greater density of planting (4,500 vines per hectare, compared with 3,500 on *patamares*); the minimization of soil erosion if kept well tilled; the elimination of the use of herbicides; and a more aesthetic treatment of the environment.

Experimentation with other solutions continues, some of which will be mentioned under individual quinta entries.[48]

Another issue closely related to the shortage of labour arouses passions scarcely less intense than controversy over the respective merits of *paramares* and vertical planting: that is, the respective merits of *lagares* and fermentation tanks. The latter have been established for about three decades and take the form either of autovinifiers (where the colour and tannin are extracted from the must by using the pressures of CO_2 released during fermentation) or pump-over tanks (in which the movement of the must is controlled mechanically).

This is not an issue which can be discussed in detail here: there are wide differences in the use of *lagares* (where, after a small amount of treading, the must is often circulated by use of a variety of pumps, such as a *movi-mosto* pump) just as there are now considerable variations in the use of tanks (with cooling systems and other design modifications) for pumping over.[49] Opinions on both sides have adherents who are respected old-hands in the port business. The supporters of *lagares*, however, are somewhat embattled. 'We'll go on with *largares* as long as we can,' they say, 'but that will only be for as long as we can find people to get into them.'

Experimentation

Experimentation is in the air. The Centro de Estudos Vitivinícolas do Douro (CEVD), at Régua, has its field station at the Quinta de Santa Bárbara[50], at the mouth of the Rio Torto. It played an advisory part in the large-scale replanting which has been carried out during the 1980s. Much of its research has been carried out on selected quintas, in conjunction with shippers, and with academic organizations such as the oenological department at the University of Vila Real, itself within the Douro region. Another important research organization is ADVID (Associação para o Desenvolvimento da Viticultura Duriense). It is an

Previous page
5
Dovecot at Quinta da Terra Feita. Dovecots are a feature of the landscape in many parts of the Douro

Opposite
6
Quinta do Tua, with one of the most elegant façades of any quinta house in the Cima Corgo

association of both shippers and growers whose members cooperate in viticultural research, and comprises Barros, Cockburn, Cruz, Ferreira, Quinta dos Murças, Quinta do Noval, Sandeman and Taylor. Cockburn and Ramos-Pinto also carry out much independent research.

PDRITM

An ambitious project for replanting *mortórios* and other areas capable of producing top grade port was started in 1985. Known officially as PDRITM (Projecto de Desenvolvimento Rural Integrado de Trás-os-Montes), it is commonly called the World Bank Scheme, having been financed from that source. Basically, under the scheme a grower could plant or replant up to 24 ha per vineyard provided two main conditions were met: Firstly, only land designated as Class A or B under the Cadastro[51] could be used – essentially in the Cima Corgo and Douro Superior – but it would receive a guaranteed *benefício*; Secondly, only five grape varieties, assessed by CEVD as the top class port vines, could be used – Touriga Francesa, Touriga Nacional, Tinta Roriz, Tinta Barroca and Tinto Cão – and these had to be planted on *patamares* in a specific way (though vertical planting was allowed in a handful of cases).

The aim of the scheme was to replant 6,200 ha, thereby increasing the percentage of high grade musts. The incentive provided was a loan from the World Bank, free of interest repayments for seven years, after which accrued interest and the loan itself have to be repaid within a further ten years. The scheme (closed three years later) was fully taken up.

It remains to be seen what the outcome will be. An assumption of the scheme was that the extra top quality port produced would be absorbed by increased sales of vintage, LBV and premium grade ports. However, after over ten years of regular increased port sales, 1989 saw a down-turn of about 2 per cent. This has induced a note of caution, and a second PDRITM is to be used, not for further expansion, but to correct mistakes and finance improvements in the plantings done under the first scheme.

Clearly, a downturn in sales accompanied by a reduction in prices paid to growers by the shippers, coinciding with the start of repayments of both principal and interest on the loan, could lead many farmers into financial difficulties. Many observers think that this could happen, and already, at the beginning of 1990, much of the 1989 vintage remained unsold by the growers, who had asked for higher prices than most shippers were prepared to pay.

The law of 8 May 1986

There has been a long-standing sense of grievance on the part of some growers that the complete monopoly which the shippers have had over the export of port is contrary to their interests. Until recently all port, by law, had to pass through Vila Nova de Gaia before being sold abroad. But by a law of 8 May 1986, independent growers may now sell their port without this happening. They are excused certain of the legal conditions imposed on shippers, such as having to have a minimum stock of 150,000 litres; however, like the shippers, they have to maintain a stock equivalent to three times their annual sales, and are subject to such conditions as not selling in bulk (only in bottle), and not buying in grapes or wine.

Had this legislation not come about, independent port producers would have been the only wine producers within the EEC unable to sell their wine independently. Even now they face a very limiting restriction, namely that they are not allowed to sell to Portuguese agents for export by them since they have to export directly to foreign handlers.

The consequences of the law of the 8 May 1986, are of particular interest within the context of this book. It has stimulated a number of independent producers to market their own quinta wine under their own label and to seek export markets for it. Shortly after the new law came into force some of these independent producers, in conjunction with producers of single quinta table wines, formed an association called AVEPOD (Associação dos Viticultores-Engarrafadores dos Vinhos do Porto e Douro). There are at the moment nineteen members, and the aims of AVEPOD include the promotion of 'the concept of estate-bottled wine of VQPRD quality with a regional appellation'.

Developments on this front have so far been very modest: but only four years have elapsed since the new law, and it takes time to mature stock and to prepare to enter the market. Evidently what we see at the moment is only the tip of an iceberg. All independent producers wishing to market their own wine, either internally or abroad, have to be registered with the Instituto do Vinho do Porto.[52] In May 1989, the list of registrations (the latest available at time of writing) amounted to eight for the home market, and thirty-seven for the export market. These registrations, however, largely represent market aspirations, for, as far as I am aware, there are only five independently owned quintas which are exporting (or have exported) since 1986: Côtto, Crasto, Infantado, Romaneira and La Rosa. The others – some of which have just planted their vines – are preparing to do so. After an inevitable time-lag, therefore, we may expect the number of single quinta ports offered on the market to gain momentum.

The shippers do not see the development of single quinta ports from independent producers as any kind of threat. With control of over 99 per cent of the export market, why should they? If anything they welcome diversity on the grounds that any publicity for port benefits the majority, and it is the shippers themselves who, in the last few years, have brought the largest number of new, single quinta ports to the market.

Single quinta ports

A precise description of a single quinta port is not as easy as it may seem since, surprisingly, no exact definition has been laid down either by law or by the conventions of the trade. Discussions have been taking place between the Instituto do Vinho do Porto and the Associação dos Exportadores de Vinho do Porto (Association of Port Wine Shippers), but so far no agreement has been reached. With respect to single estate table wines the matter is, of course, covered by EEC regulations, but there are still no such regulations with respect to fortified wines.

In the absence of any accepted definition, therefore, one is forced back on the lowest common denominator: single quinta ports are ones which come from a single property. Even this simple definition is not without problems. In the Douro many properties consist of scattered parcels of land, which raises the question of how widely they can be scattered. The suggestion currently being mooted is that they should not be more than one kilometre apart.

Again, the idea of a single quinta port conjures up, perhaps, the idea of a Bordeaux château or of an estate bottled burgundy, with the guarantee of authenticity which they carry. A single quinta port, it might be thought, is the Douro equivalent. This parity is certainly what many single quinta port producers would like to achieve (particularly the members of AVEPOD), but the reality is far from this.

Not only are very few single quinta ports estate bottled, in the sense of being physically bottled on the quinta, there is also no legal requirement whatsoever that a single drop of the wine in the bottle should actually come from the quinta whose name appears on the label! And, in quite a large number of cases, ports are sold with all the appearance of being single quinta wines when, in reality, the quinta names are simply being used as brand names. To my mind this is a scandal, and one which, with the rapid appearance of more single quinta wines on the market, the trade must quickly rectify if the reputation of genuine single quinta ports is not to be blighted by the brands masquerading as such.

Throughout this book I have tried to distinguish genuine single quinta ports from those that are not, and the phrase 'single quinta port' is used to designate one which comes from (but is not necessarily bottled at) only one property. That said, the concept still allows for considerable diversity, because, thus defined, a single quinta port can be anything from a humble three year old ruby to a more than forty year old tawny, a *colheita* or a vintage wine. In fact, every recognised type of port except for crusting port can be found. This seems logical given the diversity of producers and their products, but for some time (within the British sector of the trade) the concept of a single quinta port has had a more specific meaning. To explain this properly we have to remind ourselves of the traditional meaning of 'vintage port'.

Vintage port and single quinta vintages

Shippers have for well over a century 'declared' certain years as vintages. This has happened because only in certain years does the wine of a single vintage reach the high quality which they believe is necessary to provide a wine which justifies (i.e. benefits from) being bottled at an early age and matured in bottle instead of in cask. Unlike single quinta wines there is a now universally accepted convention about what a vintage wine is: it is port from a single year which is initially matured in cask and bottled not less than two, and not more than three years after the vintage year. It normally takes from ten to fifteen years, and in the case of really great vintages, twenty or more years to reach full maturity.

Although there has never been complete unanimity between shippers about which vintages to declare, there has normally been a considerable consensus. It has usually occurred only when most shippers have agreed that there has been enough wine of sufficiently high quality from a particular year to make a declaration worth while. If a shipper has opted out of the consensus it is usually because, for some reason, he does not have wine which he considers good enough. On average there has been a general port declaration about three times every decade, and this comparative rarity has made them something of an event.

Although, as we have seen, it was quite common to ship single quinta ports last century, by the end of it this practice had all but died out, with the important and notable exceptions of Roriz and Noval. Quinta do Noval, which declared vintages more or less in line with other shippers, is, in this respect, slightly anomalous. From one point of view it was (and is) a firm of shippers; from another, it is the proprietor of a quinta.

In the domestic market a few small producers used to bottle and sell their port (mainly around Régua) until the 1930s, when increasing bureaucracy put a stop to it. The custom of shipping single quinta ports was revived, largely by British shippers, after 1950. Taylor led the way with a 1958 Quinta de Vargellas; Croft followed with a 1967 Quinta da Roêda; others have started to offer single quinta vintages much more recently with a cluster of 1978s like Warre's Quinta da Cavadinha, Dow's Quinta do Bomfim and Delaforce's Quinta da Côrte.

Such single quinta ports are produced in exactly the same way as declared vintages, but they have been offered in years in which their shippers did not declare a vintage. It is for this reason that British shippers very often refer to them as 'off-vintage' wines – a somewhat confusing term which indicates that, although they are ports of a single vintage year, they are from a year in which the shipper did not make a declared vintage.

The reasoning behind this is as follows. In a year in which a vintage is declared the shipper is putting his reputation and prestige behind his wine: it is the best he can do, and by declaring it he is guaranteeing that it is of the highest quality. He is, in a sense, selecting the highest quality on behalf of the consumer. In other years, however, smaller quantities of very good wine are often produced, and these, particularly from good quintas, can be made into satisfactory wines which, if they do not scale the heights of a declared vintage (and are not intended to compete with them) nevertheless develop into attractive, usually somewhat lighter, ports. For the British shippers, therefore, single quinta ports constitute a 'junior league' of vintage wines – secondary to declared vintages, but by no means second rate.

Apart from Noval, the chief exception to this is Forrester's Boa Vista,[53] which, although not originally a true single quinta port, has been since 1979.[54] However, this traditional British approach to single quinta ports is becoming less clear-cut as more single quinta vintages, particularly those from independent producers, come on to the market.

The changing concept of vintage port

There is, I am sure, no danger of the shippers' traditional declared vintages disappearing; but it does seem to me that the old system of identifying quality with a vintage declaration is being slowly eroded in at least three ways.

In the first place, the frequency of vintage declarations by some shippers has recently increased markedly.[55] The greater their frequency the less distinctive they can be, for there is no reason to think that over-all quality has so dramatically increased within the same period.

In the second place, whereas a shipper draws on port from a large variety of sources and can pick and choose his best lots to make the vintage blend which he declares, the proprietor of a single quinta can only draw on his own resources. Thus a shipper can distinguish between a 'declared vintage' (normally a blend from various sources) and an 'off-vintage' single quinta. The proprietor of a single quinta has only his own wine, and every year he produces it – which, of course, is not literally every year – he is declaring it. His position is indeed like that of a Bordeaux château. If the wine is poor he may decide not to bottle it under his own label; but, if he does, he does not distinguish which of these years is of superlative quality and which is secondary. He simply produces his wine and leaves the market and informed opinion to discriminate which are the better and which are the lesser vintages. It follows that the more the public starts to think about single quinta ports in 'Bordeaux' terms, the less clear-cut the concept of declared vintage years as something special will become. There will simply be better and worse vintage years.

The third reason is not unconnected with the first. Traditional declared vintage ports have, in general, been heavy-weights which take time to mature. This has been a reflection of their depth and quality. Hand in hand with the increased number of declarations by some shippers there have been marked changes in the style of some of the vintage ports being offered. Both Messias and the Real Companhia Velha, for example, have been taken to task in the wine press for producing relatively light and quick-maturing vintages in the 1980s. They have replied by pointing out, quite rightly, that, whatever the traditions of the trade, there is no intrinsic reason why a vintage wine has to be unapproachable when young or has to require long maturation. They are, they say, producing a lighter style for which there is a place in the market, not just because such wines are cheaper, but because more and more people prefer a lighter style to drink.

This is a difficult argument for the British shippers to counter. They, after all, have offered their 'off-vintage' single quinta ports as lighter, quicker-maturing versions of their traditional declared vintages. Having started along this road one can go one stage further, which is just what some of the Portuguese shippers are doing. All this tends to reduce the original connotations of quality associated with the concept of vintage, and to strip it down to meaning, quite simply, wine of a particular year.

Vintage wine and vintage quality

Some of the independent quintas have also been producing vintage ports which are lighter in character than the traditional declared vintages and which, both in style and character, are not unlike the shippers' single quinta 'off-vintages'. In some cases (e.g. Quinta do Côtto, Quinta do Infantado) this appears to be the result of a definite policy: a lighter style is being deliberately sought. For this Miguel Champalimaud has coined the apt phrase 'more readily drinkable port'. In other cases (e.g. Quinta do Crasto) it may be more a consequence of the way in which the wines have been made (in this case, with a *movi-mosto* pump). And in some cases – as with Romaneira, perhaps – it seems to have happened for no easily assignable reason.

Some of the British shippers have told me that they believe that it is inevitable that single quinta wines will be lighter. This is one of the reasons why they do not regard the independent quintas as serious competition. A 'true' vintage wine will have a complexity which results from a blend of wine from different sources, and this factor, by definition, is ruled out for the single quinta producer.

I believe that this is not a sound argument. In the first place, if a single quinta is produced in a declared year is it not likely that it will have the weight associated with such vintage years? Because the British shippers have eschewed single quinta wines in declared years it is unfair to take their single quinta ports as representative of the best that can be done in the genre. In the second place, it is by no means clear that the larger quintas cannot achieve complexity by blending contrasting lots. Both Romaneira and Quinta de la Rosa, for example, are able to draw on grapes from areas different both in terms of altitude and micro-climate. It is at least an open question whether or not such quintas are capable of competing with traditional declared vintage blends, even if one judges that they have not yet done so.

The ultimate answer, however, must surely be provided by Quinta do Noval. Consistently reckoned within the top ten shippers of declared vintage ports, it meets the required criteria from its own resources. Moreover, at least one important shipper's 1945 vintage port, celebrated for its weight, complexity and length, was, in fact, from a single quinta – although, for reasons which escape me, I have been asked not to reveal its identity. Finally, it must be significant that the Symingtons, whose firms have hitherto offered single quintas in 'off-vintages', are planning to market a single Quinta de Vesúvio in declared vintage years as well as in others, very much along the lines of a Bordeaux château.

All that said, it must be admitted with some sadness that so far the evidence of independent quintas being able to compete successfully with the shippers' declared vintages is rather thin. We are still talking, in the majority of cases, about potential rather than actuality.

The market for single quinta ports

In dealing with the recent development of the market for single quinta ports it is convenient to distinguish between those offered by the shippers, and those offered by independent producers seeking to take advantage of the recent changes in the law to market their ports both in Portugal and abroad.

The number of shippers' single quintas is increasing rapidly. The reasons for this are varied, but mainly commercial. For example, some shippers have perceived that single quintas appeal to the growing number of wine lovers looking for wines which have an identity and individuality which volume products lack, and which the wine of a single property appears to guarantee. Other shippers feel that the market for their declared vintages has become a bit over-heated — especially with the awakening of intense interest in them in the United States. Quantities of declared vintages, after all, must always be limited if top quality is to be maintained. They have been hoping that the introduction of more single quinta vintage wines, quicker maturing and less expensive, will help to satisfy some of this demand. Lastly, as more single quinta ports come to the market and become better known, many shippers feel that they cannot afford not to join the trend.

In the case of the independent producers the story is somewhat different. As some of them are rapidly discovering, it is one thing to produce a wine which a shipper is happy to buy to put into his blend, it is another thing to produce a finished port which gains ready acceptance by the public. Some producers are discovering that, quite apart from finding export markets, it is difficult even to sell in Portugal.

It is not just a question of their producing a port of the requisite standard of quality, it is more that they have no marketing experience, and no ready access to distribution networks. In the case of exporting their port the problem is even harder. Most overseas agents are looking for port which fits into existing markets and many producers do not really know, and have failed to research, what these markets require. Moreover, in many cases, export agents look for guarantees of volume and continuity which small producers are unable to give. Both the domestic and export markets are therefore in a very embryonic state at the present.

Nevertheless, within the last decade the number of single quinta wines on the market has quintupled, and it is clear that, after having been eclipsed for almost a century, they are making a come-back. The press has reported that, in England at any rate, by the end of 1990 single quinta ports had become very modish: 'after dinner the style leaders are sticking with single quintas (single-estate vintage ports)'.[56] Whether these ports will regain the pre-eminence they at one time had I rather doubt; on the other hand, it will be surprising if they do not begin to re-establish themselves as an important part of the market.

The Individual Quintas

The Baixo Corgo

The Baixo Corgo (or Lower Corgo) is the name given to the most westerly and, in terms of land area, the smallest of the three port-producing areas. All of them have very irregular shapes,[1] which makes it difficult to describe them accurately. For our purposes it will be sufficient to regard them as the regions north and south of particular stretches of the Douro. The Baixo Corgo extends on the north bank of the Douro from the mouth of the Rio Corgo (on the eastern outskirts of Régua) westwards to Barqueiros, a small village about 14 km downstream from Régua. On the south bank it extends from Barró (opposite Barqueiros) eastwards to the Rio Temilobos about 5.5 km to the east of Régua. The area reaches north to Vila Real, and south to just beyond Lamego.

The Baixo Corgo is, historically speaking, the birthplace of port, and it remains a large and important area in terms of the size of its production, if less so in terms of its quality. Covering 45,000 ha, it has 15,180 ha (35.7 per cent of the land) of vineyards, and the wine

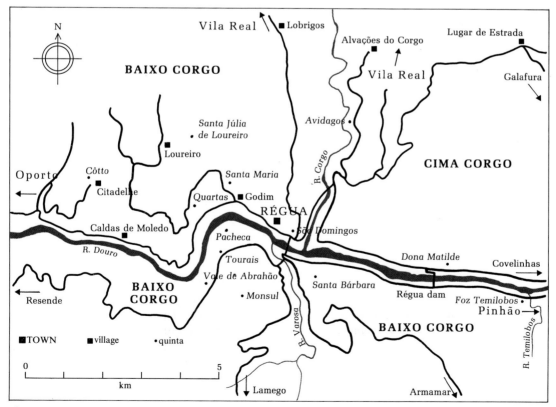

The Baixo Corgo

produced is used mainly for white port and standard commercial rubies and tawnies.

Within the Baixo Corgo, in the days of the *feitoria*, the *concelho* of Santa Marta de Penaguião was equalled only by Lamego in the importance of its wines. I know of four producers in the Baixo Corgo who believe that it is possible to make a port of traditional vintage quality, but they are exceptions.[2] Most informed people would claim little more for them, apart from the excellent whites, than that they are of good dependable quality. The glamour has moved out of the Baixo Corgo and up stream to the Cima Corgo.

Why has this reversal of favour occurred? Surely the quality of the wines, dependent on soil and climatic conditions which are essentially unalterable, cannot have changed to such a degree? Part of the explanation is historical – at the time of the demarcations the Baixo Corgo was the most accessible part of the region – but it is also to do with changes in the character of port itself. In the early days of the *feitoria*, when the addition of brandy to the wine was not yet universal and the proportion added was smaller, port was a much lighter, more fragrant and delicate wine than today, and this quality was much prized. It was precisely because such wines did not withstand the journey to England very well that fortifying the wine became so usual. We know that the wines had this more delicate character not only because contemporary writers tell us so,[3] but because different, more delicate grape varieties were generally used to produce them. We also know that the addition of brandy to the wine results in a loss of colour, so, as the custom of fortification grew, it became necessary to find grape varieties better able to withstand this change. It is now generally agreed that the varieties which provide the more robust qualities of present-day port do best in the conditions which are found further up the river, but not in the Baixo Corgo. Such considerations partly explain the switch in the assessment of the Baixo and Cima Corgo since the *feitoria* days.

Of the many quintas to be found in the Baixo Corgo few have names which are familiar even to those who know something about port – itself an indication of how far the area has declined in esteem. Of the nine selected for inclusion here, four have a long history of almost continuous private ownership going back well beyond the beginnings of the *feitoria*; the other five, all belonging to port shippers, whilst not without their share of history, show some of the diversity of the present-day port trade. All except the Quinta de Santa Júlia de Loureiro were within the *feitoria*.

Taking our start from Régua, we cross the Douro. To the right is the way to Pinhão, Resende and Lamego; to the left is the way to Armamar, and if we take this road we come, soon on our left, to the Quinta de Santa Bárbara, belonging to Manoel D Poças Júnior, Vinhos, SA.

Quinta de Santa Bárbara

Santa Bárbara[1] offers protection from inclement weather, so it is perhaps appropriate that a port quinta, where success is so dependent on sun and rain at the proper times, should carry her name. In this case, however, the name is not a primitive form of insurance policy, but due to a mediaeval chapel which stands within the quinta itself. Chapels dedicated to Santa Bárbara are not uncommon in the Douro.

The quinta stands on the shoulder of a hill, with north facing slopes looking over the Douro to Régua and the mouth of the Rio Corgo, and south-west facing slopes (which produce the best wine) looking across the Rio Varoza. It is relatively small, but its history stretches back to monastic times, having once belonged to a religious brotherhood in Guimarães. Two small quintas, Alvarelhão and Pena Chão, were incorporated into Santa Bárbara some time prior to 1980. It is also marked on Forrester's map of the Douro.

It was purchased in 1980 by Poças, a family firm which was started in 1918 and is perhaps best known for its Pousada Port, which is encountered naturally enough by visitors to the government-sponsored hotels called *pousadas* – though not, of course, only there. Previously the quinta had belonged to Sr Manuel Araújo Ribeiro. Poças, who had regularly bought its port over a long period, were on the lookout for a good quinta when they were approached by Sr Ribeiro, who, with his wife, wished to move to Lisbon. Poças acquired the property in the knowledge that a lot of investment would be required to put the quinta back into first class condition. It had been badly planted; the vines were too old; the buildings, including the house, were run-down.

The buildings are still run down: only the tiny chapel, standing sentinel over Régua, has been restored (a propitiation?). Naturally, the vineyard is the first priority, and a third of it has now been renewed. Most of the planting is continuous, with a little traditional terracing and, now, some vertical planting – but the mechanization of the quinta is as yet insignificant. Poças, however, intend to mechanize further, so it is likely we shall see *patamares* opposite Régua before long.

The new vines, which are block planted, and vinified separately, are just coming on stream. The wine is made on the quinta and kept there briefly until it is transferred to the Quinta das Quartas in Régua, after which some of it may go to Vila Nova de Gaia. Most of the wine goes to be blended, though in good years the best is now being reserved. Thus 1989 saw the release of a single quinta 1980 *colheita*, to be followed in due course by an '82.

From the Quinta de Santa Bárbara, by following the signs for Resende for a couple of kilometres, we find a road to the right at the Quinta de Tourais which takes us to one of the oldest quintas in the region, on flat land close to the river.

Quinta da Pacheca

The first documented mention of the Quinta da Pacheca is in 1738, when it was inherited by Pedro Pacheco Pereira from his aunt. It had been created from parcels of land leased over almost two centuries by the Pacheco Pereira family, already established in Oporto in the reign of Dom Pedro I. The first vineyard of which we have a record was acquired in 1551 from the Convento de São João de Tarouca at an annual rental of 250 *réis* by Bastião Pereira, and there are records of a further fourteen acquisitions up until 1738. More small vineyards were acquired after that date, and many within the quinta, such as 'Cerrado', 'Margaridas' and 'Vinha Grande', still retain their original names.

The quinta remained in the family until 1903 when circumstances forced João Gonçalo Pacheco Pereira to sell to José Freire de Serpa Leitão Pimentel, the father of the present owner. The Pimentel family, which comes from this area, were already rich landowners by 1385, with properties between Poiares and Lamego, and have been closely associated with the production of port for many generations. For almost two and a half centuries the Pimentels owned the Quinta de Santa Júlia de Loureiro.

By 1903 Pacheca had already reached its present size (in five separate but closely situated parcels). It was, however, rather run down, and the 1904 vintage yielded only 13 pipes. Extensive replanting was undertaken until, by 1916, production reached almost 47 pipes. Unusually for this time, much of the planting was carried out in blocks of a single variety, or of two varieties planted in alternating rows. In 1922-3 a new *armazém* was built. The original house, dating from the sixteenth century, was altered in 1910, and again between 1975 and 1983. It retains its chapel dedicated to Nossa Senhora de Conceição.

Sr Eduardo Mendia Freire de Serpa Pimentel, a much respected senior member of the wine trade, took over the quinta from his mother in 1952. A further programme of replanting was carried out between 1953 and 1974, and also under PDRITM; 20 ha are now mechanized.

Sr Serpa Pimentel's main efforts and greatest successes have been in the field of table wines. Apart from producing red wines from traditional Douro varieties he has specialised in producing white wines from foreign varieties, and in 1979 he began to sell them as estate bottled wines. Sr Serpa Pimentel also produces port and table wine at the nearby Quinta de Vale de Abrahão, of equal antiquity and marked on Forrester's map. Using only his own grapes, he is now probably the largest private producer of table wines in the Douro.

At the Quinta da Pacheca 30 per cent of the total production is made into port, all of it red (though some white is also produced at the Quinta de Vale de Abrahão), and this has been bought for a number of years by Cockburn. No single quinta port is produced, and Sr Serpa Pimentel is adamant that vintage port is not successful in the Baixo Corgo. However, two of his five sons are in the wine trade, and it is with them that the future of the Quinta da Pacheca will rest. Perhaps Sr Serpa Pimentel has a secret hope that they will decide to commercialize the quinta port. 'In 1987 I bottled 105,000 litres of table wine. For the moment that is enough to do. My sons must do something also.'

Shortly after rejoining the main road, continuing towards Resende, a small road on the left leads to one of the oldest, and surely one of the most romantic quintas, in the entire Douro.

Quinta de Monsul

Passing through the green entrance gates of Monsul, flanked by deciduous conifers (*Taxodium distichum*), you immediately enter an enchanted kingdom. To left and right the vines form a miniature valley on either side of the road, which is lined by pear trees, and which a granite marker informs you is the Rua Santo António. Over the vines on the left you see the tops of the cypresses which surround the property, whilst the slope on the right is surmounted by the strange and romantic quinta house itself. The road gently climbs in a curve towards the house: the Rua Santo António, bearing to the right, gives way to the Rua 25 Abril, which in turn becomes the Avenida Ignês, rather exotically lined with palm trees. Finally, going through more green gates, you enter a long courtyard with its white and yellow buildings – the chapel and quinta house on the left, the farm manager's house, *adegas*, and other domestic offices on the right.

Afonso do Vale Coelho Pereira Cabral[1] married Inês Guedes de Carvalho on 25 April 1881. For the rest of his life he remained ardently in love with her, as the Portuguese say, 'like a groom towards his bride', and it was they who lavished so much care on the beautification of the quinta and who stamped it with the very special character it has today.

From the main entrance another road, the Rua Affonso, leads to the house. Thus, the two roads named after Afonso and Inês are linked by the streets named after the date of their marriage and Santo António, the patron saint of engaged couples. To the east of the house is an arboretum, and it, like the rest of the property, is laid out with avenues and streets, in this case named after their children, each with its granite marker. The grandchildren, too numerous to have individual streets, were given an olive-grove and the Avenhaga dos Bisnetos (Lane of the Grandchildren). The layout of the quinta is, therefore, a celebration of the love of Afonso and Inês for each other and for their family.

The first owner of the Quinta do Paço e Torre de Monsul,[2] to give it its original full name, was Dom Afonso Henriques, the first king of Portugal. The king gifted it to his friend Pedro Viegas in 1163, and in the same year, with the king's agreement, it was sold for 480 *merabetinos* to Dona Teresa Afonso, who was the widow of Dom Egas Moniz (knight and friend of the king) and wet-nurse to the king's children. Dona Teresa Afonso founded the Mosteirô de Santa Maria de Salzedas, south of Lamego, in 1156, and in due course she gave the Quinta de Monsul to the monastery as a gift.

On 25 July 1331 the monastery leased the quinta to Dom Afonso de Vasconcelos e Menezes, Lord of Penela – an influential nobleman in the region north of Coimbra – thereby initiating a (fully documented) series of leases which ended only with the expulsion of the monks in 1834. Moreover, ever since 9 July 1469, with the exception of the nine years before it was purchased by Afonso Cabral, Monsul has remained in the possession of the same family. If, as seems likely although unproved, the lessee in 1469, Gonçalo Afonso, was related to the Coutinho family who had been the previous leaseholders,[3] the family ownership of Monsul goes back beyond 1469.

It is impossible to do justice in so short a space to the rich history of the owners of Monsul throughout the centuries; but perhaps the gap of nine years in the family ownership should be explained. The representative of the ninth generation after Afonso de Vasconcelos e Menezes was Luís Guedes de Vasconcelos. He was married to the daughter of the *Capitão-Mor* of Lamego, Gaspar Leal Gomes, who owned the Quinta de Tourais (previously a nunnery of the order of Santa Clara) next to the Quinta da Pacheca. After his death, and the death of Luís Guedes de Vasconcelos in 1754, one of the latter's sons, Rodrigo, succeeded to Tourais, and another, Bernardo, succeeded to Monsul.

Thus, the two properties were held by collateral branches of the family for nearly a century and a half. In 1888, when, 'owing to the vicissitudes of life', Bernard's great-grandson Afonso Guedes de Carvalho e Sousa sold Monsul,[4] Rodrigo's great-great-grand-daughter, Inês – who had married Afonso Cabral in 1881 – was a part-owner of Tourais. The family was devastated by the sale, and Afonso and his wife Inês decided to buy back Monsul as soon as possible. Like their lives together this was to be a shared effort, and as a tangible demonstration of her part in the purchase, rather than because the money was needed by her husband, she sold her interest in Tourais to help pay for Monsul. They succeeded in re-purchasing it in the year 1897.

Apart from the layout of the estate already described, Afonso and Inês added substantially to the house and farm buildings. Of the original tower and palace[5] little if anything remains, but the oldest part of the house is certainly of considerable antiquity. As one enters the courtyard, a separate small chapel, built in 1599 and still in use, stands on the left. Between the chapel and the house is a water *tanque*, resembling a small *lagar*, and bearing the date 1469 – the date of the first lease, not of the *tanque*! Steps lead up to a porch which shields the entrance to the *andar nobre* of the oldest part of the house. Below this are two *armazéms*, almost half subterranean for coolness.

At the front door one is confronted, astonishingly, by a gigantic, white stove-enamelled 'Stephens Inks' thermometer. Inside, the hall has a low, whitewashed beam roof. Apart from a discreetly covered ping-pong table, not much has changed here or in the rest of the house since the days of Afonso and Inês. Family mementos abound and, indeed, Afonso's study is much as he left it. His glass-fronted escritoire still contains his letter balance, old seals and pill boxes, a Wills tobacco tin, a magnifying glass, roller blotter and bottles of inks (Stephens, of course). Added to this part of the house is a lofty, turn-of-the-century, tile-clad extension built by Afonso and Inês.

A plan of the quinta shows that in 1904 it consisted of 22 ha, of which only 9.8 ha were under vines, and today these figures remain the same. The ratio of red to white vines is 3 : 7. The Monsul port used to be made on the quinta and for some time was sold to Taylor. For the last twelve years, however, apart from a very small amount of port for domestic use which continued to be made until 1985, the entire grape production has been sold to Taylor and vinified at their Casa dos Alambiques at Salgueiral, near Régua.[6]

Afonso died in 1946, and Inês four years later. Of their children only one daughter is still alive, and she and their many grandchildren (over forty of them) now own the quinta jointly, using the house on a rota system. The house and farm are managed by two of the grandsons.

All the planting at the moment is continuous, but eventually mechanization will have to come. One hopes that it will not spoil the unique character of the quinta, and that Monsul will continue to flourish for another eight hundred years.

All the remaining Baixo Corgo quintas to be considered are on the north bank of the Douro, so we now retrace our steps to Régua to visit two quintas in the town itself. The first, near the railway station, belongs to Adriano Ramos-Pinto, Vinhos, SA.

Quinta de São Domingos

Strange as it may seem, this quinta is situated in the centre of town and its vineyards, set amongst encroaching suburbia, are reached (since 1976) from the quinta buildings by an under-road tunnel. Acquired from Sr António Costa Gouveia e Cunha in 1915, the quinta was then only a vineyard, but now an attractive avenue lined with plane trees leads to a creeper-clad reception centre for visitors beside a rose garden. Next to the reception centre are two *armazéms* dating from 1916 and 1925, with vinification facilities and wine storage in wood, stainless steel and concrete.

The wine produced in the quinta is used for tawny port. A brand previously sold under the quinta name has now been discontinued.

The quinta is managed by Sr Acácio Monteiro, who has worked here for fifty-eight years, continuing in the footsteps of his father, who also worked here and at another of the firm's properties, the Quinta do Bom Retiro, for fifty-four years.

On the other side of the town, in the little suburb of Godim behind the built-up sprawl of Régua, we find the little Quinta de Santa Maria belonging to Cockburn Smithes & Ca, Lda.

Quinta da Santa Maria

This quinta is not important principally for its production of port – though it does produce some – but as a wine storage centre and Douro guest-house for Cockburn.

Cockburn acquired the quinta in 1973. For many centuries it had belonged to the Melo Sampaio family, whose splendid coat of arms adorns the chapel at the front of the house. In the nineteenth century the blood line of the family ceased because, although António de Melo Sampaio, who married in 1815, had nine children, none of them had any issue. One died as a child; six never married; and the other two, though married, had no children. One, however, had two adopted sons, of whom only one married, and it is through him that the succession of the quinta passed.[1]

Apart from dynastic problems, the family's fortunes dwindled. Land was gradually sold off to meet debts and the estate, which last century had been many times larger, had shrunk to only 6.5 ha when the family decided to relinquish it.

The house, which (judging from the date on a pillar in the under part of the house) may date back to 1798, has been remodelled many times, most recently and drastically in 1976, and certainly gives little clue as to its age apart from the tiny but beautifully maintained chapel which is situated to one side. Demurely tucked away behind some trees sheltering a small paved area with seats and an old mill-stone table, the house, with its windows guarded by green-painted grilles, is relatively small. It backs on to the vineyard, with views over Régua, and behind it in addition to a garden, there are, in the true quinta tradition, vegetables, chickens and ducks. The attractive interior contains a collection of Davenport 'seaweed' faïance which originally belonged to Martinez Gassiot (a firm incorporated in Cockburn), and some charming drawings and watercolours by Joseph Forrester which testify to his artistic ability.

The vineyards on gentle gradients have traditional continuous, unmechanized plantings. In the last few years the few vines of lesser quality have been re-grafted with noble varieties. Apart from the disused *lagares* in the *armazém* under the house, there are no wine-making facilities on the quinta, so the grapes are taken to the company's *adega* in nearby Lamego.

On a slightly higher level than the quinta house, and mercifully out of sight of it, is the warehouse building. Apart from office space, it consists essentially of two large halls which between them provide storage for the equivalent of 11,000 pipes of port. The cask hall, the broad span of its roof supported by its walls and a single central row of slender pillars, contains 5,000 oak pipes. Despite the fact that it has an aluminium roof it is very cool, the temperature and humidity being carefully monitored.

The second hall, at a lower level, contains one of the largest formations of immense vats in Europe. There are seventeen of them in all, made from Memel oak, the largest holding 397 pipes. The vats, originally belonging to Guinness in Ireland, had been acquired by Coates, the English cider manufacturers, from whom Cockburn were able to buy them at the accounting figure of one pound each. These vats, holding the equivalent of 6,000 pipes, are convenient for storing ruby ports because, with the small ratio of wine in contact with the wood, their colour is not affected. From time to time Cockburn receive organized groups of tourists, and it is here, beside the vats, that they are entertained to dinner, followed quite often by a display of folk singing and dancing by members of Cockburn's staff.

Opposite
7
In the Rio Torto valley. These stainless steel cylinders have a disturbing effect on the landscape

Overleaf
8
Quinta do Porto, overlooking the Douro and adjacent to the Quinta de la Rosa

From Godim the road towards Fontelas climbs westwards along the hills north of the Douro, affording good views of the river and Régua. Here we find another property belonging to Manoel Poças Júnior, Vinhos, SA – the Quinta das Quartas.

Quinta das Quartas

Purchased in 1923, Quartas originally belonged personally to the founder of the firm (and grandfather of the present owners). 'It was the apple of his eye', says Manuel Poças Pintão, the firm's export manager, and remained his personal property after the business was made into a company.

In 1981 Poças decided to centralize its Douro stocks by developing the quinta as a storage depot, and a large warehouse was commissioned in 1987. This warehouse dominates the site, and has a vast hall containing storage in wood. There are also two stainless steel tanks for recovering wine from the lees resulting from racking, and four external 100,000 litre stainless steel tanks for storage prior to transit.

Although the warehouse has a double roof to assist in maintaining a cool temperature, since maturation is quicker in Régua than in Vila Nova de Gaia, port destined for vintage or LBV wines cannot be kept here. On the other hand Poças find that, whereas traditionally the first blends of wines used to be made at Vila Nova de Gaia, the facilities at Quartas enable them to carry out the initial blending here before sending the wine down the river.

Under the main storage hall and facing the vineyards, are associated facilities: a room for experimental micro-vinification; a plant room catering for the filtration of the lees tanks immediately above, and electronically programmed barrel cleaning in the cask hall; a small canteen; and space for a future bottling line.

The warehouse gives a present total storage capacity of 5,000 pipes, but there are already plans for a second stage development of the site to raise the storage capacity to 11,000 pipes, and to make it into a modern vinification centre.

For all this a price has had to be paid. Not only has the family atmosphere vanished, but 6,000 vines had to be sacrificed to provide space for the warehouse. Moreover, those remaining, all on traditional terraces, do not really constitute a viable number, though it is hoped that future purchases of adjacent land (presently small-holdings) will remedy this.

Flanking the entrance gate are the old buildings of the quinta, now meticulously restored, with a house for the manager, the *adega* where the quinta wine is still made, and, on the usual lower level, the original earth-floored *armazém* with its *toneis*.

The entrance court also contains a bust of Manoel Poças Júnior, erected in 1988 to celebrate both the centenary of his birth and the seventieth anniversary of the founding of the firm. Although he might not approve of what has happened to the 'apple of his eye', he would certainly endorse his grandsons' foresight in starting a development which will consolidate the firm's future position.

Previous page
9
Quinta de la Rosa. The old vineyard looking towards the old *caseiro*'s house (now rented under the *turismo de habitação* scheme)

Opposite
10
The Quinta do Infantado with, in the foreground, an old bullock cart of the type used within recent living memory to transport pipes of port down to the Douro

From Fontelas we continue climbing on the same road until we reach a small roundabout (with a decorative cross), from which a winding road on the right leads towards Loureiro.

Quinta de Santa Júlia de Loureiro

'This quinta has always been very happy with ladies', says Eduardo da Costa Seixas, its owner. Originally called the Quinta de São Gião de Loureiro (the name of the *freguesia* in which it stands), in the eighteenth century it became known simply as the Quinta de Loureiro,[1] or, after its owners, as the Quinta do Pimentel. Later still, in 1844, on the marriage of José Freire da Serpa Pimentel[2] to Dona Júlia Petronilho Pereira Leitão de Carvalho, it was decided to change the dedication of the chapel to Santa Júlia in her honour, and since then the property has been known as the Quinta de Santa Júlia de Loureiro.

Although situated in the *concelho* of Santa Marta de Penaguião, this quinta is nevertheless just on the border of the 1761 *feitoria* demarcation of Loureiro.[3] It was originally owned by the Mesquita Ferreira family of Romesal,[4] who moved to Santa Júlia at the beginning of the eighteenth century, and then passed to the Pimentel family, in whose possession it remained until 1981, through the marriage of Dona Luisa Teresa Pereira de Serqueira Mansilha to José Inácio Pimentel de Mesquita e Vasconcelos.

It was another lady, Dona Maria Emília da Oliveira e Maia, the second wife of their great-grandson, José Pimentel Freire de Machado Mesquita e Vasconcelos (created first Visconde de Gouveia in 1848), who undertook much of the development of the quinta. Of considerable independent wealth, during the 1850s she planted some woodlands, laid out the vineyards and gardens, and developed the farm buildings and installations. The designs and bills for these projects still survive. When Dona Maria Emília da Oliveira e Maia married, she paid off her husband's considerable debts in exchange for which she took a mortgage on the quinta. Subsequently, however, by an arranged marriage, her niece married his nephew, later the second Visconde de Gouveia, and by mutual consent he settled the quinta on his nephew while Dona Maria forgave the debt.[5]

The grandson of this couple, Manuel de Serpa Pimentel Pereira Leitão, married Dona Maria Leonor da Rocha Leão da Costa Seixas. Dona Leonor, who inherited the quinta from her husband in 1959, treasured it rather as Dona Maria da Oliveira e Maia had done. It was, she said, her 'little oasis', and, having no children, she left it on her death in 1981 to her nephew Eduardo da Costa Seixas.

From the entrance the road leads first through woods, then through the vineyards, sloping gently on broad terraces from left to right, ending in a completely enclosed courtyard shaded by an immense lime tree which was planted in December 1842. The house is a traditional *solar*, the oldest part of which dates from the origins of the quinta in the seventeenth century, but it was extended eastwards to form a symmetrical façade, probably in the nineteenth century, when the present chapel was built. The house is two storeys high and is fronted by an old verandah with cast iron supports and a glass roof. Sitting here one looks over a charming little terrace garden with clipped yew hedges, below which is an orchard, beyond which one gazes down to Régua.

Apart from some *patamares* made under PDRITM, some traditional terraces have been replanted for mechanization, and by 1994 40 per cent of the quinta will be mechanized. About a third of the production is made into port – largely with grapes from Romesal (about a fifth of the total planted area) – which is sold to Sandeman, and the remainder is made into table wine which is sold under the name of the quinta. Sr da Costa Seixas interests himself deeply in the quality of his product, and for his table wines he is experimenting with national grape varieties which were popular in the past but are now out of fashion. He has no intention, however, of producing a single quinta port.

To visit the Quinta de Avidagos, belonging to C da Silva, Vinhos, SA, we return to Régua and cross the Rio Corgo, turning left towards Vila Real, and left again towards Alvaçoẽs do Corgo.

Quinta de Avidagos

The Quinta de Avidagos stands on the left bank of the Rio Corgo some 4 km from its confluence with the Douro. Despite the fact that it is east of the Corgo it does not count as a Cima Corgo property. This is because according to the rule which governs the division between the two areas, the rainfall has to drain into the Douro before it can be included within the Cima Corgo.

The quinta's importance to its present owners, da Silva, the producers of Dalva Port (not to be confused with A J da Silva & Ca, as the proprietors of Quinta do Noval used to style themselves) is as a vinification centre rather than as a vineyard. Pictures of the attractive but relatively modern quinta house taken fifty years ago,[1] when the property belonged to João Maria de Sousa e Paiva, show it to have been smart and neatly maintained. Today the house, hidden behind trees which have grown up in the meantime, is used only for storage. At the side of the house are the other quinta buildings, including a small detached chapel. The *adega* contains unusually embossed granite *lagares* which are still used for making the quinta wine.

The quinta is intersected by the road from Régua to Alvaçoẽs do Corgo, and on the side of the road nearer the river, we find the main centre of operations – a vinification centre which was built just after da Silva purchased the quinta from the heirs of Sr de Sousa e Paiva in 1971. Da Silva prefer to purchase grapes rather than port from their farmers, and in this centre they have both autovinifiers and concrete pump-over tanks, used in conjunction with a cooling plant with a capacity of 60,000 litres an hour. The quinta has storage for 5,450 pipes in concrete, but three months after the vintage the wines are normally removed to Vila Nova de Gaia, where the company has recently built new storage facilities and a bottling line.

The vineyards, a mixture of terraces and continuous planting, reach down to the river and up behind the house. In the best years the production is used for vintage port: otherwise, depending on quality, it may be used for a single quinta ruby or LBV.

To reach the Quinta do Côtto we take the road from Régua westwards down the river towards Mesão Frio. After passing through Caldas de Moledo a small road on the right, signposted to Citadelhe, takes us to our final destination in the Baixo Corgo.

Quinta do Côtto

The Quinta do Côtto has several claims to our attention. It is one of the oldest properties in the Baixo Corgo; its house is certainly one of the most strikingly beautiful in the whole of the Douro; its proprietor, Sr Miguel Champalimaud, is undoubtedly one of the most outspoken critics of the port establishment; and, not least, Quinta da Côtto was the first property (and, from the Baixo Corgo, so far the only one) to export port, bottled in the demarcated region of the Douro, direct from the Douro under the new law of 8 May 1986.

'Côtto' (variously spelt 'coto' and 'couto') indicates a reserve or sanctuary, and in the early middle ages the quinta had the unusual privilege of a *direito de côtto* (a right of sanctuary), possibly under monastic auspices, whereby those fleeing from the king's officers could find refuge there. This right appears to have been first granted to Araújo Cabral Montez, a native of the bishopric of Tuy, and the estate has been in the possession of the Montez family ever since the thirteenth century. Two members of the family – Francisco Araújo Cabral and João Baptista de Araújo Cabral Montez – were executives and members of the Administrative Council of the Old Company.

Paulo José Champalimaud de Nussane, born in Limoges in 1730, settled in Portugal. His son, Lieutenant-General José Joaquim de Sousa Lyra e Castro Champalimaud, was the most famous of the Portuguese generals in the Peninsular Campaign, rising to Field Marshal. He distinguished himself particularly in the defence of the Minho against Marshal Soult, and in commanding the brigade of the 9th and 21st Regiments at the Battle of Bussaco.

The direct male line of the Champalimauds was extinguished in 1915, but through the marriage of General Champalimaud's daughter, Dona Carlota Casimira, to João Baptista de Araújo Cabral Montez the name continued within the direct Montez male line – first for two generations as Montez Champalimaud, then latterly simply as Champalimaud. Thus Montez, over three generations, became transmuted into Champalimaud – such are the confusing convolutions of Portuguese family names.[1]

The quinta sits on the hill behind the tiny village of Citadelhe, between Mesão Frio and Régua (as the crow flies rather than as the road winds). Citadelhe, which means 'citadel' in Portuguese, stands on the old Roman road which connected Lamego and Braga, and is sufficiently high up on the curve of the hills to make it difficult to catch more than a glimpse of the Douro. The striking, neo-classical south façade of the house dominates the village, with its estate over the crest of a hill towards the east, surrounded by forest, olive groves and other vineyards,

The house, the third on the site, dates from the seventeenth century. Square, with a central courtyard, its main façade is of monumental proportions. The chapel is incorporated in the house at one of the rear corners. The main *adega*, which is downhill to the east of the house, was built at the beginning of the century, but it was extended and modified in the 1960s. Eight autovinifiers were installed in 1964, a new bottle store was added in 1988, and there is a cold stabilization system. The old *adega* now contains the large wood vats and *toneis* moved from the *armazém* when concrete vats were installed. A small laboratory and a small bottling line complete the picture.

The quinta has vines in five detached parcels of land. Côtto enjoys relatively gentle gradients so almost all the old (mixed) plantings, which were done by Sr Miguel Champalimaud's grandfather, are continuous. The new plantings are mainly on *patamares*, with less than a hectare planted vertically. It is intended, however, to adopt vertical planting as the norm in the gradual renewal of the old vineyards. In some of the old vineyards a row of vines has been removed to make tractor mechanization possible, and about 40 per cent of the vineyard can be worked by tractor.

Miguel, one of three brothers, took over the running of Côtto from his father at the end of 1976. Apart from making wine, he is a tireless publicizer of the idea of estate-bottled single quinta port – 'personalized wines' – and not only campaigned for the reforms of the law of 8 May 1986, but was instrumental in the founding of AVEPOD.[2] Believing, however, that the name 'single quinta port' has become sullied by indiscriminate trade use of the term to market wines of poor quality not originating from a single quinta, he prefers to use the term 'classic vintage port' to describe his own product.

Although traditionally a producer of port, it is perhaps for its red Douro table wine that Côtto is more immediately famous. Of the total production about 45 per cent is Douro wine (red and white) and 55 per cent port. Quinta do Côtto has been bottling and selling its red table wine since 1964. A reserve version of this wine, called Grande Escolha, first appeared in 1980, and it is particularly on this wine that the reputation of Côtto rests.

This is particularly relevant to the Côtto port for two reasons. First, because the base wine for the ports and for the table wines is exactly the same. Secondly, and more importantly, Sr Champalimaud believes that port should in all essential respects be made in the same way as red table wine, except for the malolactic fermentation. 'Basically I don't treat port differently from the [table] wines', he says. This undoubtedly makes many of the things he does unique in the Douro, and is one of the reasons that the traditional port producers (i.e. almost everyone) regard him as a heretic. Indeed, being passionately against the oxidization of wine in any way, he goes so far as to reject tawny port as a valid part of the port tradition. 'The days of drinking old wine are over: now is the age of fruit and freshness.' It is in this area that he sees the biggest opportunity for independent estate producers.

Unlike an increasing number of makers, Sr Champalimaud is not dissatisfied with his autovinifiers. As for *lagares*: 'good for folklore – for journalists!', he says.

What, then, are the principal ways in which the Côtto port is treated differently from usual? The first thing is that five or six days after the brandy has been added to the must the wine is racked by pumping it off the lees (most shippers do not rack the wine until the beginning of the following year). Secondly, each year, whether it is to be bottled or not, the port is cold stabilized as part of a process involving all the Côtto wines, starting in January with the white wines and ending in June with the reds and the port. After this they are moved to the wood.

So far Côtto has produced only one vintage port, the 1982. Since then the entire port production has been sold to shippers. It is hoped, however, that there will be a 1989 vintage and that all the port will be bottled on the quinta within the next five years.

The Cima Corgo

The Cima Corgo (the Upper Corgo) is the central part of the demarcated region. It extends from the Rio Corgo on the north of the Douro, and the Rio Temilobos on the south bank, eastwards to the gorge of the Cachão de Valeira. Like the other sub-areas of the region, it has a very irregular boundary which runs just north of Murça and slightly south of Sendim. At 95,000 ha it is just over twice the size of the Baixo Corgo, but, with only 13,035 ha (13.7 per cent) of vines, it nevertheless has a smaller production. Despite this it has taken the place of the Baixo Corgo as the heart of the wine country.[1]

As in Pombaline times, the quintas of present renown are situated very close to the Douro, or in valleys of its affluents, especially the Rio Torto and the Rio Pinhão. Above Pinhão, which is at the centre of the region, the north bank of the Douro as far as the Rio Tua has traditionally been divided into two *costas*: the Costa de Roncão, from the Ribeiro da Póvoa roughly as far as Carrapata, and the Costa de Castedo from Carrapata to Tua.

From Régua a road goes eastwards along the north bank of the Douro as far as Covelinhas, and from Pinhão a road goes westwards, more or less keeping to the north bank of the river, as far as Gouvinhas. Unhappily, despite its being only a matter of 3 km, these roads do not meet – though it is possible to continue to Régua on the Gouvinhas road, taking a detour away from the river. There is, however, a good road from Régua to Pinhão along the south bank of the Douro.

There is no marginal road between Pinhão and Valeira on either bank, but it is possible to make a circuit of the area by way of Alijó, across the Valeira dam, São João da Pesqueira, and back to Pinhão through the lower part of the Rio Torto valley.

These roads, with several short detours, will determine the order in which the quintas of the Cima Corgo are dealt with in this section, thus:

1   Régua to Pinhão – south bank
2   Régua to Pinhão – north bank
3   The Rio Pinhão Valley
4   Pinhão to Valeira – north bank
5   Valeira to Pinhão – south bank
6   The Rio Torto Valley

Reference to the map on pages 58-9 should help the reader to orientate himself.

1 Régua to Pinhão – south bank

From Régua, heading towards Pinhão on the south bank, we pass the

Régua dam and the mouth of the Rio Temilobos. We are now in the Cima Corgo. Past the Quinta dos Frades and Folgosa we come to the mouth of the Rio Tedo. A road on its left bank takes us to the Quinta de Nápoles, belonging to Niepoort & Ca, Lda.

Quinta de Nápoles

According to tradition this is one of the oldest of the Douro quintas, its name deriving from the family to which it belonged for almost five hundred years. According to Augusto Leal, the Nápoles family came originally from Sarzedo in the *concelho* of Moimenta da Beira (hence the Quinta do Sarzedo, once an alternative name), acquiring the property in 1496 on the expulsion of the Jews from Portugal by Dom Manoel.[1]

Undoubtedly within the 1757 *feitoria*, Nápoles was demoted to wine at 19,200 *réis* in 1758.[2] However, after its owner Luís Joseph Machado Ferreira had petitioned in 1759,[3] it was reinstated in 1761. A stone marker in front of a mill whose ruins are still within the quinta has now disappeared, but another, which was in the custody of Luís Ferreira, survives in the neighbouring Quinta de Castelo de Borges. Forrester marked the quinta on his map.

Leal, writing in 1886, tells us that the quinta is 'completely infected with *phylloxera* and in ruin, and, being poorly administered and badly tended, has not for many years produced a third of the wine it could and should produce'.[4] At this time its proprietor was José de Lemos de Nápoles Manoel.

It seems that over the last hundred years the quinta has been condemned to periodic decline. In 1941, when it belonged to Dona Felismina do Carmo Barboso and her husband, we learn from Cordeiro that the quinta was 'presently being replanted due to the state of abandon to which it was consigned for several years'. He continues: 'it was acquired two years ago[5] by the present owners who have spent a lot of money on its renovation; at the moment, however, it has a much diminished production'.[6] Whether this programme of renewal was fully carried out is doubtful. If so, a further decline appears to have occurred. From about 1953 until 1961 Mackenzie & Co (now absorbed into J H Andresen Sucrs, Lda) rented the quinta house and the *lagares*, but seldom bought the quinta wine which, by then, had no reputation whatsoever.[7]

Thus, when the quinta was purchased by Niepoort from Dr António Mesquita Carvalho de Magalhães in 1988, it was again extremely run down, its idiosyncratic house empty and decaying. Niepoort, however, are determined to turn the quinta round and re-establish its erstwhile reputation, and they have lost no time in carrying out the first stage of a total restructuring of the vineyards to make them completely mechanized.

Had you looked across the Tedo at Nápoles in 1989 you would have seen a charming picture of olive trees, woodland and a few traditional walled terraces, surmounted by the quinta buildings on the crest of a small knoll. In 1990 the picture was quite different.

Opposite, above
11
Quinta de Vargellas seen from the top of the quinta. The quinta house is on the centre right; the new *refectório* and living accommodation are on the centre left; and the *adega* is the long building with the white roof on the extreme left

Opposite, below
12
Quinta do Panascal. The house stands amongst almond trees and old terraces

Overleaf
13
The Rio Pinhão where it joins the Douro, with the Quinta da Foz on the right

There were fewer traditional terraces, and, where previously there had been *mortórios*, you would have seen *patamares* newly carved out of the hillside.

The quinta buildings stand by the entrance to the quinta. To the left is the *adega*, its *lagares* with slate bottoms and granite sides. In front is the quinta house, with a large *armazém* at ground level. Its old casks, having been empty for years, have been reconditioned and now share their quarters with pump-over cylinders installed for the 1989 vintage. The house has heavily fretted overhanging eaves, which give it a vaguely alpine look. Present plans are to renovate and enlarge it for public relations use. The *patamares* have just been planted, one quarter of them experimentally (perhaps a surprisingly high percentage) with varieties other than the five now almost universally adopted for new plantations. No decision has yet been taken about how the wine they produce will be utilized. What can be said is that a start has been made on the renovation of the quinta – one which, it is to be hoped, will last longer than some previous ones.

Returning to the Douro, we continue towards Pinhão. Shortly a sign on our right indicates the entrance to the Quinta de São Luiz, belonging to Barros, Almeida & Ca, Vinhos, SA.

Quinta de São Luiz

Large letters on the wall of the *armazém* proudly proclaim 'Founded in 1638', leading one to suppose that this must be another venerable Douro quinta. It seems all the more surprising, therefore, that there are no references to it in the nineteenth-century literature on quintas. Even Vila Maior hurries past with a bland excuse: 'our attention is arrested by many Quintas . . . but . . . we cannot tarry long'![1]

The mystery is solved when one discovers that São Luiz was previously owned by C N Kopke & Ca, Lda, a firm purchased (with the quinta) by Barros in 1952. The year 1638 was when Kopke was founded, and has nothing at all to do with the quinta!

When Barros acquired São Luiz it already incorporated the Quinta de Dom Pedro and the Quinta da Fonte Santa, which had been purchased by Kopke in 1937. Through the latter we can learn something about São Luiz in the mid-eighteenth century.

Although it is presumed that the south bank of the Douro between the Rio Tedo and the Rio Távora was included in the *feitoria* in 1757, in 1758 this part of the river was demoted to wine at 19,200 *réis*. Amongst the protesting petitioners in 1759 were Luís Joseph de Almeida, the owner of Fonte Santa, asking for reinstatement on the grounds that, the previous year, he had sold his wine for 25,000 *réis*, the highest price which the purchaser had paid within the district.[2] Another petitioner was Joseph António da Costa, the owner of a quinta next to Fonte Santa, asking for recognition because he had always sold wines of good repute to foreigners.[3] Both properties were included in the *feitoria* in 1761.

It is clear from the schedule of the 1761 demarcation that the

Opposite, above
14
Quinta da Terra Feita. Behind the buildings is Terra Feita da Cima which Taylor has recently acquired

Opposite, below
15
The house at Quinta de Nápoles prior to restoration

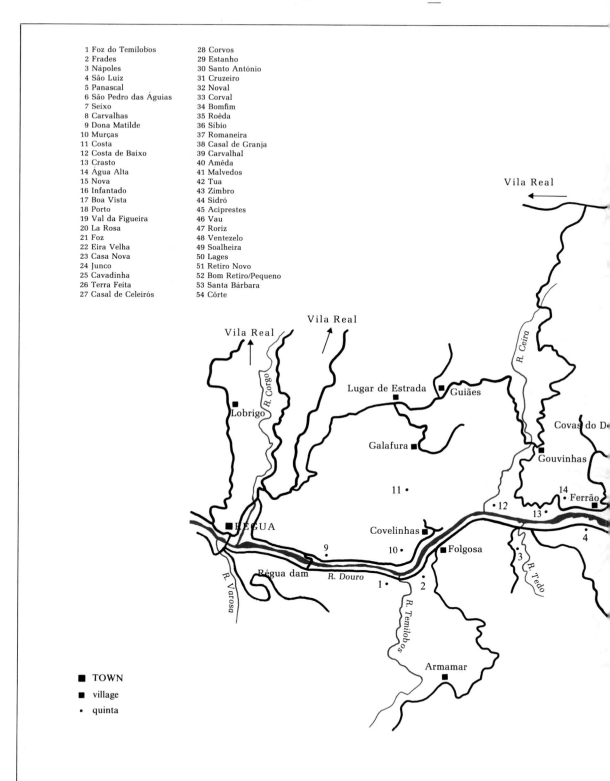

1 Foz do Temilobos
2 Frades
3 Nápoles
4 São Luiz
5 Panascal
6 São Pedro das Águias
7 Seixo
8 Carvalhas
9 Dona Matilde
10 Murças
11 Costa
12 Costa de Baixo
13 Crasto
14 Agua Alta
15 Nova
16 Infantado
17 Boa Vista
18 Porto
19 Val da Figueira
20 La Rosa
21 Foz
22 Eira Velha
23 Casa Nova
24 Junco
25 Cavadinha
26 Terra Feita
27 Casal de Celeirós

28 Corvos
29 Estanho
30 Santo António
31 Cruzeiro
32 Noval
33 Corval
34 Bomfim
35 Roêda
36 Sibio
37 Romaneira
38 Casal de Granja
39 Carvalhal
40 Amêda
41 Malvedos
42 Tua
43 Zimbro
44 Sidró
45 Aciprestes
46 Vau
47 Roriz
48 Ventezelo
49 Soalheira
50 Lages
51 Retiro Novo
52 Bom Retiro/Pequeno
53 Santa Bárbara
54 Côrte

■ TOWN
■ village
• quinta

The Cima Corgo

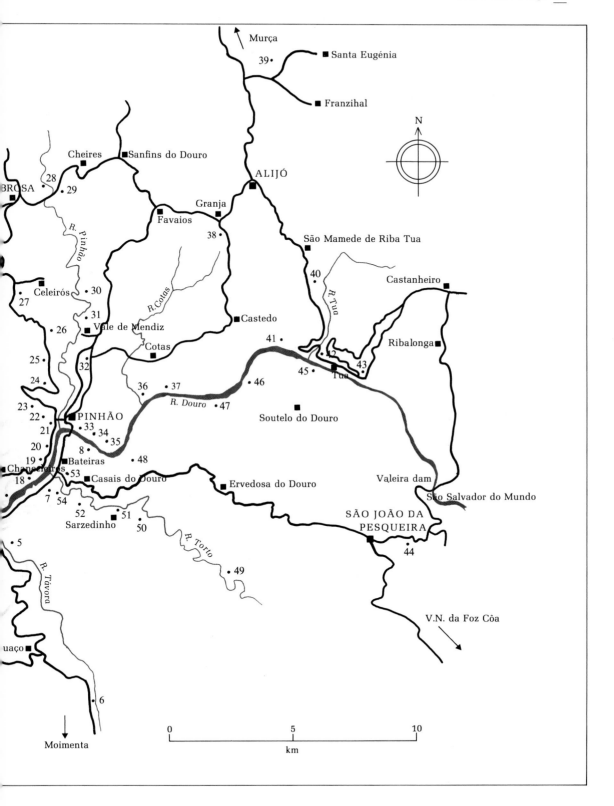

Murça

39 •

■ Santa Eugénia

■ Franzihal

N

■ Cheires   ■ Sanfins do Douro

BROSA •
28 •
    • 29

ALIJÓ
■

Granja
Favaios   • 38

São Mamede de Riba Tua

R. Pinhão

40 •

Castanheiro ■

Celeirós
27 •   • 30

31 •
Vale de Mendiz
26 •

R. Cotas

■ Castedo

41 •

Ribalonga ■

Cotas

R. Tua

25 •
     32
24 •

36 • • 37

• 46

45 •
42 •
43 ■
Tua

23 •
22 • PINHÃO ■
21 •   • 33
       • 34
20 •   8 • • 35

R. Douro   • 47

•
Soutelo do Douro

19 •
Chanceleiros ■ • 48
18 •   53 • Bateiras
                Casais do Douro

■ Ervedosa do Douro

Valeira dam

São Salvador do Mundo

7 • 54 •
     52 • • 51
Sarzedinho   50 •

R. Torto

SÃO JOÃO DA
PESQUEIRA ■

• 5

R. Távora

• 49

44 •

V.N. da Foz Côa

uaço ■

• 6

0   5   10

Moimenta

km

boundaries of the vineyards it cites in this area do not correspond to today's realities,[4] from which we must conclude that São Luiz did not exist at this time as a single quinta. By the end of the century, however, São Luiz had come into being and its first recorded owner, from 1800 until 1830, was João Varandas.[5] Thereafter it entered the period of obscurity remarked on above, to emerge again in 1922, when it was acquired by Kopke, who continued to own it until it was sold to Barros.

The quinta house, though almost two centuries old, has been twice remodelled since the Second World War, and this has masked its original character: a parapet hides the traditional tile roof, and the windows are modern in style. To compensate, however, there are pots and troughs of flowers scattered all over the quinta. Their vivid hues, thrown into bright relief against the whitewashed walls, make São Luiz perhaps the most riotously colourful and floral of all the quintas in the Douro.

The house, with some charming old painted Alentejo furniture, provides a comfortable and unpretentious setting for company entertaining. Outside there is a big terrace for relaxing in the cool of a summer's evening whilst looking down the river or across to Crasto and Água Alta.

Behind the house is the tiny chapel, which is still in use. The quinta no longer has its own private chaplain, though within living memory it did. Apparently the priest, who had to travel some distance, was thoughtfully furnished with a horse. When he relinquished his post he disappeared, having sold the horse and pocketed the proceeds. Fortunately his successor had a motor car!

At a slightly higher level, behind the chapel, are some storage *balões*, and the *adega* and *armazém*. The concrete autovinifiers, installed by Barros between 1958 and 1960, shortly after acquiring the quinta, are used with a circulation pump and heat exchange temperature control. It is planned, however, to replace these in the very near future with stainless steel pump-over tanks with temperature control. The *lagares*, last used in 1973, have now been destroyed. There is extensive storage in the quinta, but the new wines all go down to Gaia within the year.

The quinta vineyards are quite steeply sloped and undulate along the river bank. When Barros acquired the quinta it had some 120 ha of very crowded plantings. However, with the acquisition of the Quinta da Mesquita in 1972, the Quinta da Lobata in 1974, the Quinta da Alegria in 1982, and the Quinta da Galeira in 1987, the area of São Luiz has now been considerably extended.

Conversion of the original, traditional terraces for mechanization was begun in 1977. Presently about a third of the whole (mainly recently acquired land) consists of *patamares*, while in the old Quinta da Alegria there is some vertical planting. There are plans for the extensive replanting of the original quinta to increase mechanization further. (Barros are particularly proud of the sophistication of their mechanization.)

Kopke produced a vintage port on whose label the quinta name appeared, and Barros resumed the tradition with their 1970 single quinta vintage. When not used for this, the wine is aged separately to become an old tawny, or occasionally a *colheita*.

Continuing towards Pinhão, we come to another river, the Rio Távora. A road on the right bank of the river leads to the Quinta do Panascal, belonging to Fonseca-Guimaraens, Vinhos, SA.

Quinta do Panascal

De Roncão e Panascal vêm os melhores vinhos do Portugal. 'The best wines of Portugal come from Roncão and Panascal' – thus a local saying reflects a long established pride in the wine from the Rio Távora. Indeed, its reputation was already established in the eighteenth century, when Rebello da Fonseca wrote that 'in the whole of this territory there are not to be had more agreeable and delicate table wines'. Vila Maior, speaking of their 'estimable qualities'[1] concurs, and Fonseca-Guimaraens (no relation, of course, to Rebello) are entirely of the same opinion. All of which explains why, in 1978, Fonseca were delighted to be able to purchase the quinta.

Panascal was the second quinta to be acquired by Fonseca: Cruzeiro came in 1973 and Santo António the year after, in 1979. Unlike some other shippers who have recently bought quintas with which they have not had any long-term connection, Fonseca's purchasing philosophy is to acquire only quintas which have supplied them for many years, and on the quality of whose port their own high reputation rests. They had previously bought from Panascal for some twenty years, though the quinta was purchased in the knowledge that it would require almost complete renovation.

Prior to 1979, Panascal had belonged to the Pacheco family (cousins of the owners of the Quinta da Côrte) for forty-seven years – latterly to Coronel José Pacheco. Before that nobody seems to know. Situated on land just outside the *feitoria*, the quinta appears to be of comparatively recent foundation. Vila Maior mentions Panascal in 1869 only as a district with five small-holders,[2] and the quinta is probably a later amalgamation of their vineyards.

Kol d'Alvarenga, writing in the 1920s, gives a brief description of Panascal, still with *mortórios* and half-ruined houses, but with 'well-cared-for new buildings, with a patio in front, and the name of the quinta in black on a wall'. The wine, which he says was of great renown before *phylloxera*, he describes as being one *com tripas* – with guts.

The typically bumpy road to the quinta passes under a depressing *mortório* – one of the many to be seen along the banks of the Távora. Here the river is narrow, its bank rising steeply on the opposite side. Entering the property, the road snakes up to the eighteenth century quinta house, recently renovated for the farm manager – d'Alvarenga's 'new buildings'! – its *adega* and *armazém* placed, contrary to tradition, side by side under the upper domestic floor. Its situation, overlooking the Távora, is a pleasant one. Beneath the house there is a granite water tank which is reckoned to be over 200 years old. It is fed from a spring and holds 400 pipes, so the quinta is never without water.

Since acquiring the quinta Fonseca have undertaken a big programme of renovation and development, and the purchase of the Quinta do Val dos Muros in 1985 has added a useful 15 ha. Of the original vineyards only some terraces by the river remain, and these have been re-grafted. Apart from a small amount of vertical planting, the rest of the vines are on *patamares* and fully mechanized.

To get a proper impression of the extent of the property you should take the road on the other side of the Rio Távora. Reaching Santo Aleixo, the road curves left following a bend of the river, and from here you have the best view of all. The farm buildings are down below: opposite and above are the *patamares*.

In 1989 it could not have been claimed that this was the most beautiful sight in the Douro, but it was certainly one of the most arresting: raw, stark-looking *patamares*, their shoulders not as yet disfigured by weeds and chiselled out of the hill-side like a gigantic piece of modern sculpture the colour of burnt sienna. A carbuncle? Perhaps; but impressive, nonetheless, as powerful evidence of man's ability to shape nature to his own needs.

The *lagares* have not been used since 1978 because of problems caused by the intense heat at Panascal during the vintage. From 1979 (except between 1985 and 1988, when it was made at Salgueiral, in Régua[3]) the port was made at the Quinta de Vargellas. However, with the use of a cooling pump, it is intended to bring the *lagares* back into use for the 1991 vintage. Small quantities of single quinta vintages ('77 and '78) were made experimentally, before the purchase of the quinta, from grapes grown in the old vineyard, and, proving successful, they have been released on the market, as has an '83.

Taking the road to Tabuaço on the opposite bank of the Rio Távora, we continue towards Moimenta under the granolithic cliff face of the Penedos do Fradinho, until, just within the southern extremity of the demarcated area, we reach our next destination.

Quinta do Convento de São Pedro das Águias

A little road on our left winds down to a charming, detached cluster of buildings dominated by the monastic church. A black metal gate set in a tall, creeper-covered wall, and beneath a stone cross, opens onto a courtyard: to our right, a large *tanque* constantly being filled with water, whose splashing gives an air of cool tranquillity to the scene; to our left, a little rose garden, bordered by clipped box and yew hedges, behind which is the low, white quinta house built in the style of a *solar*; in front, the church, built of granite, its central green door surmounted by a niche containing an ancient painted statue of St Peter.

A low tower to the left of the church connects with a wing of the house, under which a door leads into a small, paved cloister. Through its arches we see another garden of clipped hedges, a pool at its centre mirroring a large wall sun-dial. A more peaceful scene it would be hard to imagine, unless, perhaps, it is the setting of the monastery itself, with its view across the river of bracken-covered hills devoid not only of all human habitation, but, alas, of *águias* (eagles).

The first monastic foundation under the order of São Bento, in the eleventh century, was actually in the neighbouring *freguesia* of Paradela, about a kilometre upstream. After the Bernardine reform the monastery was moved to its present site[1] and flourished until the expulsion of the religious orders in 1834, when all but the church, *lagares* and *armazéms* were destroyed by fire. According to a local tradition the removal of the statue of St Peter would lead to the destruction of the quinta, and, when it was removed by peasants in 1834, it is said that the walls of the church began to tremble. The statue was quickly restored.

São Pedro das Águias was rated for wine at 10,500 *réis* in the 1758 demarcation.[2] Prior to the fire it appears that the quinta was rented for a while, in 1818, by António Bernardo Ferreira (uncle and father-in-law of Dona Antónia Ferreira) then at the outset of his career.[3] After the fire the monastery remained in ruins until the last part of the nineteenth century, when it was rebuilt purely as a farm, with 'the church adapted to the noble functions of an *adega*'.[4] In December 1986, it was acquired, in a run down state, by its present owners, Quinta do Convento de São Pedro das Águias, Lda, a subsidiary of the French owned Vranken-Lafitte Group, proprietors of Charles Lafitte champagne.

The quinta, which now includes the Quinta do Paço and the Quinta Monte Redondo, has a frontage along both banks of the Rio Távora of some 11 km. The vineyards in front of the monastery are on broad terraces, descending quite steeply towards the river, but most of the vines are on new *patamares* upstream, where much of the land is on relatively gentle gradients.

The wine-producing installations are on the river side of the monastery, and they are at present undergoing reconstruction and enlargement. Although there are *lagares*, the wine is presently made in fermentation tanks at the neighbouring Quinta da Aveleira. As a departure from tradition, it is being matured in *barriques* of Limousin oak purchased from Château Margaux.

After only three years' activity, the quinta wine is not yet ready for marketing, but tawnies not from the quinta – ten and twenty years old, and without indication of age – are being sold under the São Pedro das Águias, do Paço and Monte Redondo names. They are exported only to France.

Returning to the Douro and continuing towards Pinhão, we come to a third river – the Rio Torto ('Twisted River') – where we find the Quinta do Seixo, belonging to A A Ferreira, SA.

Quinta do Seixo

The Quinta do Seixo crowns the hill on the left bank of the Rio Torto, where it joins the Douro. As one can see from old engravings, it is a dominating position and 'the handsome and snowy edifices of this Quinta'[1] have always been a landmark. What catches the eye today, alas, is an ugly array of stainless steel tanks and a new *adega* built in 1980. It is a sad change. Even the handsome old gateway, illustrated by Vizetelly, has now been by-passed.

It appears that there was no Quinta do Seixo at the time of the Pombaline demarcations. That part of the present quinta facing the Douro, whether or not it was in the 1757 demarcation, was rated at 19,200 *réis* in 1758, the demarcation listing the owners of four vineyards. One of them, the Reverend José Ribeiro Monteiro, unsuccessfully petitioned for inclusion in the *feitoria* in 1759, and the 1761 demarcation confirmed the status quo. As for the slopes facing the Rio Torto, they were rated at 10,500 *réis* in both 1758 and 1761.[2]

The quinta, which is marked on Forrester's map, was either formed or renamed by the Barão de Seixo, to whose family it belonged in the mid-nineteenth century,[3] and from whom it was acquired by the firm of Miguel de Sousa Guedes,[4] probably in the late 1880s, shortly after the Quinta das Carvalhas.[5]

There is a story that Sousa Guedes was one day in the company of C N Skeffington, a partner in Taylor, Fladgate and Yeatman, and, as they passed Seixo, Skeffington remarked that he was thinking of purchasing it for the firm. He subsequently found that Sousa Guedes had beat him to it – the consequence being that, instead of Seixo, Taylor purchased Vargellas. Whether the story is true is another matter.

Vizetelly went to the quinta in the Barão's time, passing through the 'imposing gateway, surmounted by the armorial bearings of its owner'.[6] His visit coincided with the vintage, during which he heard a song called *Marianinha* which, he tells us, had been banned by the Oporto authorities for the impropriety of some of its verses. I am told that it is still sung today. He also reported that *phylloxera* was rife, with the yield much down from its erstwhile 300 pipes.

The buildings, apart from the new *adega*, have probably changed little since Vizetelly visited Seixo. They are built in a line down the slope, with, at the top, the pretty little eighteenth century chapel and quinta house which, he says, 'has a certain air of pretension about it' (the interior has massive carved wooden doors and wooden ceilings), and the humbler offices ranged below.

The vineyards, on the other hand, have changed beyond recognition. Having been reconstructed by Sousa Guedes,[7] they have once more been radically revamped by Ferreira, who purchased the quinta in 1979 from the heirs of José Maria de Castro Sousa Guedes, who was Miguel's son. Only a third of the old walled terraces remain, and, with over half the quinta now vertically planted, Seixo is one of the comparatively few large quintas planted in this way.

Sousa Guedes marketed a port with the quinta name, but, except for a single year, Ferreira have not continued this tradition. Currently the best grapes are used for port, which contributes to their vintage and top grade blends, while the balance of the harvest is amalgamated

Opposite
16
Quinta do Junco, its white buildings dominating the skyline

Overleaf
17
A worker carries a *gigo*, one of the large baskets used at harvest time to transfer grapes from the vines to the *lagares* (or to intermediate transport). When full, these baskets weigh about 60 kg

with locally purchased grapes to produce a red Douro table wine called 'Esteva'.

From Bateiras, where the Rio Torto joins the Douro, it is a short distance to Pinhão. On the right, just before crossing the bridge over the Douro, is the entrance to the Quinta das Carvalhas, which belongs to the Real Companhia Velha.

Quinta das Carvalhas

The Quinta das Carvalhas has a prominent position on the left bank of the Douro facing Pinhão. Its frontage stretches from opposite the Quinta da Roêda down to where the river sweeps round in a left-hand curve opposite the Quinta da Foz. It covers the whole of the hillside facing the Douro, extends over the summit – which is crowned by the dominating Casa Redonda, visible for miles around – and occupies part of the upper slopes of the right bank of the Rio Torto. It is almost certainly the largest quinta in the whole of the Douro region,[1] and it is undoubtedly the jewel in the crown of its owners, the Real Companhia Velha.

Dating back at least to the beginning of the eighteenth century, it was originally called the Quinta da Deveza and belonged for a time to the influential Castro e Sande family of São João da Pesqueira. In 1759 Manuel Leme de Castro e Sande unsuccessfully petitioned to have his wines (at 19,200 réis) placed in the *feitoria*.[2] Carvalhas is marked on Forrester's map.

Vila Maior tells us that in 1869 it was owned by the Barão de Chanceleiros,[3] but by 1876 its owner was a Sr Borges of Lisbon;[4] Vizetelly, the following year, says that its production (usually purchased by Sandeman) 'does not exceed 70 pipes',[5] but by 1880 the ravages of *phylloxera* had created 'conditions of true decadence and destruction',[6] and the production fell to 26 pipes.

In this year Carvalhas was purchased by Miguel de Sousa Guedes,[7] who, predictably, mounted a long, radical, and formidably expensive rescue operation. *Phylloxera* had not yet run its course, and in 1883 production plummeted to 8 pipes.[8] Thereafter, as work on new terracing and plantations progressed, and access roads were installed throughout the quinta, the figures show a rapid turn-around. By 1885 there were 34 pipes, and ten years later 211 – and all this without recourse to grafting. Monteiro remarks that the universal reputation of the wine on foreign markets was a matter of 'justifiable pride to Sr Sousa Guedes, who, in his fierce zeal to preserve the admirable and genuine qualities of his famous product, maintained the cultivation of indigenous vines over tens of years without grafting them with *americano* rootstock, thanks to expensive treatment using carbon disulphide'.[9]

Work on the improvement of the existing installations, and the provision of new ones, was carried out simultaneously – stables, an *azenha* dated 1898, then and possibly still the best in the Douro, *cardenhos*, additions to the old quinta house, an office, quinta kitchen,

Previous page
18
An *ajulejos* (tile) panel in the *casa dos lagares* at Quinta da Foz showing a vintager carrying a *gigo*

Opposite
19
The gatehouse of the Quinta de São Luiz

a remodelled *adega* (with three large *lagares*, now removed) and an *armazém*. These are essentially the buildings in use today.

Not content with this, Sousa Guedes continually added to the size of the quinta by incorporating others, starting with the Quinta das Baratas in 1886. Its old *armazém*, at the end of the bridge spanning the Douro, is now the gatehouse and main entrance to the quinta. Thereafter came the quintas das Covádas, do Zeferino (or de Santo António) in 1899, das Monteiras in 1926, and later still das Galgas, da Cascalheira, da Plombeira and, lastly, da Cruz de Ventozelo in 1972.

In 1975 Miguel de Sousa Guedes & Irmão Lda (as the company was known after 1909) became part of the Real Companhia Velha, whose dynamic president is Sr Manuel da Silva Reis. The task of replanting 150 ha of largely traditionally terraced vineyards is, however, a daunting one, and so far only a tenth have been renewed (some with vertical planting), with less than half of that mechanized. The remaining vines date from the Sousa Guedes era and much, clearly, remains to be done.

Nevertheless, since 1985 more than 500 pipes of port have been produced each year, with a record 533 pipes in 1987, made in the quinta's autovinifiers. The quinta wine goes into the Real Companhia's vintage blend; otherwise it is used for other premium ports, and some is aged to produce the single quinta tawny which made its first market appearance in 1989 – though a sweet tawny with no indication of age was also marketed under the Quinta das Carvalhas label some years ago. Apart from this, a port under the name Quinta da Cruz is marketed exclusively in France.

Seen from Roêda, across the Douro, the main cluster of white quinta buildings cannot claim much architectural distinction. With its strong horizontal emphasis, it looks like something between a ship moored against the river bank and a bathing lido. (There is indeed a swimming pool – the largest of any quinta I know.) This effect is caused by the adjacent *cardenhos*, whose tiered galleries give the ensemble a deck-like aspect. Behind the buildings, on the relatively steep slopes, rise the many vineyards intermixed with olive groves which, closer to the summit, give way to woodland.

From the main gate to the quinta house is exactly one kilometre, along a drive lined on both sides with orange trees (replacing the eucalyptus trees noted by Monteiro). As you reach the house the first thing to strike the eye is the spectacular *azulejos* (celebrating the centenary of the founding of Sousa Guedes's company in 1851) on the side of the two-storey chapel, which stands to the west of the house.

The house is both airy and spacious, with its first floor rooms opening on to a broad terrace facing the river. It is very much a family house, full of family pictures and photographs, and fascinating collections of bric-á-brac. Here there are old painted and gilded curtain cornices, wooden chests, pottery jugs and teapots; over there we find small collections of flat-irons and wooden shoes; all contributing to a highly personal and informal atmosphere.

Probably to any new visitor to the region, the most fascinating aspect of Carvalhas is the Casa Redonda. This large, circular building looks from the distance as if it could be a meteorological station, set in a commanding position on the Cabeça das Monteiras at the top of the quinta. From its surrounding terrace there are spectacular panoramic views over a sizeable part of the vicinity – the Rio Torto valley, much of the Douro, and up the Pinhão valley to Quinta do Noval and beyond. Contrary to popular belief, the twenty year old Casa Redonda is no longer used as a house. It has just undergone a huge transformation intended to cater for special sight-seeing trains with the installation of a glassed-in panoramic floor on top, and a restaurant to seat five-hundred people below. It appears, therefore, that many more people will in future have the opportunity of visiting the quinta and of seeing for themselves these marvellous, bird's-eye views of the port country.

2 Régua to Pinhão – north bank

Back in Régua, we leave by the road we took for the Quinta de Avidagos, but after crossing the Rio Corgo we turn right for Covelinhas. Just after the Régua dam we come to the Quinta Dona Matilde, belonging to Barros, Almeida & Ca, Vinhos, SA.

Quinta Dona Matilde

The Quinta Dona Matilde, formerly the Quinta do Enxodreiro, was bought by Manuel Moreira de Barros in 1927. He had married Matilde, the sister of his employer (later partner) Manuel Almeida, and it was in honour of his wife (and mother of the present head of the firm) that he later renamed the quinta.[1]

Dona Matilde is, in fact, a very old quinta which was within the original *feitoria*,[2] Owned at this time by Manoel de Silveira Pinto, it is described as being oval in shape and walled.

The quinta, which is marked on Forrester's map, has always had the reputation of being difficult to work. In 1875, Leal tells us that 'the wine of this quinta is very fine [although its cultivation] . . . being situated on the terrible slopes of Pedro Caldeira,[3] must be very costly on account of the steepness of the terrain and its being composed of schistous rock'.[4] At this time the quinta belonged to another Manuel da Silveira Pinto – presumably still the same family, which also owned the neighbouring Quinta dos Murças.

The quinta house was in ruins when acquired by Barros, and the present house is modern. The Barros family has always used Dona Matilde as a family retreat, and it has unusual recreational features. Behind the house and down-river there is a little arboretum, perfect for an after-lunch walk, while a reservoir tank, with water pumped from the river, doubles as a swimming pool. At the top of the quinta, adjacent to the Canelas road, there is an old *miradouro*: the view, sadly, has been spoiled not so much by the dam as by the hideous, derelict silica-processing factory between the dam and the property.

The quinta has something of an 'S' shape, having both a re-entrant and, on the west, a spur of land. About 4 ha of existing terraces have just been re-planted, most of the other planting having been carried out in 1972. Since 1980 the quinta has included the Quinta da Carvoeira, as yet undeveloped.

Economic necessity now dictates that the grapes are taken to be processed at the Quinta de São Luiz. Some wine is brought back to Dona Matilde for a year, and is mostly aged for tawny port, especially for the seven to eight year old tawny sold under the Quinta Dona Matilde name. This does not claim to be a single quinta port, though the back-bone of the blend does come from the quinta. It is sold mainly in Portugal.

Continuing to Covelinhas the road climbs, offering good views across the Douro. One passes the vineyards of the Quinta dos Murças on the left before the road comes back down almost to river level, where its quinta house is situated.

Quinta dos Murças

The Quinta dos Murças borders the Quinta Dona Matilde and extends, up-river, to the Quinta da Capela at Covelinhas. Opposite are many quintas, of which the most noteworthy are the Quinta dos Frades and the Quinta da Foz do Temilobos.[1] Originally in the 1757 *feitoria*, the land occupied by the quinta, except for a small area, was demoted in 1758 to wine at 10,500 *réis* or excluded altogether, and this was confirmed in 1761.[2]

The quinta is mentioned briefly by Vila Maior: it produced, he said, 'about 40 pipes of wine of superior quality' and belonged to Manuel da Silveira Pinto, whose family continued to own it (and the neighbouring Quinta do Enxodreiro) until the beginning of this century.[3] The family of the present owners purchased the quinta in 1940 from a firm called Tait & Co, which it may be presumed had acquired it from the Silveira Pintos. Over the years it has incorporated a number of other quintas, notably the Quinta do Vale de Figueira (not to be confused with the quinta of the same name belonging to Sr Hoelzer) and the Quinta do Campo Redondo, with the result that it is now one of the very few quintas in the Douro to have 300,000 or more vines and a *benefício* in excess of 500 pipes.

The quinta's owner, Sra Maria de Conceição Pinto de Azevedo, has had Eng° João Nicolau de Almeida (of Ramos-Pinto) as her consultant since 1977, and, under his guidance, the quinta is note-worthy for the extent of its vertical planting. Eng° de Almeida told me; 'The first vertical planting in the Douro was done here about forty-five years ago by a Swiss man who had been invited to do it by the owner. It was not a success, but it triggered my interest.'[4] A revival of this method was started in 1978, and now four fifths of the quinta is planted this way – even, with Eng° de Almeida's persuasion, some PDRITM plantings.

The combined *adega* and *armazém*, which is situated close to the railway and away from both the vineyards and quinta house, dates from the beginning of the century. Since 1956 the wine has been made in autovinifiers – the first ever in the Douro. Priority has so far been given to investment in the vineyards, but redevelopment of the *armazém* in the near future envisages the provision of a bottling line, laboratory, office and stockroom.

The quinta house, down by the riverside, is a U-shaped chalet with a terrace overlooking a small garden, the water, and (alas) the railway. Rather insignificant from the outside, it is surprisingly commodious within, and most charmingly decorated with numerous pictures and engravings.

The quinta sells about 85 per cent of its wine to shippers, but retains the remainder for a single quinta wine. A 1987 LBV was recently launched on the market, and others are to follow. The quinta is also experimenting with various grape varieties with a view to making table wine in the future.

As the road stops at Covelinhas we have to return to Régua and, staying on the left bank of the Rio Corgo, we take the road to Vila Real by way of Lugar de Estrada, beyond which a road on the right is signposted to Galafura. This takes us to the Quinta da Costa belonging to Aida Coimbra Aires de Matos & Filhos, Lda.

Quinta da Costa

This quinta is redolent of tradition and is remarkable in a number of ways, not the least of which is the extreme difficulty of reaching it. Galafura stands at the head of the valley which goes inland from Covelinhas, on the Douro, but, despite talk of linking the two during the last thirty years, nothing has so far been done. This leaves the many vineyard owners in the valley without adequate road communications.[1]

To get to the Quinta da Costa I was taken down a very broken and rocky track, which according to local tradition is an old Roman road (though, if it is, it has been much altered). It leads down towards the Douro from Galafura through the Vale de Aveleira, along the steep slope of the left bank of the Ribeira de Covelinhas. Even when driven at a snail's pace, our Land Rover pitched and tossed, and frequently scraped its underside on the rocks in the ridge between the ruts which, when they had not disappeared in a sea of mud, served as an apology for a road.

Down this road, otherwise negotiable only by tractors, then back up it again, the vineyard workers daily make their way. All materials have to be brought along it, and, at the harvest, the grapes have to be brought up it. This is done in Land Rovers modified as pick-ups. I must say that I have seldom felt such a sense of adventure (or remoteness from civilization) when going to visit a quinta! Nothing has changed, if not from Roman times, at least from the not very far-off days when bullock-carts brought the wine down this road to the river.

The Quinta da Costa is about half-way down this valley, on the steep slope between the track and the little *ribeira*. It was in the original *feitoria*, its status being confirmed in 1761 by two marker stones which still stand at the northern limit of the property – one of them on the side of the road I have just described.[2] Its owners since before 1785, the Aires de Matos family, claim that it has 'the old configuration of Douro quintas in the time of the Marquês de Pombal'. Not for much longer: within the year its terraces will have become *patamares*.

What makes this quinta so fascinating, however, is not so much its remoteness as that it has, at its centre, the Armazém das Giestas Negras, which is almost certainly the oldest *adega* in the Douro. Illustrated on its owner's 'Valriz' label, its stone lintel bears the date 1575. The *adega* is roofless, but inside are the remains of an old slate *lagar*. The wine is now made in the modern *adega* which they built in Galafura in 1966. Part of their port production is sold to Sandeman, and the rest is retained for their own use.

Close to the Quinta da Costa are the quintas do Vermelho, Condessa, do Velal, da Cruz, Barroca, Laceira, Lamas and Fojo which, with some other vineyards, form the agricultural estate belonging to the family.[3] The estate extends to some 53 ha, with a production of 250 pipes, three fifths of which are made into port. Aida Coimbra Aires de Matos & Filhos have been bottling their table wines and port since 1984. Their ports – currently marketed only in Portugal – range from two dry whites to a more than forty year old tawny.

Back on the road to Vila Real, we take the next turning on the right to Guiães. Continuing down the east side of the Rio Ceira valley to rejoin the Douro, we find the Quinta da Costa da Cima, with its little chapel, and turn down a track to our right.

Quinta da Costa de Baixo

This quinta (Costa is the name of the area), which is almost midway between Régua and Pinhão, was always in the *feitoria* and has a granite marker of the 1758 demarcation within its bounds. It appears, however, that the marker may have been moved, for it is engraved with the name 'Melo', and this probably refers to the Quinta do Melo, marked on Forrester's map and incorporated in Costa de Baixo many years ago.[1]

The quinta belongs to a brother and sister, José Afonso and Maria Gabriel Bulas Cruz, having previously belonged to their father, and, prior to 1951, to Dr Emília Magalhães de Brito Ermida. It extends up the hill to border the Quinta da Costa da Cima, with a separate parcel of 5 ha on the other side of the public road. Since 1990 it has incorporated the Quinta da Foz Ceira, down the hill at the confluence of the rivers.

Entering the quinta through elaborate iron gates set in a massive granite arch surmounted by the date 1886, we have the 50 m long *armazém*, dated 1840, on our left, and the quinta house, presently being remodelled for *turismo de habitação*, directly in front. To the left of the new house is the *adega* and, behind it, the old very traditional quinta kitchen and *caseiro*'s house. On the Douro side of the house is an uncommonly well-preserved threshing floor, measuring about 17 metres square.

Just under half of the quinta is on block planted, mechanized *patamares*, the remainder being on old mixed planted terraces. Some of the old vine stock has been improved, but about 6 ha still need modernization. When Dr Bulas Cruz (who teaches computer science at the University of Vila Real) and his sister took over the quinta (prior to the new law of 1986) they decided they would like to sell some of their wine under their own label in Portugal. A tawny is now available, and as the new plantations mature it is hoped to offer a much bigger range. Only the best wine is kept for maturation on the quinta, the rest being sold to shippers.

A short distance along the road we see on the right a charming group of buildings on a neck of land leading to a small promontory which juts into the river.

Quinta do Crasto

With its natural strategic command of the river both up and downstream, it is not difficult to imagine this as the site of a Roman fort — for 'Crasto' is a corruption, it is said, of the Latin 'castrum', and the remains of a Roman road can still be seen at no great distance from the quinta.

Roman origins apart, Crasto is of considerable antiquity, There are references to it as far back as 1615, but it did not, it appears, belong either to a monastery or to a noble family. It was included from the start in the *feitoria*,[1] when it belonged to João Pacheco Pereira, a Customs House Judge in Oporto. Last century, according to a 150 year old letter still extant, the quinta wine was sold to Ferreira — a firm with which there is still a cordial relationship. In the present century, Crasto was bought in 1910 from the Sottomayor family by Constantino de Almeida, whose grand-daughter Leonor and her husband Jorge Roquette now run the quinta. Sr de Almeida was proprietor of the Sociedade dos Vinhos do Porto Constantino Lda, now part of Ferreira, and it is due to him that the present house and installations exist.

The quinta buildings are ranged picturesquely along the ridge of the promontory. Nearest the river is the chapel, built in 1811 and dedicated to Nossa Senhora das Necessidades: then comes an old *pombal*, now a water reservior; and next is the house, built shortly after Constantino de Almeida's acquisition of the quinta as a temporary residence, but still in use.[2] Next we find the *adega*, built in 1923, where the wine is made in the built-up *lagares* with a *movi-mosto* pump. Sr Roquette says he does not think that this method realizes the full potential of the wine, and he intends to change in the near future to pump-over tanks with cooling facilities, whilst retaining the *lagares* for his best grapes. Between the *adega* and the road we have, successively, the *armazém*, built a year after the *adega*, the *lagar de azeite*, and the *caseiro*'s house and quinta kitchen. The new *cardenhos* are in another part of the quinta.

Crasto now incorporates the Quinta do Reitor ('rector'), the Quinta do Sampaio, and the Quinta da Sobreira do Osso (or Quinta da Pasteleira).[3] None of these was in the *feitoria*, though the Quinta da Sobreira was raised from 10,500 to 15,000 *réis* in 1761.[4] In the nineteenth century this last also, coincidentally, belonged to the same proprietor as Crasto. Crasto and Pasteleira both appear on Forrester's map of the Douro.

The old terraces have mixed plantings while the new plantings, mainly in Reitor and Sobreira, were started in 1986. These – partly on *patamares* (to Sr Roquette's regret, for he is an enthusiast for vertical planting) done under PDRITM, and partly vertical – are block planted.

In the best years the production is kept for the quinta's own wine, and in other years it is sold to shippers. Although, in the past, the quinta has occasionally made vintage wines for family use – 1927 is still in the cellar – 1978 was the first single quinta vintage produced for commercial purposes, followed by '82, '85 and '87. Tawnies from the same years are also maturing, and it is hoped to extend the range by 1994.

Although a shipper offered to market the Crasto port as a single quinta, the decision had already been taken to enter the market independently. The project has begun modestly, though the quinta wines are already being exported to the United States.

Crasto is one of the quintas illustrated in the famous blue and white tile pictures which adorn Pinhão railway station.

No sooner have we turned out of the gate of Crasto than, on the left, we have our next quinta.

Quinta da Água Alta

The Quinta da Água Alta is up-river and slightly inland from the Quinta do Crasto. It is situated on both slopes of a re-entrant through which flows the Ribeiro do Bom Dia (also called the Ribeiro das Águas Altas). The quinta, which has been in the family for two centuries, now includes a number of others which were purchased by the grandfather of the present owner, Sr António Borges de Sousa: the Quinta do Carvalho; the Quinta de Espinhal da Cima, which is behind Água Alta; the Quinta do Vale de Nogueira, which is on the opposite side of the stream behind Crasto; and the Quinta do Vale de Sesões, which is behind Vale do Nogueira. Finally, the Quinta do Bom Dia, a separate property which came into the family from his mother's side, is situated behind Vale de Sesões.

There is no mention of a Quinta da Água Alta in any of the Pombaline demarcations, although, in 1757 there is mention of a Quinta Nova belonging to João Lopes de Carvalho which appears to have been on the site of Água Alta. This was, and continued to be, within the *feitoria*, but the area of Bom Dia was not: the intermediate quintas were rated for red wine at 15,000 *réis*. In 1758 the only change was that Bom Dia and the intermediate quintas all became 10,500 *réis*. In 1759 *two* quinta owners in the Bom Dia area had unsuccessfully petitioned for inclusion in the *feitoria*, but in 1761 they were rated at 15,000 *réis*, as were the intermediate quintas.[1]

Água Alta is marked on Forrester's map of the Douro. The quinta buildings, visible from the road, are simple and traditional. A track leads up to the *armazém* and *adega*, and from there a path leads to the *caseiro's* house, refectory and modern *cardenhos*. The *lagares* which are in use are situated in the Quinta de Espinhal da Cima, but the *lagares* which hold most interest are those in the ruined farm house at Bom Dia. Here there are two *lagares* fashioned out of huge, four metre slabs of slate, complete with a chestnut beam press *in situ*. Doubtless a few others survive in the Douro,[2] but these are the only examples with a beam which I have seen. Such presses were becoming obsolescent in Vila Maior's time. Sr Borges de Sousa intends to restore this *adega*, which is of considerable historical interest.

A third of the plantings are on *patamares*, the rest being on traditional terraces. Sr Borges de Sousa is keen to proceed with further mechanization, but he is far from convinced that *patamares* provide the final answer. The quinta enjoys a very hot micro-climate, and picking usually starts early.[3]

The Borges de Sousa family are large vineyard proprietors, particularly in the Celeirós area,[4] and it was through meeting Sr António's father, Sr Jorge Borges de Sousa, that John Graham found himself in a position to establish his shipping firm, Churchill Graham, Lda, the first new shippers for over fifty years. Having previously been bought mainly by Cockburn and Taylor, the port from Água Alta and other Borges de Sousa properties is now purchased by Churchill Graham. They offer the Quinta da Água Alta as a single quinta vintage, chosen to show a contrasting style to their declared vintage.

The road continues down to the railway station at Ferrão and then starts to climb again, and shortly we reach the entrance on the right to the Real Companhia Velha's Quinta Nova.

Quinta Nova

The Quinta Nova is in a shallow re-entrant down-stream from the Quinta da Boa Vista (Cachucha) and opposite the mouth of the Rio Távora and the Quinta de São Luiz. The land it occupies is more extensive now than it was at the time of the Pombaline demarcations. What was then the quinta was completely included in the *feitoria* in 1757 and 1758, but in 1761 the *feitoria* area was restricted to the immediate margin of the river. The part of the present quinta up-stream towards Cachucha was excluded in 1757 and 1758, but was rated at 10,500 *réis* in 1761.

Despite a misleading inscription *1764-1954* on the wall of one of the buildings, the quinta was clearly in being at the time of the 1757 and 1758 demarcations, in both of which it is specifically mentioned. The 1758 demarcation says that 'all of the quinta of the said João Lopes de Carvalho called the Quinta Nova is included in this demarcation'.[1] A 1758 stone marker still exists in the quinta.

The quinta is marked on Forrester's map, but it seems to have had an uneventful history during the nineteenth and twentieth centuries, having remained in the hands of the Carvalho family until its then owners, the heirs of Joaquim José de Carvalho, sold it in 1987 to the Real Companhia Velha.

The farm buildings form an attractive group, the most distinctive building being the tiny detached chapel, which is dedicated to Nossa Senhora de Carmo and bears the date 1795 over its door. The *lagares* are no longer in use, and the wine is autovinified. Apart from some PDRITM *patamares*, the rest of the quinta, being on very gentle slopes, has continuous planting.

The road now climbs out of the valley behind the Quinta Nova and, cresting a hill, descends into Covas do Douro, sitting at the head of another valley. Further on is Chanceleiros, where, on the right, is the adega of the Quinta do Infantado.

Quinta do Infantado

This area, called Gontelho, was on the fringes of the *feitoria* of 1757. In 1758 and 1761, however, it was rated for wine at 15,000 and 10,500 *réis*. Infantado dates from 1816, when the fine existing *armazém* was built, and, as its name suggests, it was owned by the Infante Dom Pedro (later one of the two brothers in the civil war of the same name). Forrester marks it on his map of the Douro.

At the beginning of this century the quinta was purchased by João Lopes Roseira, a Covas man with some vineyards in the locality. At that time Infantado consisted of about 40 ha, of which only 5 or 6 were planted. He also purchased the Quinta da Serra (now incorporated in the quinta), but then died suddenly at a young age. Fortunately his wife Dona Margarida Alice was a woman of very strong character and tenacity. As well as raising their three boys, whom she sent to college, she took over his debts and the running of the quinta. It was a struggle, but she even managed, when she had a little money, to buy some new parcels of land. She ran everything with rigorous precision, and died, in 1984, at the age of ninety-three.

Two of her three sons have had most to do with the quinta, the third, João, having moved south. António, whose son, also João, presently runs the quinta, had been in charge for four years when he went to Oporto to practice medicine and his brother Luís, another doctor, took over. A keen politician, he fell foul of the Salazár regime, but after the revolution he served as the Douro deputy on the council which framed the new constitution.

He had the idea of producing port like a Bordeaux château, and in 1979, when the outlook for independent producers was not that bright, he persuaded his mother and brother António to begin bottling a proportion of the quinta's wine with a view to selling it on the home market. Some other producers wanted to do the same thing, and out of this evolved the idea which, after a few years, took shape as AVEPOD.[1]

It was in 1979 that João, who is a trained agronomist, became involved in running the quinta. At the same time more purchases of land were made to make provision for enlarging the business, and today Infantado comprises about 110 parcels of land in the *freguesia* of Covas do Douro alone. In addition to vines, the Roseiras grow olives, fruit, and cereals and have land devoted to forestry and horticulture.

Much effort is going into the increased mechanization of the vineyards. About 10 ha of *patamares* have only one row of vines per terrace – to obtain maximum quality – which is almost new to the region. The policy is to avoid the use of herbicides as much as possible.

The *armazém* nestles within a small valley. It still has its original, traditionally constructed, oak roof, but the most impressive thing about it is its *cubas* and *toneis*, which have an average age of a hundred years, the oldest *tonel* being dated 1786. All the wine is kept in wood, and all the *toneis* bear the names of members of the family, in accordance with a charming custom of naming the *toneis* as children are born. One *tonel*, however, is named after Mário Soares, the President of the Portuguese Republic; he baptised it with a glass of port and signed it in chalk during a visit to Infantado on 21 July 1988.

Attached to the *armazém* is the *adega*, with granite *lagares* with embossed sides in which the wine is still made. João says, 'I think it makes the best quality, but I do not know for how long it will be possible to continue making the wine in this way. After working twelve hours in the vineyards people have to come and work another four hours in the *lagares*, and that has got to stop one day.' There are a few other out-buildings – the bottling is done in one of them – but, surprisingly perhaps, there is no quinta house of any description. The family has always lived in Covas.

The quinta wine used to be sold to Taylor and Sandeman. Exceptionally, some of it is still sold to shippers, but most is matured for the quinta's own produce. This is available across a wide range as an extra-dry white aperitif, ruby, tawny, twenty year old tawny, a 1977 *colheita*, a 1983 LBV, and five vintages from 1978 to 1985. A few numbered bottles are available for collectors. At the moment Infantado is exporting to the United States, Sweden, Spain, Germany, Holland, and a little to Great Britain.

Asked about the character of Infantado port, João pointed out that it is drier than normal. The different vineyards also give complexity to the wine, but, João continued, 'All our grapes come from Gontelho, which gives our wine a unity – an individuality. That is what is in danger of being lost when you blend grapes from many different places, however good they are. For us the individuality of our port is the most important consideration.'

Also in Chanceleiros, a road leads between two houses to the Quinta da Boa Vista, belonging to Forrester & Ca, Lda.

Quinta da Boa Vista

'The Quinta with the Fine View' – well, perhaps; though there are certainly finer views to be found. Boa Vista looks across the river at the Quinta do Pego and the Quinta do Espinheiro. Nevertheless it must be admitted that they do not enjoy quite such a good reciprocal view, for the dominant feature of the Boa Vista quinta buildings is a large, square and ugly *adega* built in 1977. It draws the eye, and, seeing the quinta from across the river, one is apt to overlook the charm of the traditional buildings alongside it.

The property as it now is comprises three quintas: Boa Vista, Cachucha and Ujo. Part, at least, was within the Pombaline demarcations. Ujo was within the 1757 *feitoria*, but only rated for wine at 10,500 *réis* in 1758. Its owner, Domingos Alves, unsuccessfully petitioned for reinstatement in 1759, but the rating was raised to 15,000 *réis* in 1761.[1] All three quintas appear on Forrester's map.

Having belonged to the firm of Offley, Webber and Forrester in the nineteenth century, the property passed out of its hands earlier this century and was only bought back again by Forrester (as the firm now styles itself) in 1979.

Prior to being acquired by Offley, Webber and Forrester last century, the Quinta da Boa Vista belonged to the Barão de Viamonte, and the Quinta da Cachucha to the Barão de Soavedra.[2] According to a verbal tradition within the firm, it had been buying the Boa Vista production for fifty years or more when it was decided to purchase the quinta from the Barão de Viamonte in the 1820s. It may therefore have belonged to the firm before Joseph Forrester joined it in 1831.[3]

It is amazing how little is really known about Joseph James Forrester, who perhaps did more than any other Englishman for the port trade, and who, even now, is more famous in Portugal than he is in England. Arriving in Oporto in 1831 to join his uncle's business, he soon made his presence felt. Talented in many directions, he published books and pamphlets about port (rather controversially, he originally opposed the fortification of the wine); he was a gifted artist and draughtsman, and was the first person to draw and print reliable maps of the Douro; he was an authority on *oïdium*; and for his services to port he was created a Portuguese *Barão* in 1855. Ironically, he was drowned in 1861 in the river to which he had devoted his life when, coming downstream to Régua with the famous Dona Antónia Ferreira on board, his boat capsized in the rapids of the Cachão de Valeira. As testimony to Forrester's enduring fame in his adopted country, during a three day progress down the Douro, on 20 July 1988, Dr Soares, the President of the Portuguese Republic, unveiled a commemorative bronze plaque fixed to one of the cliffs of the Cachão, after which he cast a wreath on the waters of the river.

It is rather odd, therefore, that, given Forrester's celebrity, Vila Maior does not even mention Boa Vista by name. On the other hand, when Vizetelly visited the quinta in 1877 he was clearly quite impressed by it.

The Quinta da Boa Vista ranks among the best quintas of the Upper Douro. Neither pains nor expense have been spared in its planting and cultivation and improving the primitive system of vinification which commonly prevails in this comparatively inaccessible region . . . Unfortunately the Boa Vista vineyard, which in good years used to give fifty or sixty pipes of fine wine, was attacked some five years ago by the phylloxera, and its production has now fallen off considerably.[4]

Two of Forrester's four sons – Frank and William – were by this time in charge of the firm. Sellers reports that 'the replanting of the vines has had the attention of the proprietors, who have devoted a very considerable amount of time and money to benefiting this celebrated Quinta'.[5] By all accounts it was a heroic task. 'Great importance [was] attached to deep trenching (*roteamento*), the schistous soil being turned over with a pick, shovel, and crowbar to the depth of 8 to 10 ft., resulting in many instances in the merging of five or six of the old terraces (*jeios*) into one, thus economizing space, and rendering cultivation more easy.'[6] This, in turn, had the effect of creating possibly the highest terraces in the Douro – 9 m high, as opposed to a normal maximum of 3.75 m, and without cement or binding material of any sort.[7]

In 1924 the last member of the family to be connected with the firm, John Offley Forrester, decided to sell out his share and leave Portugal. Three quarters of the company was purchased by an English consortium, whilst the other quarter remained with the Portuguese partners, of whom Dr Jacinto da Silva Pereira Magalhães had the biggest share of 62 per cent. It was a condition of the deal that the quinta (incorporating Cachucha and Ujo) remained with the Portuguese partners. Thereafter the history of its ownership became thoroughly confused. One partner, Manoel Maria Lucio, who had had a 14 per cent share in the quinta, left it on his death to the Seminário do Sagrado Coração de Jesus de Gaia, to which it still belongs. The principal share was inherited by Dr Jacinto Magalhães's daughters, the Marquesa da Foz and the Condessa de Cabral. They and the other Portuguese shareholders later sold to Eulalio José Fonseca of Amarante, although it later transpired that because he purchased through an attorney, he had failed to register the title to the quinta in his own name.

It was thus that matters stood in 1962 when Offley-Forrester (as the company then was) was acquired by Sandeman and Martini Rossi.[8] It was decided to buy back the quinta, but the intractable problems of sorting out the old deeds led to considerable delays. One attempt at purchase fell through at the last minute, and even when it was eventually purchased in 1979 – apart, that is, from the 14 per cent still owned by the Seminário – the title was still incomplete. José Bras was brought back from retirement to try to resolve the matter, and after months of unremitting hard work, combing through all the notaries in Lisbon, he was successful.[9]

The quintas of Cachucha and Ujo may have been added to the property towards the end of the nineteenth century after being bankrupted by *phylloxera*.[10] Cachucha sits downstream from Boa Vista (with Ujo further inland) and, according to Sr Bras, originally produced good sweet white wine. Its quinta house, which bears the date 1842 and has six *lagares*, is now in ruins.

Boa Vista sits in a curved, shell-like indentation formed by a recession of the hillside. Heat is accumulated in the shell, with a temperature which is generally 4–5 degrees higher than that at Pinhão, 5 km further up the river. This gives the quinta its own micro-climate, and Boa Vista is usually the first quinta to be harvested in the Upper Douro.[11] The traditional terracing has mixed plantings, and there has been no replanting here since Forrester took over. Part of the *patamares* are *mortórios* reclaimed under PDRITM. The part of the vineyard belonging to the Seminário is maintained by Forrester, who buy the produce.

The quinta buildings are quite close to the river, with the vineyards fanning out behind them, and the older buildings are being restored. Facing the river is the very prototype of a traditional Douro farmhouse as described in the Introduction. It is planned to use the restored building as a company guest house. Alongside, at right angles and separated from it by a pergola, is the modest building said to have been used by Joseph Forrester himself. Although this was restored externally in 1987, it remains a shell, but will become an annexe to the main farmhouse.

Just behind these buildings are the *caseiro's* house, old stores and outbuildings, and an old distillery (with two further *lagares*), whilst a little further back are the *cardenhos*. All are scheduled for re-development, and will provide a new kitchen, canteen and accommodation for permanent and temporary staff.

The modern *adega*, built in 1977 by the previous owner, contains pump-over tanks, originally autovinifiers. There is short-term stainless steel storage for the new wine, which is moved down to Vila Nova de Gaia as soon as possible after the vintage. This *adega* deals exclusively with the produce of the quinta, though for some time after Sandeman acquired the company the grapes were taken to be vinified at their *adega* at Celeirós.

Until 1979 the 'Boa Vista' label was only a trademark, but since then it has indicated a single quinta wine. Forrester are unique in releasing an LBV in the same years as they declare a vintage. Boa Vista used to be thought of as a lighter and quicker maturing vintage port than most, but the company claims that since it has all come from the quinta the vintage wine has become weightier.

Amongst its claims to fame, the quinta has possibly the first woman quinta technical manager in the Douro. When I asked Maria Rosário Janeiro if she had encountered any chauvinistic prejudice when she came to the Douro, she admitted that things had not been easy to begin with. The first time she visited Boa Vista on her own after her appointment as manager, the *caseiro* introduced her to his wife as the *wife* of the new manager! She had difficulty in persuading him to overcome his disbelief.

As we approach Pinhão, the next quinta we come to, on our right, is the Quinta do Porto belonging to A A Ferreira, SA.

Quinta do Porto

Just down-stream from the Quinta de la Rosa, and exactly opposite the Quinta do Seixo, stands the Quinta do Porto. To judge from its farm house, the quinta was probably founded in the eighteenth century. The ground on which it now stands was included in the *feitoria* in 1757, excluded altogether in 1758, and rated for wine at 10,500 *réis* in 1761. The quinta appears on Forrester's map.

Its modern history starts in 1863, when it was purchased by Dona Antónia Ferreira, one of the legendary figures of the nineteenth-century port trade. Born in 1811, she was the daughter of a wine merchant. In 1834 she married her cousin, António Bernardo, who also worked, though reluctantly, in the family wine business. His restless and artistic temperament drove him to foreign travel, and in 1844, at the age of thirty-two, he died suddenly in Paris. His widow, encouraged and supported by his father, began to take an active and successful part in running the family firm.

Her increasing social prominence, and the tenacity of her character, are well illustrated by the curious episode, starting in 1854, which resulted in her exile to England. Dona Antónia was approached by the Prime Minister, the Duque de Saldanha, Marechal of Portugal, with a proposal that her daughter, Maria da Assunção, aged twelve, should marry his son, although she was to remain in her mother's care until of legal marrying age. Dona Antónia declined, but invited the duke to wait until Maria da Assunção became of an age to make her own choice. The duke resorted first to bribery, by promising her the title of Condessa de Vesúvio, and then to threats. Dona Antónia fearful of her daughter's safety, heard one day that, on the duke's orders, Maria da Assunção was to be abducted that very night. While she and her daughter took refuge in the Convento das Chagas at Lamego, armed soldiers surrounded the Casa de Travassos, near Régua (where she had been born and still lived). The duke's men gave chase, and from Lamego Dona Antónia fled first to Vila Real, then, after a six days' trek through the mountains avoiding the roads, she and her daughter arrived in Vigo, to be welcomed by her agent Francisco José da Silva Torres, who had arranged a boat to take them to England.

After living in Brentwood for three years, she returned to Portugal not only with her daughter safely married to the Conde de Azambuja (grandson of Dom João VI), but herself married, a second time, to Francisco da Silva Torres, the faithful agent who had helped her in her hour of need.[1]

From this point Dona Antónia's affairs prospered. She continued the steady acquisition of quintas initiated by her uncle and her first husband, while constantly renovating existing ones and introducing innovations in all of them. Her reputation for fabulous wealth (she was certainly a multi-millionairess) was matched only by that of her charity. When she died in 1896 she was universally known by the affectionate diminutive, the 'Ferreirinha', still used today to refer not only to her but to Ferreira, the port firm which her heirs founded to carry on the work she had started.

Although other quintas are seen as her most significant achievements, the Quinta do Porto has a special importance for Ferreira because it is the only one still under their direct control. For this reason they have recently restored its charming old farm house to welcome their trade guests. Standing at the top of the quinta, the eighteenth-century part of the building is connected to a nineteenth-century addition by a large and traditional farm kitchen, now used as the main guest dining-room. The original part, with rooms with traditional octagonal wooden ceilings, contains some bedrooms, a small dining-room and a stylish and comfortable drawing room. Intriguing artifacts, books and china associated with the firm provide an effective and atmospheric décor.

Underneath these rooms is the *armazém,* containing the *toneis* in which some of the quinta wine is matured, and ajoining the house is the chapel. Until recently this was used as a dormitory for the *roga,* but it still retains its naïve ceiling painting and is at present undergoing a full restoration. The gallery of the chapel connects with the adjacent upstairs bedroom, and is a source of astonishment for the guests who open the door expecting to find a cupboard!

Behind the living accommodation, in traditional fashion, is an *adega* where, until 1988, all the quinta wine was made. Now, with labour shortages and an inevitable concern for cost efficiency, only a small amount continues to be made in the quinta, the rest of the grapes being vinified at the Quinta do Seixo. The wine is sold as a ten year old tawny quinta port.

It seems possible that the quinta was smaller when Dona Antónia bought it, or possibly the yields were still suffering from *oïdium:* only 6 pipes in 1865. Thereafter things began to improve, with the recorded yield building up from 16 pipes in 1866 to 52 in 1873, a record not exceeded before the end of the century. *Phylloxera* struck in 1878, and the next recorded yield was for 1881 – a mere 3 pipes. In 1883 the Commission for Phylloxera (*Comissão Filoxérico*) actually made the Quinta do Porto its Douro base. For the ten years thereafter the recorded figures fluctuate between 4 and 9 pipes, with 10 in 1891, '95 and '98, 11 in 1894, 13 in 1892 and '97, 16 in 1893, and an exceptional 28 in 1896. As can be seen, it took a long time for the effects of *phylloxera* to work themselves out.[2]

The vineyards, which stretch below the house almost down to the river, are a mixture of traditional terraces, beautifully and solidly constructed, and *patamares.* Tucked into the hillside beneath the approach drive to the farm house is a new and, at present, very unsightly house for the *caseiro.*

Outside the quinta house is a well-kept lawn and, still unusual in the Douro, a swimming pool. Inside, the presence of Dona Antónia, whose indomitable personality is still very much part of the Ferreira image, can still be felt. Her photograph surveys the drawing room from above the fireplace, and I believe she would be pleased with what she can see.

Not far along the road, on the left, is the Quinta de Val da Figueira.

Opposite
20
Quinta do Crasto. Standing on a promontory, the quinta buildings are seen across the Douro strung out on the horizon

Overleaf
21
The house at Quinta do Vesúvio, with the exotic palm tree which dominates its front court

Quinta de Val da Figueira

The Quinta de Val da Figueira, which Forrester marks on his map, goes back at least to the middle of the eighteenth century. In 1759 its owner, Pedro da Silva, petitioned for inclusion within the *feitoria*. Although the deputies favoured the request, it is curious that of all the many dozens of such petitions this is the only one of which we do not know the result![1] For almost a century and a half thereafter the quinta recedes into the mists of history, until it again had a brief moment of prominence. A tile plaque, placed on the wall of the *adega* in 1940, records that 'after the destruction of the vineyards of the Douro by *phylloxera*, it was at this Quinta de Val da Figueira that the first American vines were experimentally planted by Dr Joaquim Pinheiro de Azevedo Leite Pereira, the true saviour of the Douro Region'. The plantings were made in 1878.[2]

The quinta was purchased from one of his sons in 1936 by the parents of the present owner, Sr Alfredo Eugénio Cálem e Hoelzer. The old quinta house is now occupied by the *caseiro*, the Hoelzers having built a charming new house further up the hillside in 1939. A solitary cypress tree beside it makes it conspicuous for miles around. Designed by Leandro de Morães, it has an adjoining chapel dedicated to Nossa Senhora do Rosário.

Sr Hoelzer has no plans to expand the area of his vineyards, but he plans to mechanize further by transferring some of his old vineyard to an olive grove adjacent to the Quinta de la Rosa, whilst saving where possible those terraces which can still be ploughed by a mule.

The main nucleus of quinta buildings is halfway up the winding road which leads from the entrance to the house. Beneath the *caseiro*'s house is the main *adega*. From a production of about 16 pipes when the quinta was first acquired, the average is now around 100 pipes. There are further buildings, some rebuilt in 1945, others more modern, which contain the *armazém*, *cardenhos*, and usual offices.

Sr Hoelzer is related to the Cálem family through his mother, and his association with their firm has been a close one. Having joined it in 1933 he officially retired in 1988, but still works part-time as a taster. In a curiously parallel way, the *caseiro* who was working on the quinta when his parents purchased it in 1936 only retired in 1988. For many years the wine has been sold to Cálem, but now part is kept for ageing on the quinta and a ten year old single quinta tawny has just been released on the market.

And further along the road, this time on the right, we have the Quinta de la Rosa.

Quinta de la Rosa

The Quinta de la Rosa announces itself across the river with black lettering on its *armazém*'s white walls which is quite the most elegant to be seen in the entire Douro.[1] But, Quinta *de la Rosa* does not sound like a Portuguese name and, indeed, it is Spanish. This quinta, which used to be the Quinta das Bateiras,[2] was renamed earlier this century by Albert Feuerheerd,[3] whose daughter Claire was given it as a christening present from her English grandmother. The name commemorates a successful brand of sherry which his firm in Jerez had launched at the turn of the century. Both names appear on the main gate of the quinta.

Outside the Pombaline demarcations which, nevertheless, recognized the Quinta da Foz upstream and the Quinta do Porto downstream, Bateiras is not mentioned in the older books although it appears on Forrester's map. At the beginning of this century it belonged to Dr António Reis, the local doctor, from whom it was purchased for Claire in 1906. Since then it has grown with the addition of the Quinta Amarela nas Bateiras,[4] the Quinta de Lameiro do Rego, and, in 1985, the Quinta das Lamelas.

In 1911 Albert Feuerheerd made extensive alterations and additions both to the house and to the *armazém*. Dating from the seventeenth century, the house, which is painted white with green shutters, is rather rambling inside, and boasts a priest hole excavated into its rock foundations. It must be one of the most charming quinta houses in the entire Douro, and contains some remarkable furniture, including Lord Melbourne's bed and a reproduction of Nelson's dining table from the *Victory*.[5] Happily there is now no trace of what might have been a real disaster when, in 1976, a landslip caused a large part of the front wall of the house to collapse on to the railway, which runs just underneath, blocking the line for three days.

A secluded garden on the downstream side of the house affords a lovely setting, and contains what is thought to be the first *filtered* swimming pool in the Douro, converted from a duck pond in 1955! There is also the old house of the Quinta Amarela nas Bateiras, neglected by Albert Feuerheerd, but now restored, complete with its own pool, for *turismo de habitação*.

It was in the improvements made to the vineyards and the wine installations that Albert Feuerheerd made his most important contribution to the quinta. When he built new terraces in 1911, he anticipated the shortage of labour which the First World War was to make a reality, and replaced the steps with ramps to facilitate the use of mules. These, unfortunately, are not quite wide enough for tractors. More *lagares* were installed, and the *armazém* was extended to make it into a mini shipper's lodge, with a total storage capacity in excess of 700 pipes – most unusual for a quinta so modest in size. His idea was to buy local grapes, make the wine in the new *lagares* and store it on the quinta. Several of the *toneis* still in the cellar were brought from Jerez, the oldest of which is dated 2 January 1891.

Nevertheless, the quinta remained small, with a production of around 30 pipes. Interestingly, Feuerheerd sold a single quinta port from La Rosa, though his last vintage – 1931 – never reached the market. In the uncertain conditions of the 1930s his business failed (it was bought by Barros Almeida), and, when he died shortly afterwards, Claire Bergqvist was, in her own words, 'left with the quinta knowing nothing of the vine or how to run the place'.[6]

Thereafter, the quinta sold its port to various shippers (Morgan, Croft, Delaforce, and latterly to Sandeman).

It was just after the Second World War that Claire Bergqvist, having separated from her husband, decided to make her home at the quinta. She wrote: 'Owning a quinta in the Douro does not mean that one makes a fortune. Far from it. But it is a way of life and I, for one, would choose no other'.[7] In due course La Rosa passed to Claire Bergqvist's son, Tim, whose main job now is running the family's pulp paper business, founded in Portugal by his Swedish great-grandfather. For some years the quinta was used by Sandeman, who not only bought its grapes, but made about 600 pipes of wine from neighbouring quintas in the *adega*. The La Rosa wine went into the Rebello Valente port sold under their Robertson Brothers label. Then, in the light of the new legislation of 1986 and after much thought, the decision was taken to market La Rosa as a single quinta port once more.

Tim's elder daughter, Sophia, was working at the time as a top-level management consultant. Now, using these skills, she is marketing the quinta port in a novel, and so far unique, way: by selling what are called Advanced Port Purchases. The basic idea is that, by making an initial cash investment, a participator in the scheme purchases a certain amount of the port made in the five subsequent years. Taking price rises and inflation into account, this should provide either drinking port at a modest price or an investment profit. Additionally, there is always the possibility that the vintage of the century could happen within these five years. The scheme, started in 1988, has apparently begun well. In due course the surplus production will be marketed separately as Quinta de la Rosa port.

The quinta has recently been the subject of considerable investment. It is convenient to consider the planted part of the quinta as consisting of two areas of roughly the same size. The original vineyards, which have walled terraces, stretch along the Douro towards the Quinta do Porto. Here an experiment in mechanization is taking place. A mini terrace is being created in the centre of some terraces by levelling the inclination and replanting. Tim Bergqvist is adamant, however, that he does not wish to alter everything. 'I put down the complexity of our wine to my old grandfather's planting philosophy. In the old part of the vineyard we have anything up to twenty different varieties which will be maintained for their exceptional overall quality, despite their unknown statistical mix.'

The upper part of the Quinta, where the quintas de Lameiro do Rego and Lamelas are situated, is mainly on the northwest side of the valley through which the Ribeiro de Lameiro do Rego flows, with Cálem's Quinta do Vedial on the opposite side. When it was purchased in 1985, Lamelas was in a state of complete abandon, but now it consists of block planted *patamares* and is providing a timely boost to the quinta's production as its new marketing scheme develops. Moreover, its situation being so different from the rest of the quinta, it is likely that Lamelas will contribute further to the complexity of the quinta wine.

Changes are also taking place in the *adega*, where five of the *lagares* were built up by Sandeman to create open pump-over tanks. Tim Bergqvist was unhappy with this system and has now brought three unmodified *lagares* back into use. Two 9,000 litre Silase auto-vinifiers have just been installed and he plans to install tanks like those at the Quinta da Cavadinha.[8] Storage capacity in wood has been brought up to 900 pipes, and a small bottling line will be installed in 1992.

The La Rosa port has the reputation of being a shade drier in style than most, and some detect an underlying hint of walnuts in its bouquet. The 1988 port is to be declared as a vintage, but it is otherwise too early to say how the new single quinta wines will develop.

The road takes us over the railway level-crossing and, coming round a bend, we see Pinhão across the Rio Pinhão. On our left is the Quinta da Foz, belonging to A A Cálem & Filho, Lda.

Quinta da Foz

The Quinta da Foz, so named because it is at the *foz* or mouth of the Rio Pinhão, has belonged to Cálem for just over a century. In the 1758 Pombaline demarcation the quinta was referred to as 'the quinta of Capitão António Borges Ribeiro, situated at the mouth of the Pinhão on the banks of the Douro', and despite the existence of a document which appears to include its wine in the *feitoria*, the principal evidence suggests that it was so classified only for white wine, the red being rated at 15,000 *reis*.[1] Full *feitoria* recognition was granted in 1761.

The same would also have been true of vineyards in the immediate vicinity of the Quinta da Foz and now part of it, though precisely where the demarcation ran it is not nowadays possible to say. Interestingly enough, it was here that one of the earliest frauds concerning the demarcation was detected. A letter, dated 18 August 1774, probably from the Conde de Oeiras to António de Mesquita e Moura, one of the Old Company's officials, gives the details of 'the abominable and criminal fact'. Apparently five locals, three of them priests, had falsified the demarcation either by moving the official markers, or by putting up bogus ones (it seems odd that the law officers should have been uncertain which!). Given that some infractions of the wine law could attract such extreme punishments as public flogging or transportation to Angola, the punishments for 'this prejudicial and scandalous fraud' were relatively mild. The main culprits were exiled forty leagues beyond the boundaries of the provinces of Trás-os-Montes and Minho, and their wines were purchased by the Company for three years at a price well below that at which they were officially rated. All the offenders had to pay the cost of replacing the false marker and putting up more markers 'to avoid all confusion'.[2]

The quinta subsequently passed into the hands of the Beleza de Andrade family,[3] and, in 1885, it was sold to António Alves Cálem, who had established his port shipping business in 1859. Over the years the size of the quinta was increased by the incorporation of small neighbouring quintas: the quintas do Sagrado, do Vedial and da Sangra – all of them west of Foz, going down the Douro – were bought by the founder's son, another António; while the Quinta de Santo António – on the right bank of the Rio Pinhão, just beneath the Quinta da Eira Velha – was purchased more recently by the founder's grandchildren, José and Joaquim (father of the present head of the firm).

Regrettably the Cálem archives were destroyed in a fire at Vila Nova de Gaia in 1976, but it is surmised, from a date above the door, that the quinta house was built in 1872. Still very much a family home with beautiful antique furnishings it, like the rest of the quinta, has been subject to later modification and development. Most noteworthy is the creation of five ground floor bedrooms out of part of the old *armazém*, partly under ground level and therefore marvellously cool in the heat of the summer. There is also a chapel, consecrated in 1922, which is decorated, like some other parts of the quinta, with *azulejos* painted by Maria Madalena Cálem – sister of the firm's founder. Apart from the usual offices there is a modern *azenha de azeite*, the olive oil production from the quinta being quite appreciable. The most notable building, however, is the large and airy *adega*, also decorated inside with *azulejos* of Douro scenes and with its four granite *lagares* arranged untraditionally in a square. Lastly, there is a restaurant specifically for the entertainment of groups of visitors. Foz is one of the few quintas to welcome tourist groups and individual visitors on a regular basis.

The quinta's old vineyards are on traditional terracing, and Cálem have no plans at present to change them, though they would prefer to have more *patamares*. The problem at the moment is that the conversion would necessitate five years' loss of *benefício* – something not even the largest proprietor can realistically contemplate. In the meantime, it is hoped that the savings made in the running of the mechanized part of the quinta, when the new plantings come into production, will help to balance the costs of maintaining the traditional part.

All the quinta wine is made in the *lagares* – 'and will continue to be as long as my father lives', Maria Assunção Cálem assured me. In due course the production from the new vineyards will be vinified by individual varieties. The wine from three quintas in the Rio Torto valley, acquired privately during the last decade by Dr Joaquim Manuel Cálem,[4] is also made at Foz.

The wine from the quinta is used for all the company's premium ports – vintage, LBV, *colheitas*, aged tawnies, and for the single quinta – sold in attractive painted bottles – which first appeared with the 1982 vintage, followed by the '84.

3 The Rio Pinhão valley

Here we leave the Douro and, instead of taking the bridge on our right into the town, we continue straight on towards Sabrosa, coming in a short while to the Quinta da Eira Velha.

Quinta da Eira Velha

The Quinta da Eira Velha — 'the Farm of the Old Threshing Floor' — sits on the shoulder of a hill just above Pinhão, and has one of the most majestic panoramic views of any quinta in the Douro — across to the Quinta das Carvalhas, upstream to the Quinta de Ventozelo and downstream to the Quinta do Seixo. It is also one of the oldest established quintas, and, unlike most, has a well documented history. It is marked on Forrester's map.

The quinta as it now exists was originally two properties known as Eira Velha da Cima and Eira Velha de Baixo, the former being the larger of the two. Both belonged to the See of the Archbishop of Braga, Primate of the Spains, who leased them separately to lay tenants. It is from the surviving leases that our information about the early history of the quinta comes.

In 1582 Pedro Correa, as third life,[1] surrendered his lease of Eira Velha de Baixo for a new one in favour of his wife. We may, therefore, suppose that his family had been tenants for two previous generations — back probably to the beginning of the century or beyond. The new lease specified that Sra Correa was to pay a yearly rental of 100 *réis* and one good chicken for the Archbishop's table. The vineyard (called in the lease Aleira Velha) was described as being 47.5 rods wide by 107 rods long,[2] bordered on the west and north by Eira Velha da Cima. It required eight men to dig and tend it, and produced 60 *almudes*[3] of wine a year.

The leasehold of Eira Velha de Baixo was held by the Correa family until some time after 1622, when it passed to Diogo Telles de Queiros of Vila Real, and, from his successors, by purchase of the unexpired portion of the lease, to the Rev. João Baptista Pereira, Abbot of São Pedro, Vila Real, in 1766.

The documented history of Eira Velha da Cima goes back even further, to 1513, when it was leased to Gonçalo Pinto, an Esquire to the Archbishop of Braga, for four lifetimes. The property consisted of a house, a vineyard, cultivated land, and craggy land which had never been cultivated. A reduced rental of 50 *réis* per year was levied in recognition of the expense involved in bringing the craggy land into cultivation.

The leasehold remained in this family until, in 1659, it came by marriage into the possession of Bernardo Borges Pimentel, a prominent soldier under the King of Portugal. It was then held by the Pimentel family until 1771, when the remainder of the lease then current was purchased for 3,000,300 *réis* by the same Rev. João Baptista Pereira who already leased Eira Velha de Baixo. Thus the two parts of Eira Velha became united under the same proprietorship in 1771, and under a single, three life lease in 1781. The rental was 400 *réis* . . . and a fine, fat chicken!

The successive leases of Eira Velha Cima describe the property and provide us with details of production. By 1726 it is described as 'a residential estate'. In 1739 permission was given to Dona Anna Luisa Correa Pimentel by the Archbishop of Braga to build a chapel dedicated to Santa Bárbara in the quinta on the road leading to the Rio Pinhão. (It is presumed that this is the chapel known today by the name of Santo António, situated in Cálem's quinta of the same name.) The quinta house and many of the outbuildings which exist today were built by 1771. There was an olive grove, and a large vineyard covering half the area of the estate. The wine production, which in 1556 was 30 *almudes*, had risen by 1758 to 10 pipes of white and 6 of red wine. It was, by present-day standards, incredibly labour intensive. The number of men required to produce the 16 pipes in 1758 is not recorded, but for 8 pipes in 1781 the lease improbably specifies two hundred men.

Eira Velha was included in the Pombaline demarcations of 1757 and 1758, but only its white wine was in the *feitoria*. In 1759 Luís de Cunha Pimentel petitioned for inclusion of his red wine, and this was granted in 1761.[4]

The next period in the history of Eira Velha is more obscure. After the secularization of church property in 1834, the quinta was acquired by João Pereira Bacelar of Vila Real. Between 1855 and 1867 his heirs leased the quinta to Manoel José Borges, after which the property passed to Dr Francisco Botelho Correa Machado and his family, who in 1893 sold it to Hunt, Roope & Co. This firm had bought the Eira Velha port since 1809, and had also made it from 1828 onwards. For many years it was the basis of their famous vintage brand, Tuke Holdsworth.

Almost immediately Hunt, Roope, Teague and Co. added to the property, purchasing adjoining land at auction – Fraga de Baixo in 1901, and Sagrado (with new olive trees and *americano* vines) in 1904. Three years later the quinta was transferred to one of the company's directors as his share capital in the firm. And so Cabel Roope enters our picture: one of the most colourful characters (amongst many) in the history of port. Notorious for his 'franglais'-type poor command of Portuguese, he was also a famous dandy. When Rupert Croft-Cooke, of a younger generation, asked what was so extraordinary about Cabel Roope, he was told 'Well, he was never sober'![5] It is also recorded that, when asked what he was going to do about his floating kidney, he replied, 'Keep it afloat'.

Cabel Roope continued to improve the property, but he died in 1911 and it passed to his nephew, then a minor. Having been managed by trustees, Hunt, Roope & Co (as the firm eventually became known) bought it back again in 1938. During this period, from 1918 until 1938, the Eira Velha port was bought by Graham. Hunt Roope made further large plantings of vines and olive trees, and generally improved the property.

In 1956 the quinta was sold to Sir Ralph and Thomas Newman, part owners of Hunt Roope, which was itself then sold to Ferreira, and today Eira Velha belongs to Sir Ralph's son and nephew, Richard and Peter Newman. The Newmans are an old established trading family in the west of England. At the beginning of the sixteenth century they were already bartering wine for dried fish from Newfoundland, and from 1679 onwards, under a variety of names, the company which later became Hunt, Roope & Co was in operation. The company took port to Newfoundland both to be sold and to be matured there before being brought back to Europe – a practice which the Newmans continued, even after the sale of the firm to Ferreira, until the late 1960s.[6]

Peter Newman, who took over his father's interest in 1967, recalls that he first visited the quinta when he was fifteen. 'I don't think I knew the place existed before that. My father came out here very rarely – about once every five years, or something – and he never encouraged me to get involved. He saw no future in port. The family didn't think the quinta was a place to go for holidays.'

Since 1979 there has been an arrangement with Cockburn to manage the quinta on behalf of the Newmans. They also buy the quinta wine (which is used mainly for their Special Reserve brand), and market the single quinta port which made its first appearance with the 1978 vintage, followed by the '82 and, in due course, the '87.

The quinta began to take its present shape at the beginning of this century. In 1901 a new, square *adega* was built adjacent to and uphill from the house. It was one of the first to depart from the traditional arrangement of *lagares* in a straight line in favour of a more functional, square, layout.[7] Pipes lead under the house to take the port to the *armazém*, which is some distance away. In 1949 the walls of the *adega* were decorated with six splendid tile pictures depicting scenes connected with Hunt Roope.

The quinta house is on two floors, with a covered terrace which lends it something of the air of Regency Cheltenham. The inside was considerably remodelled in the 1970s and now provides a simple but agreeable house which the Newmans use from time to time for family holidays. Between the *adega* and the Newmans' end of the house, is the part occupied by the *caseiro*. The main *armazém* is a separate, purpose-built store on a lower level, with an adjacent *azenha*, modernized in 1953 but no longer in use. Between the house and this *armazém* there is a charming, shaded little garden.

Through the quinta and along its top runs the old Pinhão-Gouvães road, its other boundaries being provided by the Quinta da Foz (Santo António), the Quinta da Casa Nova, and the Quinta de la Rosa. The original part of the vineyard has some vines thought to go back a hundred years, and the traditional mixed plantings include about twenty-five varieties of vine. Until 1974, when the present *caseiro* arrived, there were no roads through the vineyards, but now all parts of the quinta have easy access. Apart from some PDRITM *patamares*, all the vineyards are terraced. Some parts of the vineyard, however, have a remarkably gentle gradient, with as many as twenty-five rows of vines on one terrace. Here, by delaying the replacement of dead vines, it is proving possible to effect a gradual change to wider spacings between rows which are suitable for tractors. Some 4,000 to 5,000 vines are being renewed each year, with individual rows or blocks of one variety being planted. Eventually it is hoped that the whole quinta can be mechanized by a combination of such wide rows and *patamares*.

To end on a less serious note, the quinta still has its traditional animal compound on whose gate, untraditionally, hangs a miniature animals' post box! Inside one finds ducks and chickens; but, alas, there are no longer any pigs to enjoy the incredible luxury of the pig shower installed by Sir Ralph Newman. Horseshoe in shape, and decorated with painted tiles of pigs with curly tails, it provides not only a cold douche from the sides but a warm one from the top. Quinta de Vargellas please note![8]

Only a little further along the road we come to the Quinta da Casa Nova, belonging to the Banco Borges & Irmão.

Quinta da Casa Nova

Situated between the Quinta da Eira Velha and some small vineyards just below the little town of Gouvães do Douro, the Quinta da Casa Nova looks directly across the Vale de Fontão at the Quinta do Junco (in the same ownership). It belongs to the Banco Borges & Irmão. This bank (founded in 1937) was, like the Sociedade dos Vinhos Borges & Irmão, Lda (founded in 1918), the outcome of the multifarious trading activities of two remarkable brothers, António and Francisco Borges, who first went into business together in 1884. On the founding of the bank, the trading assets of the brothers were transferred to it – which explains how Casa Nova, which they had acquired in 1926 for 50 *contos*, comes to belong (like their other quintas) to the bank rather than to the wine firm. The wine firm is in any case almost entirely owned by the bank, and it buys the wine produced at Casa Nova, as it does from the bank's other quintas.[1]

From the main road a track winds up through an avenue of eucalyptus trees, then past terraces and *patamares*, to the quinta buildings, which back on to the old Pinhão-Gouvães road. The *caseiro*'s house, with its immaculately scrubbed wooden floors, is typically eighteenth century, and there is the usual range of installations. The wine, however, was last made here some sixteen years ago, and the grapes are now taken across the valley to Junco. The separate *adega* and *armazém* are now just stores.

Casa Nova has a *feitoria* stone marker quite close to its boundary with Eira Velha. Originally in the *feitoria* for white wine in 1757, it was excluded in 1758, when the marker was erected, defining the line of the boundary down the hill towards the Ribeirinho de Fontão, where there was another marker. Casa Nova was on the wrong side of this line.[2] A petition for inclusion in the *feitoria* made in 1759, by Felix Botelho Pimentel of Vila Real, was turned down, though in 1761 its red wine was rated at 15,000 *réis*.[3] At this time its production was between 8 and 10 pipes a year.

In the first decade of the century, when Monteiro visited the quinta, it belonged to the firm of J H Andresen, Sucrs, Lda. (which still exists as an independent company). With 'land for almost 300,000 vines, and containing close to 6,000 olive-trees, besides three groves of 5,000 chestnut trees and five pine woods', he found it 'enviable'.[4]

Cordeiro reports that in the 1940s the quinta was producing about 150 pipes a year, two fifths of it white. Between 1974-6 the vineyards were extended and *patamares* created, using hitherto uncultivated land and former olive groves. Most of the vines are now of red varieties. According to Sr João, the *caseiro*, the quinta grapes produce a wine with good colour, but with less refinement than that of Junco.

Sadly, when I visited the quinta in 1989, I found it less enviable than did Monteiro. A slight air of dereliction hung over the place. Sr João, who started working at the quinta in 1941 at the age of eighteen, looked rather wistful as he remembered earlier times.

Skirting round the little re-entrant of the Vale de Fontão we start to climb and shortly come, on our left, to the Banco Borges & Irmão's other property in the immediate area.

Quinta do Junco

Not much seems to be known about the earlier history of the Quinta do Junco. It stands on land which was included in the *feitoria* for white wine only in the 1757 demarcation, then additionally in 1758 for red wine at 15,000 *réis*. In 1761, it achieved full *feitoria* status.

Its modern history begins with its purchase, according to Monteiro 'in a state of extreme abandon',[1] by the Borges brothers for their Casa Bancária (now the Banco Borges & Irmão) in 1906.[2] It was purchased in conjunction with the Quinta do Muro, and was for a time called the Quinta do Junco e Muro, but the Quinta do Muro, which consisted of woodland, was disposed of by the bank after the Revolution of 1974. According to Monteiro, by 1910 it had greatly benefited from new installations, a new road and tracks, and by careful and substantial replanting. The new buildings were at the top of the quinta and consisted of houses for the owner and *caseiro*, *lagares*, *armazéms*, and *cardenhos*. The Borges and their families used to use the house for short stays in the Douro.

Since then both the vineyards and the buildings have undergone substantial changes. A new *adega*, incorporating a house for the *caseiro* at its east end, was built in 1965. The *lagares* were replaced with autovinifiers, and both here and in other *armazéms*, including one built in 1967, there is a large wine storage capacity in concrete and wood. There is also an *alambique* where *bagaceira* is made for in-house use. A new quinta house, combining accommodation for guests and the quinta manager, was completed in 1966. It has good views across the Vale de Fontão to Gouvães and the Quinta da Casa Nova. It also has that rarest and most desirable of amenities in the Douro – air conditioning.

Below the new house is the old coach house, the oldest building on the quinta, with pipes of ports dating from 1908 which are very occasionally refreshed with high quality wines. Two further ranges of buildings – the first used for stores and farm animals, but also including an *azenha* last used in 1973, and the second with the *cardenhos* – date from before the 1960s.

Patamares were first introduced at Junco in 1973 and now account for about a quarter of the whole, the remaining vineyards being on traditional terraces with the most recent plantings in varietal blocks.

The port is sold to the Sociedade dos Vinhos Borges & Irmão, who market a Quinta do Junco *colheita*.

Continuing towards Sabrosa, just opposite Quinta do Noval, across the valley, we reach the Quinta da Cavadinha, belonging to Warre & Ca, Lda, which is itself owned by the Symingtons.

Quinta da Cavadinha

Until quite recently this was effectively three properties, though collectively known by the name of the first: the Quinta da Cavadinha (which means 'well-tilled'); the Quinta do Lameirão (which means 'marsh'); and the Quinta Renova (which means 'renewed').[1]

Although white wine from this area was included in the 1758 Pombaline demarcation, followed in 1761 by the red wine,[2] little is known about Cavadinha until well into this century. During the 1930s the quintas do Lameirão and Renova were purchased in the name of António Joaquim Borges Fernandes Vinagre by his father, himself the grandson of António Borges, one of the founders of the Banco Borges & Irmão.[3] The Quinta da Cavadinha at this time belonged to Dona Maria Etelvina Machado Cascarejo, but she was unwilling to sell to the Vinagres. As there was only one house for the three quintas, this was in joint ownership: two thirds belonged to Eng° António Vinagre, and the remaining third to Dona Maria Etelvina. Apparently their respective parts were even painted in different colours.

The Vinagres did not use their part of the house, however, less because of this odd circumstance than because of their family connection with the Borges, which gave them access to the almost neighbouring Quinta do Junco. So, until 1967, when Eng° António Vinagre acquired the Quinta da Romaneira, the family would visit their part of Cavadinha only as an occasional after-lunch excursion from Junco. But despite the family connection, Eng° Vinagre never sold his wine to Borges & Irmão. From the 1920s, before the quinta came into his possession, until some time in the 1960s the wine had been purchased by Fonseca; thereafter by Sandeman and Ferreira; then, latterly, by Warre.

When Warre acquired the quinta in 1980 it had become one property, and since then they have added some small parcels of neighbouring land to it. The quinta buildings are immediately on the left of the Pinhão-Sabrosa road, but the main vineyard is on the opposite side of the road, and descends steeply in a series of broad and narrow terraces to the Rio Pinhão. A bend in the river gives the hillside a gentle curvature which helps to produce a concentration of summer heat beneficial to the ripening of the crop. The quinta shares a boundary (on the north-east) with the Quinta da Terra Feita.

As part of a gradual programme about a fifth of the vines have so far been renewed, some of them block planted. Although the remaining vines are over thirty years old, what they lack in quantity of yield they make up for in quality. Within the last year it has been possible to construct some *patamares* amongst the otherwise traditional terracing, but, unfortunately, the nature of the terrain is such that there is little prospect of further mechanization in the future.

The quinta house, with an adjacent *alambique*, remains empty. Opposite, and next to the road, there is a separate house for the *caseiro*, whilst behind are the *adega* and three *armazéms*. The *adega* was extensively remodelled in 1988 to accommodate the Symingtons' new 'secret weapon' – a special 'hybrid' double system, stainless steel fermentation tank, designed by Peter Symington (the company's production director) and his wine-making team, António Serôdio and David Baverstock. The Symingtons claim that it is amongst the most advanced wine-making equipment in the Douro.

The tanks, of which there are four at Cavadinha, each with fully automatic temperature control, combine the features of autovinification and pump-over systems in order to have the best of both worlds. In addition to having a smaller than usual capacity (12 pipes each), they have a larger diameter than normal in order to reduce the thickness of the *manta* and thus ensure a higher saturation of it by the must. First used for the 1988 vintage, their combination of optimum control and flexibility have given very encouraging results, and a decision has already been taken to install them in the new *adega* at the Quinta dos Malvedos, and eventually at the Quinta do Vesúvio.

Warre's ports have traditionally come from the Rio Torto valley, and wine from the Quinta do Bom Retiro Pequeno[4] has been, as Paul Symington put it, 'the heart of the blend . . . the basis for Warre's for a tremendously long time'. The company has announced, however, that 'in the great years when Warre's declare a Vintage, the wine from Cavadinha will be used to form a substantial part of the Warre's Vintage blend'. So I asked Paul Symington whether changing from a Rio Torto quinta to one in the Pinhão valley might not result in a radical change in the style of the wine. 'Not necessarily,' he replied. 'If, suddenly, we stopped making Bom Retiro Pequeno for the Warre's blend it would certainly change the style, which would be sad, but we would hope that that would not be the case. There will certainly be a higher proportion in the blend of Cavadinha than there might otherwise have been, but it is the job of the blender to maintain the style of Warre's.' It will be for future port drinkers to determine how well the blender manages his task.[5]

In most years when a traditional vintage blend has not been declared, Cavadinha is offered as a single quinta wine, sold only when it has matured enough to be ready to drink. 1978 was the first Cavadinha vintage to appear, and, having been sold out, is currently followed by the 1979.

Next door to Cavadinha is the Quinta da Terra Feita, belonging to Taylor, Fladgate and Yeatman, Vinhos, SA. It is reached by an unsigned track on the right of the main road, or from Vale de Mendiz, which is on our return route to Pinhão. Neither road is particularly suitable for ordinary cars.

Quinta da Terra Feita

Terra Feita sits within a curve of the Rio Pinhão, on its right bank directly across the river from Cruzeiro and upstream from Cavadinha. It is very easy to recognize, being essentially a knoll which has had its top levelled.

Until this century there were at least four Terra Feita vineyards – two upstream, in the *freguesia* of Celeirós (called 'da Cima' and 'de Baixo'), and two downstream, in the *freguesia* of Provezende. As the boundary between the *freguesias* played a crucial part in the Pombaline demarcations, in terms of the land on which they stand, these two pairs would have found themselves in different categories. In 1757, the former were fully in the *feitoria* while the latter were rated only for white wine; in 1758, both were in the *feitoria* for white wine, whereas the former were rated for red wine at 10,500 *réis* and the latter at the higher 15,000 *réis*; 1761 brought no change for the former, but the latter were fully within the *feitoria* – almost completely the converse of the original demarcation.[1]

Terra Feita was traditionally popular with British shippers, and, until they acquired Terra Feita de Baixo and one of the Provezende quintas in 1974 – both from the widow of Artur de Couto Ferreira – Taylor had bought wine here for their vintage blend well back into last century. Within fifteen years, by buying adjacent land and vineyards, Taylor trebled the size of their original purchase. Then, in 1990, Taylor was able to buy Terra Feita da Cima from the Cavaleiro family, making the resulting combination a very substantial quinta.

The quinta is formed mainly by one large hill, with secondary hills behind the Terra Feita de Baixo buildings, which are deep in the valley of a stream which flows into the Rio Pinhão. One feels a certain remoteness about their situation. They consist of two blocks, the lower containing the *lagares*, *armazém* and the manager's house, and the upper block the *cardenhos* and other offices. The chapel, sadly, has been converted into dormitories for the workers. Terra Feita da Cima also has a house and *lagares*, but at the time of writing Taylor did not yet have access to them.

The summit of the main hill was levelled in 1983 by removing 19 m from the top and replacing it with 3,400 tons of top soil. One wonders if such a Herculean effort could really be worth while. Indeed, nature took her revenge in 1989 when lightning destroyed 35 vines.

With the new acquisition, the quinta still has one third of its vines on walled terraces. Although keen to mechanize, Bruce Guimaraens told me that 'we are not going to be in too much of a hurry to knock down old vineyards at Terra Feita until we get the new ones well established. In any total vineyard situation mechaniz-ation must be a long-term policy because you've got to think of maintaining the average age of your plants.'

The wine here, as at Vargellas, is still made in the *lagares*. In vintage years it goes into the Taylor blend; otherwise, it contributes to LBV and aged tawnies. It has been decided, however, to release the 1986 vintage as a single quinta port when it reaches maturity, although whether this heralds a future run of single quinta Terra Feita ports remains to be seen.

Continuing towards Sabrosa, on the right, just as we reach Celeirós we find the Quinta Casal de Celeirós.

Quinta Casal de Celeirós

The Casal de Celeirós is a smallish walled enclosure on gently undulating ground. Vizetelly remarks that in 1877 it had not yet been touched by *phylloxera*, and writing in 1896, the Visconde Vilarinho de São Romão calls it 'a truly model quinta' and 'the only example we know of a viticultural property to get through the *phylloxera* crisis unscathed'.[1] During this period it belonged to Arnaldo Alves de Sousa, a prosperous land-owner with many properties not only in the Pinhão valley but in the Costa de Roncão and the Rio Torto valley.

In 1880 Sr de Sousa, fearful of *phylloxera*, consulted several eminent foreign experts and had a French chemist, M H Joulie, analyse his soil and his vines. Vilarinho de São Romão prints these analyses in some detail.[2] They are of too specialist a nature to repeat here, but, it would seem that either they worked to some extent, or Sr de Sousa was just lucky. Oddly enough, Vizetelly reports on another of Sr de Sousa's enlightened experiments – training the vines on wires and pruning them 'in accordance with Dr. Guyot's theories'. He goes on: 'The result, however, has scarcely proved satisfactory, for although the yield has been greater, the bunches of grapes, suspended too high above the ground, have never attained the requisite degree of ripeness [and] Senhor Souza has satisfied himself that the Guyot theories are not applicable to the Alto Douro'.[3] He might therefore be surprised to find, if he were to return to the Douro, that Guyot pruning predominates in the vast majority of the quintas dealt with in this book, and that it has been mandatory in all the PDRITM plantations. He might be pleased, however, to find that at Celeirós the traditional spur pruning is preferred; and, in fairness, it ought to be added that at high and cooler altitudes the ripening of the grapes does benefit greatly from ground heat. In high-lying areas of the Douro vines are sometimes still cultivated without wires (although not for port).

Vizetelly and Vilarinho de São Romão vie with each other in their enthusiasm for Sr de Sousa's *adega*, designed by an English engineer called Rouse with a practice in Oporto. It is described by the former as 'probably the finest in the Alto Douro',[4] and by the latter as 'to our way of thinking, the prototype of the *lagares* to use for making the very special wines of the region'.[5] Next door was the *armazém*, 'a vast and lofty apartment, its roof supported by light iron columns'. This building, at a corner of the vineyard and on the outskirts of the town, exists still as a store for Sandeman's wines, although the *lagares* are now derelict, the roof over them having collapsed.

It was here that Vizetelly witnessed the sight of female *lagareiras*, unusual then if less so now. One lot wore their husbands' and brothers' worn-out clothes with a great variety of headgear to shade 'their scarcely lovely faces' and sang the outlawed bawdy song *Marianinha*[6] with 'not particularly melodious voices'. Others, he adds primly, 'danced among the grapes with the frenzy if not the grace of a troop of wild Bacchanals. The sight was certainly amusing, although the proceeding was, perhaps, not exactly a decorous one'.[7]

Almost opposite is Sr de Sousa's 'large white house built in the modern style' which Vizetelly appreciated as 'a gleam of civilization in those outlandish parts'.[8] Sellers was equally complimentary: 'To find so grand a house in so wild a part of the country comes as a pleasant surprise to the weary traveller. Add, then, to these *solatia* [sic] the acquisition of a butler thoroughly up to his duties; a cellar replete with bottles of wine representing the most famous vintages of the Douro, of France, of Spain, and of Germany; while the culinary arrangements are of that nature to satisfy a Cardinal, or pleasure a Prince'.[9]

What now? Alas, like the *lagares*, the house is now in a degraded state. It was sold to the local parish council by Sandeman in 1985, and crudely painted notices now proclaim its current uses as a school and parish council hall. Through the metal-frame doors and windows with broken, occluded glass on the ground floor one can catch glimpses of fine plaster ceilings and imagine how it once may have been. The single distinctive feature of the façade is a fine stone representation of the coat of arms of the Conde de Bolhão, the father of Arnaldo Alves de Sousa.[10]

The quinta was inherited by Sr de Sousa's daughter, and in 1941 it belonged to her husband, António Henrique Pereira da Silva Pessanha. At this time, Cordeiro notes, the quinta amounted to 50 ha and yielded 80 pipes. As this is larger than the 15 ha walled vineyard known today as the Casal de Celeirós, a name it appears to have since acquired, one presumes it also comprised the land known today as the Quinta do Confradeiro (see below). The property then passed into the possession of the firm Victor Casimiro da Costa & Irmãos,[11] from whom it was bought by Sandeman.

Sandeman had already established a presence in Celeirós as early as 1962 when they built a vinification centre just outside the village. This being very much Sandeman country it was an obvious thing to do, and it was a further logical step to acquire the Casal de Celeirós in 1974. The vineyard is planted on broad terraces, and Sandeman began to renew the old plantings in order to obtain greater mechanization and a higher proportion of better grape varieties. The wine was used for their premium ports.

The purchase of the Quinta do Confradeiro at about the same time from the previous owners of Casal de Celeirós offered an extension of this development. Just across the road from Casal de Celeirós, it provides a further useful 30 ha now fully planted out in the traditional continuous way. Wine produced by Confradeiro which was not made into port was sold as table wine under the quinta name.

In 1991 Sandeman sold the Quinta Casal de Celeirós to its new owners, the Sociedade Agrícola Quinta do Casal e do Confradeiro, Lda., but it is expected that, for the time being, they will purchase the crop and vinify it at their Celeirós *adega*.

We continue to Sabrosa, and there we take the road which crosses over the Rio Pinhão (on a bridge with Roman foundations) towards Cheires. The Quinta dos Corvos is on our left, and shortly, on our right, is another quinta in the same ownership.

Quinta do Estanho

This quinta (*estanho* means 'pewter') belongs to Dr Jaime Acácio Queiroz Cardoso, a lawyer who returned to practice in Portugal after living for twenty years in Brazil. At the same time he decided to become a port producer, and in 1975 he acquired Estanho. Within the 1757 *feitoria* for white wine, it was thereafter excluded, despite a petition from António Teizeira Denis, a farmer with a vineyard at the site of the quinta.[1] It has a ruined house and roofless *adega* – used to illustrate the quinta label – the consequence of having been devastated by *phylloxera*.

Although there are still a few vines which are more than eighty years old, within the last decade 45 per cent of the vineyard has been replanted and half of it is now mechanized. This has been achieved by replanting some of the terraces with up to eight rows, spaced so as to allow a tractor to work them. There remain some continuous planting at the top of the quinta, and some old terracing on badly made walls. Dr Cardoso is planning to revamp this part of the quinta by alternating *patamares* and terraces (e.g. by having two *patamares* between each two terraces) an idea in which the CEVD (Quinta de Santa Bárbara) is also interested. The small percentage of white grape varieties will shortly be eliminated by re-grafting with red varieties.

In addition to Estanho, Dr Cardoso has acquired five other parcels of land close by and, on the other side of the Rio Pinhão, the Quinta dos Corvos (*corvos* means 'crows'). Here he is undertaking a complete renovation, and hopes eventually to produce a single quinta port.

Dr Cardoso owns a small *armazém* on the left of the road leading to Estanho from Cheires, and plans to restore the quinta buildings at Estanho, but his main centre of operations at the moment is under his house in the village. His long-term project, however, is to extend his *adega* and install fermentation tanks.

Dr Cardoso keeps 30 per cent of his production for his own use, and the rest goes to shippers. He entered the market in 1987 with a twenty-year old tawny port and an 'Old White Special' of about seventeen years. That part of his production which goes to make red table wine is also sold under the quinta label. As yet the quinta's production is not exported.

From here we go, via Sanfins do Douro, to Faváios where, turning right, we join the main road from Alijó back down the left bank of

Opposite
24
Quinta dos Murças and Quinta dos Murças da Cima seen from across the Douro

Overleaf
25
Quinta do Roriz, looking down on the quinta buildings from the approach road. Note the steepness of the terraces on the right of the buildings

the Rio Pinhão. The road winds steadily downwards, and, at one of the curves which is identifiable only by those in the know, a track on the right (unsuitable for cars) leads down towards the river. Half-way down we find the Quinta de Santo António, belonging to Fonseca-Guimaraens, Vinhos, SA.

Quinta de Santo António

This is a small quinta without much of a history, but with a reputation for producing excellent wine. Narrowly within the 1757 *feitoria*, it was demoted in 1758 to white *feitoria* wine and red at 10,500 *réis*, to be fully reinstated in 1761.[1] Whatever its origins, the quinta had been in the hands of the same family for over a hundred years when it was bought, in 1979, from Dr António Amado Cardoso de Freitas by Fonseca. As with the nearby Quinta do Cruzeiro, Fonseca had been buying wine from the quinta for their vintage port since 1912 and were, therefore, delighted to be able to acquire it.

Santo António has a marvellous situation with superb views directly down the Pinhão valley. The quinta buildings, consisting of a small house above two *armazéms*, a traditional *cardenho*, and a separate little *adega*, are abandoned and empty. At the moment they have no purpose to serve because, being only 3 km from the Quinta do Cruzeiro, it and Santo António are run as one, and the Santo António grapes are vinified there.

The vineyards are a mixture of traditional terraces and *patamares* bordered on the south by the Quinta do Passadouro;[2] on the east by the Quinta dos Lagares, where there is a stone *feitoria* marker; on the north by the Quinta do Vedejosa; and on the west the terraces stretch down the hill almost as far as the Rio Pinhão.

Tucked almost out of sight in a corner of the farm yard is the tiny, eighteenth-century quinta chapel. Happily, this lovely building is not ruined and a thanksgiving mass is held there for Fonseca employees each year after the vintage. Both simple and appropriate, one could hardly think of a better setting.

It is possible to continue this way to Vale de Mendiz, but it is better to resume the main road towards Pinhão, and then turn off to Vale de Mendiz. From there, a short distance along the dusty road which goes back up the valley towards Santo António, on the left, is Fonseca's Quinta do Cruzeiro.

Quinta do Cruzeiro

A massive, arched, stone gate, bearing the date 1834 and four pinnacles, leads into the Quinta do Cruzeiro. Any expectations of something grandiose, to which the gate gives rise, are immediately disappointed. The quinta house, which is just inside, is a modest, one-storey affair with a verandah sheltering its front door. This is where the *caseiro* lives.

Although the quinta buildings are insignificant from an architec-

Previous page
26
Vale de Mendiz, a little village in the Pinhão valley. Sandeman's (private) guesthouse is at the top of the picture

Opposite, above
27
Concrete port storage tanks at Quinta do Bomfim, known colloquially as *mamas* or 'boobs'

Opposite, below
28
The verandah of the house at Quinta do Bomfim, the first Douro quinta house to be modelled on an Indian tea plantation bungalow

tural point of view, this is a property which is immensely valued by Fonseca. The reason is simple, for the company bought from the quinta at least as far back as the 1870s (if not before that date) and has used wine produced there for its vintage ports since 1912. It was natural, therefore, that Fonseca should wish to secure it for themselves.

This acquisition was, it must be said, not entirely fortuitous. In the earlier part of this century, the quinta had belonged to two old ladies. The survivor, Dona Antónia Adelaide Tovar, had intended to leave it to the Church, but Dick Yeatman, then the Chairman of Taylor (with which Fonseca is associated), managed to persuade her to leave it instead to her quinta manager, Luís António Carneiro. For over thirty years he continued to look after Cruzeiro, and, although the majority of its 12,000 vines were latterly of inferior varieties, he somehow managed to produce good wine even in bad years. Finally, in 1973, he agreed to sell to Fonseca.

Mainly because of its vine varieties, the Cadastro grade of the quinta at this time was only 'B'.[1] With an heroic effort, the following year Fonseca regrafted good varieties on to much of the existing root-stock, (although a very high proportion of old vines remains) and applied to have the quinta re-graded. It was raised to 'A'. (Like Santo António, it was raised to *feitoria* status in 1761, having previously been rated only for white *feitoria* wine and red wine at 10,500 *réis*.)

The quinta has a very sheltered position facing west and takes the form of a spur on the left bank of the Rio Pinhão formed by a bend in the river. The quinta buildings are on the crest of this shoulder, and the vineyards are on its north-west and south-west slopes. An adjoining 3 ha were purchased in 1988, and more planting is envisaged.

The vintage is made on the quinta in its *lagares*, and the production continues to provide the basis for Fonseca vintage port, or for Guimaraens vintage port when that is made in years in which Fonseca does not declare. There is, therefore, no single quinta port for the time being – though in many ways Guimaraens, as Fonseca's second label is called, fulfils much the same role in regard to off-vintage years for Fonseca as do the single quinta ports of some other shippers. When not used in this way, Cruzeiro port goes to Bin 27 or to aged tawnies.

Continuing our circuit of the Pinhão valley, we turn back towards the Douro to Quinta do Noval. Its vineyards are on both sides of the road, but the entrance is on the left.

Quinta do Noval

Noval may surely lay a just claim to being the most famous of all the Douro quintas. It is, indeed, quite probably through its name that most port drinkers have come to know what a port quinta is. The name literally means 'in the valley', and is said to be derived from a small valley which forms part of the quinta itself rather than, as one might suppose, from the quinta's dominating situation on the left side of the Pinhão valley.

It does indeed command an extraordinary position. Not only does the quinta afford vast panoramic views but, with its nucleus of white buildings at the centre of its vineyards, it is itself visible from so many points that the traveller in this part of the Douro quickly comes to recognize it. Rising to a peak on the horizon behind it, the vineyards have walled terraces with distinctive blocks of white paint flanking each of the periodic flights of steps which lead up from terrace to terrace. Add to this a long, oblique, white streak bisecting the nucleus — the quinta road — which leads from the public road up to the quinta buildings and beyond to the public road at Vilarinho de Cotas.

The earliest record of the quinta is in 1715 when, as a very modest vineyard, but already called Noval, a deed was drawn up whereby it was given by Manuel Teixeira of São Cristovão as an ecclesiastical patrimony to his son, the Abbot Francisco Alves Taveira.[1] The vineyard passed, in turn, to his heirs and was sold by his niece, in 1762, to Nicolau Francisco Guimarães, one of the first Deputies of the Old Company. Surprisingly, perhaps, although Noval had been in the 1757 *feitoria*, it was rated only at 10,500 *réis* in the 1758 and 1761 demarcations.

It remained in the Guimarães family for exactly a hundred years, during which time it grew appreciably in size. By 1800 it was producing 122 pipes, though production was very variable and the record 162 pipes of 1803 was not again equalled during the following half century. Indeed, by 1860 production had dropped to only 16 pipes.[2] According to Vila Maior, although the quinta was valued at the relatively high sum of 84,800 *réis* in 1811, the purchase of more vineyards and contiguous land greatly increased its value. At the same time, as the figures for production show, it fell into 'great decadence' through an 'inexcusable lack of ordinary upkeep and renovation . . . Then the invasion of *oïdium* came to increase these depradations, finally reaching extreme decay through the almost complete neglect of its owner'.[3] Thus it was when, in 1862, the Deputy's descendant Capitão José Peixoto Guimarães and his wife sold it to José Maria Rebello Valente.

It is from this period that the quinta's present day importance dates. Rebello Valente, a port shipper who bought much of his wine in the Pinhão valley, had known the wines of Quinta do Noval since 1829 and was aware how well they sold on the British market. On this basis he decided to buy the quinta, and its regeneration started immediately: the purchase of more land; the renovation of old vineyards (mainly by grafting, with the aim of reducing the number of varieties and of ensuring 'the unity and continuity of the style of production'[4]); new plantations; and the construction of the present house, *adega*, *armazém* and other offices in a position which offered a good centre of operations. It was an immense task, given the cragginess of the quinta's terrain and the lack of any viable road whereby to bring materials on to the quinta.[5] By 1868 production had already climbed back to 150 pipes, mainly from new plantations, and Rebello Valente began to keep the Noval port apart from others as a 'distinctive speciality for export'. Vila Maior estimated that, when in full production, the quinta would give 300 pipes in average years. 'The time is not far distant in which it [the quinta] must attain this degree of prosperity,' he predicted.[6]

This, however, was not to be. The quinta was inherited from her father by Dona María José Valente Álen, wife of Alfredo, Visconde de Vilar de Álen, and it was while it was in their care that *phylloxera* struck. A second renovation was out of the question, and in 1894 or 1896[7] the quinta was sold to António José da Silva Júnior, whose father had started a port shipping company under his own name. If the date is uncertain, what is beyond doubt is that the quinta had again fallen into a grievous state, with a production of a mere 6 pipes!

It was back to square one, and, as Monteiro says, 'only a heroic determination, an inflexible drive, the most industrious management, and the expenditure of a fortune could have realized the miracle which then occurred.'[8] Dynamite was used to straighten the terraces where, previously, they had been interrupted by the crags of the hillsides; posts and wires were used to support the vines in rows (by no means normal even at this late date); *americano* vines were imported from France; traditional varieties were grafted; more buildings were put up and existing ones were modified; roads were installed. Monteiro says that, of its sort, Noval had no quinta to equal it. He compares the precision of the layout to that of a well-organized museum. There were even posts in the vineyards with notices giving the names and quantities of each vine variety.[9] It is, perhaps, small wonder that Quinta do Noval was to gain the reputation of being the show-place of the Douro.

The quinta has remained in the same family since it was acquired by António José da Silva. His daughter Teresa married Luís de Vasconcelos Porto (perhaps the ideal name for a quinta owner!), a diplomat who, with a certain reluctance, abandoned his career to enter the port trade, in which he became an ambassador for port. He was made a partner of the firm in 1920, and proved to be outstandingly successful, his main achievement being the invention of the broad terraces which are still one of the most impressive sights in the Douro. I recall first seeing the broad terraces at Noval the very first day I arrived in the Douro, coming suddenly upon them as I rounded a bend on the road from Pinhão to Alijó. It was getting dark, and the half light made the huge terraces seem incredibly massive and solid, climbing up the hill like the bastions of some huge castle. That memory remains to this day as one of my most dominant images of the Douro.

Luís de Vasconcelos Porto had noticed that it was only the front row on the narrow terraces which caught the sun and decided, instead of having narrow level terraces, to utilize the slope of the hillside to build broad terraces on which up to about twenty rows could all benefit from the sun. These broad terraces have since become common throughout the area.

António José da Silva died in 1923. His only daughter Teresa and Luís de Vasconcelos Porto also had an only daughter, Rita, and she married Cristiano van Zeller, thus linking Noval to the family owning the Quinta do Roriz. They had four children: Isabel, Luís, Fernando and Cristiano. Luís, Fernando, and their cousin Frederico, entered the business under Luís de Vasconcelos Porto, which, after his death in the 1960s, was inherited by his daughter. Fernando became managing director in 1963, but left the firm in 1982 after the death of his two brothers. The firm is still a family business, with Cristiano's son, another Cristiano, as managing director. His sister Teresa and several of his cousins are involved in running the company.

The quinta includes several smaller ones: the Quinta da Obra Nova, the Quinta do Marco, the Quinta das Orgueiras and the Quinta de Abrahão (all bought by Luís de Vasconcelos Porto, or before him), the Quinta das Aradas (bought by Cristiano's uncles), and the Quinta das Canadas (bought by Cristiano in 1988). For practical purposes the Quinta do Silval, situated close to Noval, is also counted as part of the quinta.

The Noval buildings remain much as they were a century ago. From the main road the quinta is entered under a *ramada* (the contribution of the Visconde de Vilar de Álen) which leads 800 metres up to the quinta buildings, situated on a plateau. In front of them is a terrace almost entirely shaded by a magnificent hundred-and-forty year old Moroccan blue cedar. It is flanked by a couple of cypresses, one of which supports the quinta's private post box. The panorama from this terrace is memorable. It affords views across the valley of the Rio Pinhão to Cavadinha, Junco and São Cristovão, and down the valley to Pinhão, with a glimpse of the Douro between Foz and the mouth of the Rio Torto. One can also see much of the quinta undulating over the folds of the hillside. Immediately below the terrace there is an olive grove and some pine trees.

The quinta buildings are arranged in two main blocks separated by a narrow roadway. The first has the quinta house, with its handsome dark green window shutters, furnished, as Monteiro says, with 'period furniture, paintings, china, and artistic *bibelots*';[10] then the chapel, dedicated to São Nicolau, with its oval, green glass window and surmounting bell and cross; and finally the *armazém*, with family bedrooms and an office above it and, behind it at a higher level, the *adega*. The second group has the *caseiro*'s house, quinta kitchen, refectory and various farm buildings. It is here that Noval's two coopers, unusual for a quinta, have their workshop. (Also somewhat unusually, Noval makes its own vintaging baskets.) Behind these buildings one finds a rather large range of farm animals – pigs, geese, turkeys, chickens, rabbits, pigeons and a mule. The *cardenhos* are in a separate building further up the hillside, as is the chalet which contains the swimming pool, originally a reservoir for the *armazéms*.

The *ramo* from last year's vintage hangs over the door of the *adega* where the granite *lagares* are very much in use. After looking, in the 1960s, at the possibilities of built-up *lagares* and an experimental autovinifier, it was decided that for the quinta wine the traditional method could not be improved upon. Since 1990, however, a pump and refrigerator unit have been used to control the temperature in the *lagares*.

Little altered over the years, Vila Maior would instantly recognize the *armazém*, where the quinta wine is kept for six months after the vintage. The only significant change, perhaps, is that now there is a 5-pipe *tonel* for *nacional* wine.

The vineyards at Noval are still largely terraced, though there are some *patamares* made in 1974 and 1987, and about 2 ha of vertical planting. I asked Eng° Carlos Oliveira, the quinta manager, about future plans. 'It is very important at Quinta do Noval for us to keep the old terracing. It is part of our image, and we shall never destroy those terraces. We hope to mechanize them in the future, for example in the German way, but adapted for the Douro.' By way of compensation, perhaps, the whole of the newly acquired Quinta das Canadas is on *patamares*.

Possibly the most intriguing part of the vineyards is immediately behind the house, where 5,000 of the celebrated, ungrafted, *nacional* vines grow. Cristiano van Zeller explains: 'My great-great-grandfather bought the quinta when it had just been completely destroyed by *phylloxera*. The replanting process was started shortly afterwards by him and continued up to the 1930s, having been carried on later by ... my great grandfather, Luís de Vasconcelos Porto. In this replanting process he decided to renew a patch of vines using exactly the old pre-*phylloxera* way: ungrafted. So we can say that we never stopped having ungrafted vines in that particular site ... This happened at the beginning of the 1920s [so] the 1924 harvest was most surely made into a Nacional Vintage; so was the 1927 and, of course, the 1931, and all the others after that.'

How is it that ungrafted vines survive? George Robertson reports that in the late 1970s he asked Frederico van Zeller about the treatment which these vines received, and was told that 'every six to eight years a kind of "injection" of *sulfurete* (carbon disulphide) had been applied to the roots, but nothing had been done for at least twenty-five years, and the "mortality" of these vines had been far less than the normal grafted ones'.[11] When I asked Cristiano van Zeller about the *nacional* vines he confirmed that they do in fact survive very well. The main difficulties arise when they are young, when they need nursing for a couple of years until their roots are well established. The grapes of *nacional* vines are even smaller than normal, and although some wine is made every year for private use, the quantities are never very large: 5 pipes in 1987, but only 2 in 1988. When a vintage is declared, however, some of the *nacional* wine is given away *gratis* to its purchasers, and generally this is in the proportion of one bottle per five dozen.

From 1908, A J da Silva shipped all their declared vintages as Quinta do Noval, and in 1973 the company changed its name to Quinta do Noval, Vinhos, Lda. The company is in the unique position of being an established Vila Nova de Gaia shipper which has a single quinta as its declared vintage. It was not always so, of course, but for several vintages now it has been a true single quinta wine. To make this abundantly clear, the name 'Quinta do Noval' is reserved for the declared vintage, exclusively made from the quinta wine, and 'Noval', plain and simple, is used for all the company's other wines. However,

Noval LBV is a blend which contains a minimum of 90 per cent of the quinta wine, and in the last few years has been 100 per cent quinta wine.

The company therefore combines the roles of producing both a single quinta wine and other blends, and, with a view to rationalizing its operations, is making a gradual move from Vila Nova de Gaia to the Douro. This is legally possible in terms of the new legislation, and practically possible in view of the vast *armazém* and *adega* which were built in 1970. Situated on the edge of the quinta nearest to Pinhão, it has to be admitted that here is another blot on the landscape. The *adega* is used to make the wine produced from grapes bought locally, and it contains a laboratory. Already a little old-fashioned, Noval hopes to convert from autovinifiers to pump-over tanks by 1991, and plans to change from centrifugal to roller crushers. The *armazém*, on two levels, has the capacity to take all the stocks presently held in Gaia. Apart from two mixing tanks and five concrete *cubas*, all the storage is in wood. The stock is computer controlled. Two springs in the *armazém* provide natural humidity, and a fibre-glass insulated roof helps to maintain the temperature at a fairly constant 18 degrees centrigrade.

The Quinta das Canadas is situated east of Noval on the reverse side of the same hill, and its acquisition has advanced the company's intention of making itself self-sufficient. When the new plantations are in full production within the next five years this will match 100 per cent of the company's top quality wine requirements, and it is Noval's policy eventually to become completely independent in all its wines.

Quinta do Noval is a quinta with a definite personality. It is also a dangerous place for guests, the van Zellers having rather a name for practical jokes. Cristiano's father and uncles would put pepper on visitors' tooth brushes, or – worse – in the days before all the bedrooms had bathrooms (pre-1960s), fruit salts in the ladies' chamber pots. When they came down to breakfast the next morning, the victims would confine themselves to tea and dry toast. In the dining room, if a lady should be unwise enough to relax her feet by taking off her shoes, she would likely find, when she rose to leave the table, that they had been kicked by the gentlemen to the other end of the room. 'But I won't tell you about the ghost joke,' Cristiano told me. 'We still use that one.'

Quinta do Noval manages to blend tradition with a forward-looking policy. Superficially much, for example the buildings, remains unchanged, but it seems that the company will be the first shipper to take the radical step of transferring its operations entirely to the Douro. Despite this, Cristiano van Zeller is far from being an iconoclast or lacking in sentiment. When I asked him if there was anything he regretted about the present-day Douro he said that what he misses most is waking in the morning to the weeping sound of the bullock carts taking the pipes down to Pinhão – a remark which, in itself, shows how much conditions have changed within a quarter of a century.

4 Pinhão to Valeira – north bank

Completing the circuit we now arrive at Pinhão, and the next three quintas are entered from the town itself. The first is the Real Companhia Velha's Quinta do Corval.

Quinta do Corval

Opposite the Quinta das Carvalhas, and tucked between the Quinta do Bomfim and the eastern confines of Pinhão, is the tiny Quinta do Corval, acquired in 1921. With only 3.5 ha of continuously planted red vines, its importance is clearly not due to its production but to its *adega*, which is used to process the grapes purchased from farmers in the region, and for its enormous storage capacity of 4,000 pipes. Although an old installation, it is spotlessly maintained. Its *armazém*, with two rows of concrete tanks receding into the distance, their brass fittings polished and gleaming gently in the twilight, induces an almost religious awe – the feeling of standing in the nave of an immense cathedral dedicated to port.

The Real Companhia Velha markets a sweet tawny under the brand name Porto Corval.

Next door is the Quinta do Bomfim, belonging to Silva & Cosens, Ltd, the proprietors of Dow's port, and owned by the Symingtons.

Quinta do Bomfim

The Quinta do Bomfim (meaning 'good end') was purchased in 1890, when the company was controlled by George Warre. It was his third purchase of a quinta within a few years, the others being the Quinta do Zimbro and the Quinta da Senhora da Ribeira. Prices of quintas were low in the wake of *phylloxera* – Bomfim was badly hit – and Warre clearly thought that it was a good time, if untraditional for a shipper, to take a closer interest in the production as well as the selling of port.

Like its neighbour Roêda, Bomfim benefits from the gentler slope of the hills as the river leaves the Costa de Roncão and curves gently round in front of the Quinta das Carvalhas. With such an ideal site for growing vines it is all the more surprising, therefore, that so little is known of Bomfim's past. Only Monteiro and Vila Maior so much as mention it, the latter simply to tell us that in the 1860s the quinta belonged to the heirs of Padre Agostinho Ferreira of Mondrões, and had a production of 50 pipes.[1]

Until after the Second World War, Bomfim seems to have been regarded by its owners as of lesser importance than either Zimbro or Senhora de Ribeira, both of which were used to some extent by the family. As a result, information about Bomfim during this period is somewhat scanty. The Zimbro visitors' book records its early development, curiously avoiding the use of its name. *1896*: 'The excavations for the new lodge at Pinhão commenced in Feb. getting

Opposite
29
Quinta da Tronqueira. This odd house was built to resemble a French château – or a local builder's idea of what a château might be like

Overleaf
30
View across the Douro from above the Quinta do Bomfim, showing the terraces of Quinta das Carvalhas on the right and Quinta do Ventozelo on the left

on well . . . *Obras* at Pinhão getting on nicely – orders came for the laying of the rails into the lodge.'[2] *1897*: 'Pinhão Lodge is practically finished, but there is still a good deal of work to be done on the office and house . . . The bungalow after only 3 weeks is nearly up to the roof.'

Then, for the next thirty-five years, there is little mention of Bomfim, until we encounter a remark which is at once indicative of its success and rather dismissive. *1932*: 'Bomfim for the first time gave over 100 pipes of mosto, the effects of planting in recent years now beginning to be felt. No reason why the quinta wines should not be quite useful, though hardly of outstanding merit.'

Within fifteen years, however, the boot was on the other foot. In the 1950s, at a time when the port trade was in deep recession and companies began to come under siege from international distilling and brewing conglomerates, the Warre family decided to withdraw from the business (which by this time was largely owned by the Symingtons). It was a choice between selling assets to buy out the Warres' share or losing the independence of the company. A regretful decision to part with two of the quintas was taken, but it was Zimbro and Senhora da Ribeira which were sacrificed, and Bomfim which survived. Even the Zimbro visitors' book became that of Bomfim.

From then on, one might say, Bomfim has never looked back, and its progress since then has been one of continuous expansion. Work on extending the *adega* began in 1963, when eight concrete autovinifiers were installed in time for the 1964 vintage. This was the last quinta vintage to be made in *lagares*, for the autovinifiers, which processed bought-in grapes, were accounted a success. The Symingtons have always been great defenders of them. In 1968 all but two of the *lagares* were removed and more autovinifiers were put in their place. 1972 saw the start of a third phase of *adega* extension, the biggest so far, and storage in *balões* was brought up to 3,180 pipes. At the same time new *cardenhos* were built, and a new canteen was installed in the farm buildings near the top of the property.

In the following year Bomfim processed 6,500 pipes of port in thirty days. 1977 saw the commissioning of a new reception area capable of dealing with 92 lorry loads of grapes in one day without fuss, and further stainless steel fermentation vats were added. 1985 saw 8,500 pipes of port and 1,250 pipes of table wine being made – an all-time record. Today, with temperature control and new crushers which were installed in time for the 1989 vintage, the *adega* is well equipped to produce huge quantities of wine.

Development of the vineyards, with an emphasis on mechanization and the maintenance of the traditional style of the wine, has paralleled this expansion of facilities. Modernization began modestly, it seems, for the visitors' book for 1959 reports that 'a mule working a small plough between the vines was an interesting innovation'! In 1965 a start was made on making new terraces in the lower part of the quinta facing Roêda and the railway, and by 1970 a programme, not only of re-planting the older terraces, but of creating new vineyards with *patamares* in the upper parts of the quinta was under way. This

Opposite
31
Gum cystus. This delicately flowered plant grows widely in the Douro region and is said to give its perfume to the ports produced on the Costa de Roncão

programme, using block planting, which also includes some vertical planting, has now almost been completed. Various small vineyards have been bought from time to time, including, in 1979, the 10 ha Quinta do Vale das Areias at the top of the property.

A single quinta wine was launched in 1988 with the 1978 vintage, followed in due course by '79. Other vintages of the 1980s will be released when they have sufficient maturity for drinking.

It would be impossible to leave Bomfim without further mention of its 'bungalow', the first of the Indian tea-planter type quinta houses in the Douro. Surrounded by a wide verandah, its roof supported by elegant cast iron columns, and with lofty rooms inside, it exudes an atmosphere of the colonial past, emphasized, perhaps, by the straw hats hung up in the spacious, encaustic-tiled hallway. The many old family photographs contribute to its friendly atmosphere making it not only a comfortable but a relaxing place to stay.

Here countless visitors have had the opportunity of enjoying the lavish hospitality for which the Symingtons are deservedly famous.[3] For this the house has undergone deft alteration and enlargement, a model of how to preserve a special ambiance: first in 1947, to make it 'easier to cope with the rather larger parties which visit us from time to time during the vintage' and most recently in 1986, with the addition of a handsome dining-room, which contains the table from Zimbro moved here in 1947. Not least enchanting is the garden, partially enclosed by two wings of the bungalow, with the shade of two plane trees, plenty of comfortable seats, and a circular, rose-covered pergola, where guests may eat in hot weather.

The third property is the Quinta da Roêda, belonging to Croft & Ca, Lda, entered by a gate on the left of the bridge, whence a road leads along the river bank in front of Bomfim.

Quinta da Roêda

'Roêda' means 'noise' in Portuguese. There used to be a rapid in the Douro here which murmured against a stone bank, but, as at Malvedos, the rise in the water level now makes the name rather inappropriate: not a murmur can be heard.

Roêda is bounded by Bomfim to its west, whilst on its north eastern boundary are the quintas of Roncão da Cima and Roncão Pequeno. Situated on a bend of the Douro, a number of re-entrants give it an undulating character. The lower slopes are indeed very gentle, and only towards the top of the quinta, dominated by the so-called guardian's house (an old farm house, complete with *lagares*) does the inclination become markedly steeper. This, as also to a smaller extent with Bomfim, makes it atypical of other quintas in the area. Vila Maior describes Roêda as an amphitheatre facing Ventozelo, but perhaps the description given by Robin Reid, former managing director of Croft, is more apt – a 'dust bowl'. It is marked on Forrester's map.

Roêda's history dates from 1811, when it was founded by Manuel António Soveral of São João da Pesqueira.[1] Vizetelly wrongly suggests that the quinta had been in existence as early as 1744, because he saw over a gate (now vanished) an inscribed stone apparently indicating that, at that date, it had belonged to 'Sor Bartolemev Bealsley'.[2] Bartholomew Bearsley, however, was the son of Job Bearsley who founded the firm now known as Taylor in 1692. It was Bartholomew who bought the house at Salgueiral which Taylor still have, and where the stone to which Vizetelly refers can now be found. The explanation given by Vila Maior for Vizetelly's mistake is simple. 'This inscription was brought by Sr Fladgate [who owned Roêda at the time of Vizetelly's visit] from Régua, where it had been over the door of the first armazém which his ancestors had there, because, despite having nothing to do with the history of the Quinta da Roêda, it serves to show the age of the commercial house to whose head this estate belongs'[3] Unfortunately, in Vizetelly's case, this commercial ruse only created confusion.

The firm of Taylor, Fladgate and Yeatman, of which John Fladgate[4] was then in charge, purchased Roêda from the Soverals in 1844. Four years later, oïdium began to make its presence felt. By 1851 it had affected Roêda very severely, and John Fladgate struggled with remedies such as phosphate of lime, coal tar, sulphate of potash, natural magnesia, and carbon disulphide. All were at one time or another applied to the vine roots, but with limited effect.

Vizetelly reports that, in a good year, Roêda normally gave 220 pipes, but when oïdium was at its worst production dropped to just $2\frac{1}{2}$ pipes. Undaunted, Fladgate undertook the renovation of the vineyards and bought more land, thereby extending the quinta to its present size. His efforts were so successful that, 'according to its owner's estimate', under favourable conditions Roêda was capable of producing 350 pipes. Then phylloxera struck, and we find Vizetelly reporting that in 1877 it 'was merely a fraction of that'.[5] Vila Maior, however, says in 1876 that the property deserves to be noted for 'the regular amount of its production, about 200 pipes, which proves the excellent management and keeping of the vineyards'.[6]

It may have been in an effort to counter the drop in production that Roêda, like Vesúvio and Val-Mór, started one of the most bizarre attempts at diversification ever contemplated in the Douro – silk farming. It was still at an experimental stage in the mid-1870s but it failed. The building which housed the silk worms is said to have stood where the quinta house now is, but not a single mulberry tree can now be seen on the quinta to recall this ill-fated venture.

For reasons which are not quite clear, the quinta, which had been bought by Taylor, Fladgate & Yeatman in 1844 (the first year that the company became known by this name) was transferred to the private ownership of John Fladgate in 1862.[7] It consisted of just over 84 ha, of which just over 66 were planted with vines, and was managed on behalf of Fladgate by 'an old monk', Padre João José da Conceição e Silva – a not unusual arrangement in these days.[8]

It was when John Fladgate retired in 1875 that Croft acquired the quinta – one of Fladgate's daughters married Charles Wright, Croft's representative in Oporto – and it has remained their property ever since. In the early 1920s Croft's general manager in Oporto, Arthur Dagge, carried out improvements which stamped the quinta with the character it has today.

First of all he undertook a major programme of replanting which still makes up about a third of the present vineyard. (This is due for renewal in two years' time, when the present programme of planting new vineyards has been completed.) He was also responsible for an extensive rebuilding programme. A new quinta house was built in 1925 to replace the old house, which bears the date 1839 and is adjacent to it on the side facing the river, but on a lower level.[9]

The house is a smaller version of the 'tea-planter' bungalow at Bomfim, from which it was frankly copied. White-washed, with dark green woodwork and a white painted roof, the house is surrounded by a wisteria-covered verandah. The inconveniences of staying at Roêda before improvements were made in 1959-60 are recalled by Robin Reid. 'All the food used to come up [from the kitchen in the old house] in a lift, which was a fairly hazardous affair, because I remember on one or two occasions the wire breaking and our entire lunch or dinner going with a frightful crash down to the bottom . . . Whenever it got stuck, we had an old chauffeur called Américo, and George Robertson and myself, who were the young members of the company at that time, used to lower the chauffeur into the shaft and he used to jump up and down on this jammed lift until it wound its way down, and then we had to pull him out again.' Nowadays, I hasten to add, it is an extremely comfortable and smooth-running venue for the entertainment of trade guests.

Arthur Dagge was also responsible for the attractive farm buildings which were erected some distance behind the quinta house between 1921–27. Full of character, these are arranged in the form of a charming square, dominated by the baillif's house with its double staircase, which Dagge rescued from an old building elsewhere. The other buildings provide good accommodation and modern amenities for employees.

Further replanting was carried out in the 1970s, and Croft decided to sell its Quinta das Beatas (facing Junco) to finance the scheme. The new plantings started in 1973, when Roêda, (with Bom Retiro and Vargellas) began the then highly experimental *patamares*, and these have now more than trebled the size of Dagge's original vineyard. In the mid-1970s Croft adopted the policy of block planting and began the micro-vinification of single varieties. The quinta is now one of the main sources for fruiting stock, and supplies cuttings for grafting (over half a million in 1988) to the farmers whose wine Croft buys, and to government agencies.

Because of the gentle slopes in the lower part of the quinta many of the terraces are very broad, accommodating up to thirty rows of vines, which gives the impression of almost continuous planting. Although a little of it has indeed been continuous, virtually all of the recent planting has been on *patamares*, and none of it has been vertical. Like Quinta do Noval, Roêda also possesses some ungrafted vines. About 3,000 of various types were planted in 1978 to mark the company's tercentenary. This was done as a celebration rather than for any deeply serious purpose, and the company still has an open mind about the results. So far they have given no special trouble, but they appear to be lower yielding than the grafted vines and their fruit is said to be 'not markedly better'.

Roêda is one of the few quintas where it is felt that the flooding of the river has made a significant difference to the microclimate of the vineyard. There has been a build-up of fungal spores in the area, and the increased incidence of fungal diseases indicates increased humidity. A meteorological station was set up on the quinta in 1980.

Between the old quinta house and the river are the old *adega* and *armazém*, built in the traditional way on different levels, but sideways on to the river with the *armazém* upstream. A new, extremely ugly *adega* was built in the early 1970s. About fifty *balões* are scattered over the built-up area of the farm, and, all told, the quinta has storage for 10,000 pipes.

Lagares were last used in 1963 (only one survives for making samples for comparative experiments), when a remodelling of the old *adega* was completed in time for the vintage. Its autovinifiers were converted to the pump-over system in 1989, and the new *adega* has additional vinification capacity. For the time being it is felt that the considerable cost of further modernization would not be justified by any worthwhile increase in quality.

Roêda has been available as a single quinta port, with some breaks, for well over a hundred years. As Vizetelly points out, 'Taylor, Fladgate & Co [was] noted for its wines from the famous Quinta da Roêda', and a single quinta port was regularly shipped by them. After Croft acquired the quinta the custom appears to have been resumed, after a short pause,[10] then went into abeyance again until Robin Reid had the happy idea of reviving it – though not without a struggle to secure the Board's agreement to it – with a most successful 1967 Quinta da Roêda. Since then a single quinta port has been regularly produced in years in which, if there has been no declaration, the quality of the wine has justified it. Only once, anomalously, and in commercial terms rather unsuccessfully, was a single quinta wine produced in the same year as a vintage declaration – 1970.

The proprietor of a neighbouring quinta described Roêda to me as 'an absolute copy-book property'. There could surely be no greater praise than that.

There being no marginal road on either side of the Douro between Pinhão and Valeira, our itinerary takes us in a large circle by way of Alijó. But, as we head for Alijó, we take a road on our right to Cotas. Just short of Cotas is the entrance to the quintas of the Costa de Roncão. First of all is the Quinta do Síbio, belonging to the Real Companhia Vinícola do Norte de Portugal.

Quinta do Síbio

Apart from the Quinta da Romaneira, Vila Maior says that there are only two quintas of importance on the Costa do Roncão. These are the Quinta do Jordão, also called 'do Pinheiro' (pine) and 'more usually known locally as the Quinta do Síbio'; and the Quinta de Dona Rosa, which 'is the flower of the quintas of Roncão, and produces the finest and most reputed wine of the Costa'.[1] Today the Quinta do Jordão is known as the Quinta do Síbio.[2]

According to Vila Maior, Síbio (which is called thus on Forrester's map) dates from the time of the foundation of the Old Company, though it was not included in any of the Pombaline demarcations. It was planted by José Joaquim Pereira Jordão, a native of Granja.[3] In the 1860s and 1870s it was in the possession of a descendant, Dona Marianna Pereira Jordão,[4] and at this time produced 100 pipes a year. Vila Maior says, in 1869, that the wine from the part of the quinta next to the river compares in quality with that of Roêda, while the wine from the upper part 'is far from attaining the delicacy' of the former. In 1876, on the other hand, he speaks of Síbio producing 'from 30 to 35 pipes of wine of [the] first class'.[5] One of these figures may just be a mistake, or this dramatic decrease in volume over seven years may indicate that the quinta had already suffered very badly from the onset of *phylloxera*.

Vizetelly briefly mentions his visit to Síbio, 'with its large white casa and adjacent chapel' – a remark which is a further cause for perplexity, there being no evidence of there ever having been a chapel.

The quinta remained in the hands of the Jordão family until it was purchased, in 1934, by the Real Companhia Vinícola do Norte de Portugal. Over fifty years later it does not appear to have changed much. The quinta buildings are not inhabited, the farm being administered from the Casal de Granja and its grapes vinified at the Quinta das Carvalhas. No attempt has been made to mechanize the property, and its traditional terraces must look much as they did in the days of Vila Maior and Vizetelly.

At the moment no quinta wine in the proper sense is being produced, although it is intended to market one in the near future. But a 1985 vintage port is sold in England with the quinta name on the label, and a tawny is also sold in France under the brand name 'Quinta de Jordão'.

The second quinta of the Costa de Roncão is close by.

Quinta da Romaneira

Although not many people seem to realize it even in the Douro, the Quinta da Romaneira is one of the very largest in terms of area. From its entrance, some 3 km north of the Douro, a sign announces that one has a further 6.6 km to go before reaching the house; indeed Romaneira has more than 50 km of roads.

The drive to the house is spectacular. The road suddenly crests a hill to reveal the Douro spread below. One can see down to Ventozelo and Carvalhas, and up to Roriz on the opposite bank, where it curves leftwards round a shoulder of land belonging to Romaneira itself.

The quinta occupies the most easterly, and easily the greater part of the Costa de Roncão, as far as Carrapata, whose rapids have now disappeared with the damming of the river. The reputation of the Costa de Roncão has always been high, and Vila Maior singles out the port of Romaneira as 'wine of first quality, among the best of the Douro, being remarkable for body, mellowness and aroma'.[1] It is perhaps not surprising, therefore, that Romaneira appears to be the first single quinta port to have been sold at auction by the English auctioneers Christie's, who offered large quantities of 'Romeneira' Port 1861 (bottled 1866) and 1863 (bottled 1867) on 25 and 26 June 1872. They sold for £1.80 to £2.15 a dozen – a fairly modest price.[2]

The original Quinta da Romaneira, marked on Forrester's map as 'Rosmaneira', is now called Romaneira Nova to distinguish it from its upstream neighbour, Romaneira Velha. Forrester also marks this on his map, calling it the Quinta dos Reis, but it was also known as the Quinta do Abade. Vizetelly remarks that 'today it is more generally known as the Quinta da Romaneira or de Dona Clara, from the name of its proprietor, Dona Clara de Lacerda'.[3] Despite its being called Old Romaneira, the Quinta do Abade is not of monastic antiquity. According to Vila Maior, 'it was first planted by the brother of a well-known Oporto capitalist, an abbot of Gouvães by the name of Padre Manuel Villaça, from whom [it] passed by gift to its present owner, Sr Joaquim de Sousa Guimarães of the city of Oporto'.[4] His ownership, prior to Dona Clara, is celebrated by the elaborate iron gate leading into the courtyard of the quinta, surmounted by the date *1854* and his initials *JSG*.

The Quinta da Romaneira has grown enormously since the last century. It incorporates, apart from some sizeable named vineyards, thirteen other quintas. These fall into three groups. The first group comprises the quintas do Abade, do Penedo Marçal, do Malhadal Velho, de Liceiras and da Carrapata (formerly two quintas, do Malheiros and da Dona Esménia) – the last two being marked on Forrester's map. These are within the Costa de Roncão. In the second group we have the quintas do Carvalheiro (formerly da Carvalheira), do Bairral (formerly two quintas, da Cima and de Baixo), do Malhadal Novo, do Esporão, da Fonte do Mouro and da Barca (where a ferry used to run across to Vau, on the other side of the Douro).[5] These quintas are between the Costa de Roncão and the Costa de Castedo, which starts after Barca with the Quinta de Merouço and continues with the Quinta dos Malvedos. The quintas in both of these groups, which were close to the river, were within the 1757 *feitoria*, but in 1758 and 1761 were demoted to wine at 10,500 *réis*. In the third group, on high ground and closer to Cotas, are the quintas de Escravelheira and da Pulga.

The quinta grew to its present size during this century. The original Romaneira belonged to the Jordão family, which also owned Síbio and Granja. In the 1860s it belonged to Dona Marianna Emilia Pereira Jordão Ferreira da Silva: later it belonged to José Joaquim Guimarães Pestana da Silva, of the Real Companhia Vinícola do Norte de Portugal.[6] He sold it to Eng° Monteiro de Barros, who founded the

Sociedade Agrícola da Romaneira in 1942. He subsequently bought many of the quintas now integrated with Romaneira: other quintas, later integrated, were owned independently by the Fundação Monteiro de Barros.

Monteiro de Barros had a step-daughter by his first marriage who inherited Romaneira on his death; she in turn was married to Sr Sebastião de Campos, and it was from him that the quinta was purchased in 1967 by António Borges Vinagre, a noted architect and a grandson of António Borges, one of the two founder brothers of the Banco Borges & Irmão.

In 1967 the bank was owned by the descendents of the two brothers, but, as a result of a dispute about how it was being run, the descendents of António Borges sold their shares to Francisco's descendents. António Borges Vinagre offered to purchase the port quintas then belonging to the bank – Junco, Casa Nova, Soalheira, Ferradoza, Silho and Hortos – but, although this was settled, no agreement was reached about the price. When Romaneira appeared on the market at this time, Vinagre, tired of waiting, purchased it instead. It was in a fairly woeful state, and he set about putting it back in order.

After 1967 he continued the expansion of the quinta by making further purchases (including those belonging to the Fundação Monteiro de Barros). More recently, his son António Barbosa Vinagre, an economist, has supervised the property, especially the production and marketing of the quinta's port under its own label. After his father's sudden death in 1989, however, Romaneira was inherited by his sister, Maria Antónia, the wife of Sr José Manuel Soares da Costa, who has large dairy farming interests in the Minho, and they are now jointly running the quinta. António, her brother, is meanwhile concerning himself with the production and promotion of *vinho verde*.

As already remarked, the approach to Romaneira is a spectacular one. The road snakes down the hillside in wide sweeps through the vineyards, and if you come in late February or early March you may catch the almond trees which line the route in full blossom. If you come in the summer, however, you hardly dare to stop to admire the view for fear of being choked by the cloud of dust your car has churned up behind you.

Nearer the river, but high above the railway, one comes to the house, sitting against the hillside on a raised terrace. The road continues round the front of the building, leading down to the *adega* and on towards the other parts of the estate. To one side, a large gate surmounted by a bell gives access to a courtyard, from which one enters the house. Recently renovated and attractively washed in pink, it retains its character as an old Douro quinta house with period furnishings, though its billiard room, flanked by two *armazéms* in the basement, is an unusual but agreeable amenity.

The *adega* and *armazém*, closer to the river, are built in traditional fashion. The lower part has autovinifiers and storage, while an extension at one end contains *cubas* for ageing tawnies: the upper part, where the original *lagares* have been removed, provides additional

Opposite
32
Quinta da Pacheca, one of the oldest quintas in the Baixo Corgo

Overleaf, above
33
The *casa dos lagares* at Quinta da Foz. The square configuration round the red vertical press marked a break with the traditional linear layout. These *lagares* were long regarded as a model for *adegas* built during this century

Overleaf, below
34
The *adega* at the Quinta do Vale de Mendiz with two completely round *lagares*, the only examples I have discovered in the Douro

storage. The bottling line is at present in the lower lodge, but a new building is projected.

Most of the old buildings on the quinta are in ruins. The *armazém* at Carvalheiro provides further storage; two houses between Romaneira Nova and Romaneira Velha provide *cardenhos*; but, these apart, the only other buildings of significance are those of Romaneira Velha. Oddly, in view of Vila Maior's account of this quinta's history, the riverside façade is adorned with a small but beautifully worked coat of arms of the Bacelar family. Nowadays these buildings accommodate the *caseiro*, the quinta kitchen and refectory, and a modern *azenha*. The quinta has 43,000 olive trees, of which 18,000 give an average production of 6,000 litres of an oil which is remarkable for its low acidity.

Romaneira has a gently curving river frontage of 3.7 km and includes two railway stations (Cotas and Castedo) and two halts within its confines. The configuration of the land is a series of re-entrants, each of which (in very general terms) contains one or two of the original quintas. Sadly, as is very evident when seen from the river, Romaneira is a microcosm of the Douro insofar as it has a bigger area of *mortórios* than of productive vineyards, especially in Carvalheiro, Carrapata, Bairral, Malhadal and Barca. These terraces are clearly very old, many of them having the holes characteristic of the *pilheiros* method of planting.[7]

Nevertheless, Romaneira's current productive capacity is high by Douro standards. There are new *patamares* reclaimed from old *mortórios* under PDRITM in Liceiras, Malhadal Novo and Bairral, and a further 10 ha of *patamares* and vertical planting in Liceiras were completed in 1990. Sr Soares da Costa is also determined, if possible, to preserve the old terraces in the two Romaneiras, which are close to the house. He wants to find a way of replanting them so that they can be mechanized, even if this means leaving only one row of vines. 'It would be too easy to tear them down,' he says, 'but, once down, they could never be replaced. We have a responsibility to preserve them if we can.'

Under his brother-in-law's guidance, Romaneira was amongst the first independent quintas to bottle and market their own wine, which first appeared in Portugal in 1986 and on the export market in 1987 (one year after the new legislation made this possible). Within four years, Romaneira already exports to Britain, France, Holland, Germany, Switzerland, Belgium and the United States, and it is one of the few quintas to offer a comprehensive range of ports: ruby, white, tawny, *colheitas*, LBV and vintage.

Romaneira, with its great size, enjoys the advantage not just of a micro-climate, but also of a variety of vineyards at different altitudes and with diverse characteristics. Some 10 ha of vines, for example, are on a reverse slope of the quinta going down almost to the Ribeira da Póvoa, while some vineyards (like Pulga) are situated fairly high up. This ensures that in every year some very excellent wine is produced from somewhere in the quinta. Another advantage of this diversity is that, with differing dates of maturation, there is time to make the wine

Previous page
35
Tomatoes drying in the sun outside the kitchen of Quinta do Bom Retiro Pequeno. Note the old bread oven

Opposite, above
36
The so-called Guardian's House dominates the Quinta da Roêda. It was once the house of a small quinta which became incorporated in Roêda

Opposite, below
37
The house at Quinta dos Malvedos

slowly. Vintaging normally starts on 20 September and continues for four weeks.

A more recent development, indicative of the quinta's diversity, is the appearance of a three year old ruby and a tawny port in 1990, both marketed as a single Quinta da Pulga. Sr Soares da Costa is also thinking about marketing a table wine in the future.

Sr Soares da Costa, who has entered into his new responsibilities with enthusiasm, is still familiarizing himself with the quinta and is to be found exploring it on his motor cycle. Since taking over he has also reassessed the quinta's viticultural management and has appointed new *caseiros*, a new technical manager, and a new oenologist. He is determined that Romaneira will remain a leader amongst the independent single quinta ports.

It is said that the wines of Roncão, and of Romaneira in particular, have a characteristic aroma of *esteva*, a variety of dog rose which flourishes on the Douro hillsides around vintage time.[8] To my mind it smells rather like sage. Having tried to detect even a hint of *esteva* in the wines of Romaneira, I have to report that I have failed. Perhaps I am not the first person to think that descriptions of wine can be a little too fanciful.

To reach the Quinta dos Malvedos, further up river, we have to go via Alijó, so we now return to the main road. On our route, between Faváios and Alijó, is the Quinta Casal de Granja, belonging to the Real Companhia Velha.

Quinta Casal de Granja

The Casal de Granja is an enormous property. It belonged last century to the Jordão family (which also owned Romaneira and Síbio) from whom it was bought by J J Guimarães Pestana, one of a group who founded the Real Companhia Vinícola do Norte de Portugal in 1889. Even at this time it was considered vast.[1]

The company failed to flourish and almost everything was lost, including the Casal de Granja. It was bought back again in 1972 by Sr Manuel da Silva Reis for the Real Companhia Velha, of which the Real Companhia Vinícola do Norte de Portugal is now a part. If there was a touch of sentiment involved in engineering this re-marriage, the outcome has been very successful for the company in commercial terms.

The Casal de Granja has now grown to some 250 ha of gently undulating land to the east of the village. Apart from fruit and olive production of appreciable size, about a third consists of vineyards. Some are of quite considerable age, with mixed plantings, not only of different grape varieties, but of white and red ones together. A large programme of vine renewal is therefore in progress, using block planting – some 56 ha within the last fifteen years – and there is now a high and increasing degree of mechanization. Two fifths of the vines are white.

Unfortunately, at this altitude of between 520–640 m, it is impossible to make high quality port, and considerably more than half of the quinta's production is used for table wine. The vintaging is carried out in an extremely modern and well designed *adega*, built close to the original quinta buildings on the far side of the village and inaugurated in 1985. Understandably it has been designed principally for table wine and has separate production lines for red and white.

Now a detour through Alijó towards Murça, turning right after about 6 km towards Franzilhal and Santa Eugénia, brings us to the most northerly of the quintas included in this book, the Real Companhia Velha's Quinta do Carvalhal.

Quinta do Carvalhal

The Quinta do Carvalhal (the 'Quinta of the Oak Grove') is in an improbable enough location, for there are not many vineyards to be seen here, and the rather forlorn, rocky landscape needs bright splashes of broom in the springtime to alleviate its severity.

The Quinta do Carvalhal claims our attention only because it is the oldest of the quintas belonging to the Real Companhia Velha, having been acquired around 1890. A small stream (the Carvalhal) flows through a valley. On one side there is a wild scene of rock and pines, but the quinta, on the other side, is for the most part on gentle slopes, planted on traditional narrow and broad terraces, without mechanization. About two fifths of its production (vinified at Casal de Granja) is made into port. The small cluster of somewhat run-down buildings includes a tiny cottage for the *caseiro*.

Returning to Alijó, we take the road which leads back to the Douro by way of São Mamede de Riba Tua.

Quinta da Amêda

The Agrellos family has been established at São Mamede da Riba Tua since 1720, with substantial small holdings – not only of vineyards – in the Rio Tua valley. The present generation consists of four brothers, two of them actively engaged in the family port business, the Casa Agrellos. Until 1986 it was in partnership with Sandeman as the Sociedade Vitivinícola de Riba Tua, Lda which bought the crop from the family vineyards and used the *adega* of the family house in São Mamede. This, the quinta da Casa da Capela had been built by a certain Baron Richter at the beginning of the nineteenth century beside, as the name suggests, a beautiful, old chapel. Recently, in the light of the new legislation, the Agrellos brothers decided to set themselves up as grower-exporters and withdrew from the Sociedade Vitivinícola.

At the Quinta da Amêda, on the right bank of the Rio Tua, they are now developing land between the river and the public road south of São Mamede. A new *adega* is planned – the old one now belongs to Sandeman – but the *armazéms* of the Quinta da Casa da Capela, stocked with old wines, still belong to the family. An over 40 year old tawny is already being exported to the USA. In due course it is intended to produce a single quinta port from Amêda, and, it is hoped, a red Douro table wine from the vineyards at the Quinta da Casa da Capela, under that label.

Continuing down the road, within sight of the Douro, a bend in the road brings us to the entrance to the Quinta dos Malvedos, which belongs to W & J Graham & Co.

Quinta dos Malvedos

The Quinta dos Malvedos, which is marked on Forrester's map, is situated on the Costa de Castedo, just west of the mouth of the Rio Tua; downstream is the Quinta de Merouço, and across the Douro is the Quinta dos Aciprestes. The name means literally 'bad ways', a reference to the rapids in front of the property before the damming of the river. Now the murmuring of the water, which used to be so audible, is a thing of the past.

The quinta did not exist as such at the time of the Pombaline demarcation, although the demarcation documents make references to the district of Malvedos. In 1761 both Rodrigo Domingus Coelho, the Vicar of Castedo (whose vineyard produced 12 pipes), and António de Sousa (who had petitioned for inclusion in the *feitoria* in 1759) had their vineyards, which were situated at Bairral, Eira do Mano and Malvedos, included in the demarcation for wine at 15,000 *réis*.[1]

Vila Maior writes: 'the Quinta dos Malvedos was established and planted by my maternal grandfather at the end of last century, and sold twenty years ago [1849] by my father to the present proprietor, who has enlarged it with new acquisitions and improved it with important renovations.'[2] Vila Maior's mother was Dona Angélica Teresa de Sousa, and it is tempting, although highly speculative, to suppose that she may have been descended from the António de Sousa mentioned above.

The man to whom Vila Maior's father sold Malvedos was Justino Ferreira Pinto Basto (a son of the founder of the famous Vista Alegre porcelain factory whose family, curiously enough, is related to Paul Symington, a director of the present owners, through his mother). His improvements, says Vila Maior, 'approached the grandiose' in scale, and included the massive terraces near the entrance to the quinta 'forming an amphitheatre bringing to mind the start of a colossal stairway for giants to climb'.[3] These terraces were later called Fort Arthur by the Graham family, and anyone who has seen them will know that they are amongst the most massive in the entire Douro.

At this time the quinta was producing about 60 pipes a year of both red and white port, which fetched much higher prices than in the rest of the district. Vila Maior foresaw that the new plantations would raise production to 100 pipes, but that was before *phylloxera* struck. The attack was very severe, and the quinta was subsequently half planted out with about 9,000 olive trees.

In common with most of the shippers at the end of last century Graham used to send their agent to stay at one of the quintas – usually the Quinta das Carvalhas – during the vintage. But with the coming of the railway, which made access to the riverside quintas both quicker and more convenient, many of the shippers decided to buy a quinta of their own, not so much for the wine but to serve as a centre of operations. Thus it was that Graham, quickly following the example of John Smithes at nearby Tua, purchased Malvedos in 1890.

It was decided to replant the quinta with red grape varieties, largely Tinta Francisca. Unfortunately, according to Colin Graham (one of the directors before the company was bought out by the Symingtons), for a variety of reasons the quinta did not do well. The manager of the quinta appointed around the turn of the century, Jim Yates, tried to copy the experiments which were being carried out at neighbouring Tua by Cockburn. But most of Yates's theories and experiments resulted in extremely poor production – '8, 9 or 10 pipes, and as often as not terribly burnt', according to Colin Graham. 'We used to keep a few cases just for fun, and when we had visitors up we'd bring out a bottle just to show what a really burnt wine was.' At that time the backbone of Graham's vintage port came from the Quinta das Lages in the Rio Torto.[4]

Consequently, the produce of Malvedos was insignificant and even the wine from off-vintages which was sold under the 'Malvedos' label was generally a blend from the Rio Torto: only very occasionally was it a straight quinta wine. The company decided to use the name 'Malvedos', which had already been registered for olive oil and citrus fruits, only because 'Rio Torto' had been registered as the brand of another company.

When the company became financially so unsound in the 1960s that it had to be sold, Malvedos was running at a tremendous loss. This was one of the reasons why the Symingtons, having acquired the company in 1970, decided not to keep the quinta. It was offered back to the directors of the old company on very reasonable terms, and Colin Graham even contemplated buying it to turn it exclusively into a grapefruit farm![5] In the event it was bought by António Baltasar Baptista in 1971. Instead of this leading to an improvement, production diminished still further. The house and garden were abandoned, and the quinta was deteriorating still further, so the Symingtons, who continued to make the wine for the new owner, decided in 1982 to buy the property back again. Since then they have expended an enormous amount of energy and money to make it viable again, and now these efforts are being rewarded.

The quinta has a southerly exposure across the Douro and extends from the shoulder of land formed by the west bank of the Rio Tua downstream, with an oblique re-entrant running north-west behind the quinta buildings. These consist of the quinta house, a pleasant but unassuming white-washed building with green painted woodwork, flanked upstream by accommodation for staff, and down-stream by the *caseiro*'s house. A new entrance has recently been made from the Tua side of the quinta by driving a road beneath and in front of the house, though this has had the consequence of making the picturesque, original wrought iron gate leading to the house redundant. The old *adega*, which is no longer used, is some distance from the house, being downhill by the railway line which runs through the property.

Various recent purchases have considerably extended the quinta, and apart from 'Fort Arthur' almost all the quinta' vineyards are now on *patamares*. Planting is in single varietal blocks so that each variety can be harvested at the optimum time and vinified separately. The development programme, which was started in the early 1980s, is already showing gratifying results. In addition, a new winery, which will contain vinifiers of the type used at the Quinta da Cavadinha,[6] is in the course of construction. It will vinify not only the quinta's own production, but that of the neighbouring quintas from which the company has traditionally bought the crop, which amounts to a total of between 850 and 1000 pipes a year.

The house has also been modernized without changing its simple, farmhouse style. Dating from last century, it was renovated in 1910, when a similarly sized extension was added to the side away from the river. In 1947 further work was carried out to replace with stone the wooden verandah which ran along the Douro side of the house. Until the 1960s there was acetylene gas lighting, and latterly this was in a dangerous state. Colin Graham remembered that 'the old lead pipes in the wall began to leak, and when you tried to light a wall lamp the next thing you knew was a large jet of flame coming straight out of the plaster in the wall'. A second-hand electric generator was therefore installed, which was replaced by mains electricity only as recently as September 1984.

During the 1970s the house was left unoccupied, and according to Paul Symington, the contents of drawers, abandoned when the quinta was sold in 1971, were found intact when it was bought back again in 1982. Further renovations, carried out since 1982, have made the house extremely comfortable. It would be invidious to pick and choose between the bedrooms, each named after a famous vintage: 1948 and 1970, however, have the advantage of access to the verandah, whilst 1945 is the room boasting the 'loo with a view', which is perfectly positioned so that the user can enjoy the view from the window down the river. This joking feature is very much in tune with a tradition of fun which has always existed at Malvedos. One of the directors in the 1930s, Gerald Graham, had a cloakroom in Oporto which was full of fittings, including a lavatory seat, which he had removed from British train bathrooms.[7] He and his brother Max were always joking. The signatures of guests in the visitors' book before the war are systematically annotated with 'decorations'. 'MBE' – might be a *bacalhau* eater; 'OBE' – ought to be a *bacalhau* eater; 'GBE' – a greedy *bacalhau* eater! Poor Neville Reid, Jr. was dismissed with an MBE – with the added comment, 'a poor performer'; whilst Malcolm MacKinnon achieved an accolade with his GBE, being 'duly invested with the insignia of the order', apparently a miniature pottery *bacalhau* on a ribbon.

In more recent times the visitors' book records another 'joke' associated with Malvedos bathrooms, but one which is unfortunately too long to print in full here. It begins:

The Malvedos Snake Master

Brave Dave the Master of Wine
Sat down on the loo feeling fine;
While easing his bladder,
He spotted an adder,
Transfixed to the wall in mid-climb.

Malvedos is full of these jokes,
Which they play on these innocent folks.
It looks like a snake,
But it's really a fake.
It must be a Symington hoax.

The snake, however, proved to be real enough, and when it reared at poor Master Dave he fled from the smallest room in indecorous haste.

Despite the fun, the approach of the Symingtons to Malvedos is very serious. The acquisition of more land and the huge planting programme which has been undertaken represent a sizeable investment in a quinta which, despite its reputation, was never a significant producer of quality wine in the old Graham era. But that is a thing of the past. Production exceeded 100 pipes for the first time in 1987, fulfilling Vila Maior's prediction more than a century after he made it. Gone are the days of burnt grapes and the level of quality is now excellent. One can only speculate about the reasons for the change. Was it simply bad management by the old firm? If so, that is likely only to be part of the truth. Another possibility is that the flooding of the river has alleviated the fierceness of the very specific micro-climate associated with Malvedos.

Be that as it may, under the new Symington régime these problems of low production and poor quality are a thing of the past. Everything is set fair for Malvedos to realize its owner's exacting expectations well before the end of the century. These improvements mean that a single quinta Malvedos port is now in prospect. As Paul Symington explained to me in an interview in 1989, 'as soon as we get production of decent enough wine from the quinta, which we actually have over the last couple of years, we'll be calling the wine "Quinta dos Malvedos", because we don't actually particularly agree with the old Graham policy . . . It is slightly misleading to call a wine "Malvedos", for people assume it comes from that quinta, but we inherited a situation which we couldn't solve overnight. Indeed, the production of the vineyard had fallen to negligible levels, so that is why we still call the '76 and '78 "Malvedos". I don't know which wine we'll actually call "Quinta dos Malvedos" but it's one we're satisfied we can produce 100 per cent off the property and bottle it as such.' Two years later, in 1991, as the book was going to press, Paul Symington reported that 'in practice "Malvedos" vintage port has been produced in recent years *only* from the quinta, as we have acquired the adjoining vineyards from which company used to buy to make up the "Malvedos" blend. "Malvedos" can therefore [now] be considered a single quinta wine.'

Crossing the bridge over the Rio Tua we come to the Quinta do Tua, belonging to Cockburn Smithes & Ca, Lda.

Quinta do Tua

The Quinta do Tua is situated on the east bank of the mouth of the Tua, facing some of the new *patamares* of Graham's Quinta dos Malvedos to the west and the Quinta dos Aciprestes to the south. The quinta, which since 1973 has incorporated the Quinta da Chousa, occupies a cone-shaped hill between the rivers, and continues upstream taking in, with Chousa, another hill. On the east it is bordered by the Quinta do Zimbro.

At the time of the Pombaline demarcation the area round the mouth of the Rio Tua consisted of small vineyards. One of these, called Eiro do Seixo, which is part of the quinta, was included in the 1758 demarcation for wine rated at 10,500 *réis*.[1] To find the origins of the quinta we have to go forward a century to 1867, when we find Dona Antónia Ferreira buying wine at Tua. Four years later, on 21 August she purchased an *armazém* and vineyards at Tua from Nicolau de Almeida. Curiously enough, in view of future events, Dona Antónia's papers also indicate that in 1871 John T Smithes intimated that his firm, Cockburn Smithes & Ca, wished to buy the entire production of her major quintas at the next vintage.

The production figures for the next few years suggest that Dona Antónia's vineyards were probably rather small: a single pipe in 1875, although up to 6 in 1877. The following year Dona Antónia's husband, Francisco Torres, received a letter dated 7 June from Lopo Vaz:

> *The Oporto market has been terrified by the news which the Barão de Roêda brought some days ago, for he says that the great majority of the vineyards of the Alto Corgo as far as Tua have already been compromised and affected [by* phylloxera*].*

Thereafter it was the same dreary story, the production falling to half a pipe in 1888, and to nothing in 1889.[2]

Dona Antónia decided to cut her losses, and the quinta was sold to Cockburn the same year. This explains the other name by which the quinta is sometimes known to the local Portuguese, the Quinta dos Ingleses (and even, it is said, the Quinta do Smith [sic]). The house contains a map of the quinta made in 1890 on which the land which is now the old vineyard is marked 'inculto (uncultivated land) da D. Antónia Adelaide Ferreira', which suggests that Dona Antónia did not have time to develop the quinta fully. In any event, with no production and *phylloxera* rife, the new owners had to start from scratch.

The neighbouring Quinta da Chousa, now part of Tua, was in the same state. It appears on Forrester's map. Until 1890 it had belonged to the Viscondessa de Ervedosa.[3] It had never recovered from *oïdium*, for even in the mid-1870s Vila Maior laments that 'the last time we saw this property it was in complete decay . . . Previously held in great repute on account of its fine and generous wine, of which it produced 40 pipes, it was finally reduced to one tenth of that quantity'.[4]

In 1890, when it was acquired by Francisco da Rocha Leão, things were even worse. The quinta buildings had been removed to make way for the railway, and the vineyard produced only one pipe. Da Rocha Leão, however, quickly built new *lagares* and a substantial *armazém*, from which a paved road went up to a chalet. Replantation began in 1891, and within twenty years production rose to 50 pipes. With olive plantations, orange groves, and orchards, in 1911 Monteiro was able to claim, with lyrical enthusiasm, that 'the products [of Chousa] are of the most select in the Douro region'[5]

What does he say of Tua? Nothing beyond noting its existence and indicating, in a single sentence, its situation and the fact of its being terraced. This rather suggests that there was little to be very enthusiastic about, and, indeed, it is said that John Smithes purchased Tua principally to provide himself with a headquarters in the Douro.

Nevertheless, even if the vineyards were not immediately of importance in such a context, a great deal of effort was going into building them. The great-grandfather of the present manager at Tua, Sr Floriano Malheiro, worked as a stonemason for John Smithes and supervised the construction of the terraces by *Gallegos* in 1893. The terraces at Tua are undoubtedly amongst the most solid in the Douro, measuring, on average, 1.5 m thick. This massiveness was simply to use up the huge amount of stone in the vineyard, but even so, mountains of stone remained, most of which was removed by women carrying it in baskets on their heads.

Chousa, on the other hand, did not maintain the perfection which so impressed Monteiro. It continued to flourish under Sr da Rocha Leão, producing for a time about 80 pipes, but in the 1930s it was purchased by António de Castro, and within ten years it was again in decline. By the time Cockburn decided to purchase it from the heirs of António de Castro in 1973 it was very run down, and the châlet had to be demolished.[6]

Tua, by comparison with Chousa, is quite tiny and, until recently, not a great deal of wine was produced there. It was only when port sales began to increase in the 1960s that Cockburn decided to develop the quinta seriously. The purchase of Chousa in 1973 was a logical step in this plan; and subsequent development of both quintas as a single unit has raised production six-fold.

If Tua was originally not particularly useful to Cockburn for port production, it was useful in another, somewhat pioneering, way because, in the wake of *phylloxera*, it provided a venue for controlled scientific study of viticulture. Smithes used his vineyard to experiment with grafting, different methods of pruning, etc. Indeed, the company's present operations at the Quinta do Atayde at Vilariça, which started with some materials taken from Tua, continue a tradition established here a century ago.

Today the massive terraces of the original Tua vineyard contrast with the *patamares* of Chousa, where all the old terraces have disappeared and the road to Carrazeda de Ansiães now crosses it several times. Chousa has been block planted with the same varieties as Tua, but, unlike Tua, it is mechanized.

Slightly uphill from the quinta house at Tua are the offices, *adega* and *armazéms*. The *lagares* are no longer used unless the other vinification facilities cannot cope with the volume of grapes, which, since Cockburn also use the plant to vinify bought-in grapes, can sometimes happen.

Externally the house is built in the style of a traditional *solar*, with granite corner pilasters and window dressings and a central balcony. An elm, standing to one side of the front of the house, casts its shadows across the façade and shades the *caseiro*'s house, which is situated in the old kitchen to the right of the main house. In the early 1970s alterations made the house more amenable, but until then it was by all accounts quite spartan, reminding one of Vizetelly's phrase 'roughing it'. Wyndham Fletcher, who knew the quinta well, describes it thus:

> Until fairly recently concessions to undue comfort in the house would have been considered decadent in the extreme, especially as the visits of ladies were not encouraged. The beds were like boards, there was only one bath with limited hot water, so that at vintage time when there were many guests the last to bath probably emerged dirtier than when he went in. There was only one primitive lavatory, which meant that some people had to make an early morning trip to the concealing foliage of the vineyard.[7].

I am very happy to report from personal experience that all that has changed. The house is now extremely comfortable, and, in the heat of the summer, guests even have a swimming pool. If it still has one major disadvantage it is the Mirandela branch line of the railway, which passes between the house and the main road. At 6.30 a.m. one's slumbers are apt to be rudely shattered as the first train of the day sounds as if it were coming straight through the bedroom.

Fletcher's remark about the discouragement of women echoes some of the discussion in the Introduction. Writing in 1969, Sarah Bradford speaks of the 'monastic vintage' at Tua, when the 'men only' rule was temporarily suspended to enable her to pay a visit, but only in her 'capacity as a writer'.[8]

The quinta port goes to the vintage blend, or otherwise to Cockburn's Special Reserve. Although there has not, as yet, been a single quinta wine, to celebrate the 175th anniversary of the founding of Cockburn in 1815, a single Quinta do Tua 1987 vintage was bottled in 1990, to be released at a future date. Whether it will be the first of many remains to be seen.

With its vineyards next to the Quinta do Tua, and its house down by the railway, we come now to the Quinta do Zimbro.

Quinta do Zimbro

A *zimbro* is a juniper – the *Juniperis communis*, consecrated to Apollo by the Greeks and the symbol of asylum. As you might expect, therefore, there is a juniper tree next to the quinta house. In fact there are two: the original one looking very battered and feeble; and another, not looking exactly young, which was clearly planted as a potential replacement by a generation with insufficient faith in the staying power of the first. I do not know how to date trees, but at the end of last century the original tree was already so old that Charles Sellers remarked that it 'is so plastered up that it is wonderful how it has preserved its vitality'.[1] Its one remaining branch, reaching out towards the side of the house, continues to flourish, albeit supported by a rusty metal beam which was remarked upon by Monteiro in 1911.

Zimbro, in common with other quintas at the eastern extremity of the Pombaline demarcations of 1758 and 1761, was rated for wines at 10,500 *réis*. Its history, however, probably stretches much further back than that, considering that the neighbouring Zimbro da Cima has been in the possession of the family of its present owners since 1684.

The quinta house incorporates a chapel, tiny but with an elaborate stone façade surmounted by an heraldic device. Vila Maior says it was owned by 'the house of Snrs Barros of Sabrosa', and it was presumably from them that it was purchased by George Warre, the senior partner of Silva & Cosens, in or just before 1888 – his first Douro property.

Evidently badly affected by *phylloxera*, Warre immediately started to replant. The visitors' book of the quinta (now kept at Bomfim) starts in 1889 and reflects not only the ups and downs of the vines, but the air of uncertainty still hanging over the future of port. *1894*: 'Found the 88 planting infected with Phylloxera – badly . . . Am[erican] Vines very good, But Portuguese bad.' Two years later things appeared to be looking up. *1896*: 'This year's wines are I consider better than any since 1878 & will I hope and believe start a new era in the Port Wine Trade.' Then, in *1897*: 'Old Portuguese vines much affected by Phylloxera.' *1898*: 'New graftings good on the whole.' *1900*: WPR writes, 'All the new plantings of vines promises well & it is a great pleasure to come to see the Quinta again and to think that there is a fair prospect of success in the future.'

Improvements to the quinta continued, and in 1903 the visitors' book has an astonishing entry: 'Bat Fives court at Z just finished – a magnificent adjunct to the Quinta'. Only those who have actually seen the quinta buildings could appreciate the extreme improbability of there ever having been a fives court at Zimbro. Perhaps this entry was simply a drunken joke.

1905: 'Zimbro is as delightful as ever. The nightingales are alive and kicking.' *1909*: 'RT finished this particular evening with a wrestling match versus the sideboard and was carried to bed by the Colonel with a broken nose. No nightingales.'

Despite progress made at Bomfim, Zimbro maintained its position as an important Silva & Cosens property until the beginning of the war. In 1939, we read that 'the new plantation at Zimbro is looking very nice'. After the war, however, everything had changed. By 1947 references to Bomfim outnumber those to Zimbro, and its visitors' book had become transformed into the one used at Bomfim. It is clear that the order of importance of the quintas had been reversed.

This was not the only change. As recounted earlier,[2] the withdrawal of the Warres from Silva & Cosens brought about the decision to sell Zimbro (and Senhora da Ribeira.) It must have been a bitter decision to make, but in 1955 the quinta was sold to Dr João Cruz Sampaio. The visitors' book entry for 18–20 February records the sale in brief, unemotional terms: 'Went up to Carrazeda to see about sale of Zimbro and had to plough through about 4 inches of snow'. That is all.

Since then the fortunes of Silva & Cosens, owned by the Symingtons, have continued to improve. It would be agreeable to be able to say the same of Zimbro, but it has to be reported that the house, at least, is in a run-down state: its front door, like Sleeping Beauty's castle, partly obscured by overgrown shrubbery. Perhaps this is why it is difficult to understand the evident attraction which the place had for its owners in the Silva & Cosens days – though an old engraving hanging at Bomfim makes it look appealingly neat and tidy. The house appears to have been built originally as a typical Douro farm house. The lower floor contains an *armazém*, while access to the first floor, with its tall, well-proportioned rooms and graceful moulded cornices, is from a small terrace with an elegant metal balustrade. The early nineteenth century style of the interior, so much later than that of the chapel, may possibly be the result of rebuilding after a fire.

This potential attractiveness is ruined, however, by the railway which, ever since its construction in the 1880s, has passed the back of the house as if it were for all the world a signal-box. The railway, moreover, runs through a fairly deep cutting, suggesting that the original *adega* was probably built in the traditional way behind the house at a superior level to the *armazém*, but that the path of the railway necessitated its removal when the cutting was made. The present *adega* is situated on the same level as the *armazém*, on the other side of the railway and slightly to one side of the house. It was last used in 1985, though recently the original iron pipes laid under the railway line, through which the must is pumped to the *armazém*, were replaced with new plastic ones.

Apart from a few rows of vines between the house and the river, the main part of the vineyard (wholly traditional and unmechanized) is situated up-hill on the far side of the railway. The produce is bought still by Silva & Cosens, but now the grapes are taken to Bomfim to be vinified. It contributes to the Dow's vintage blend, LBV and aged tawnies.

5 Valeira to Pinhão - south bank

Crossing the Valeira dam, we climb out of the Douro Valley, past the hill of São Salvador do Mundo, with its many little chapels, and, as we head for São João da Pesqueira, we come, on the left, to the massive stone gateway of the Quinta do Sidrô, owned by the Real Companhia Velha.

Quinta do Sidrô

Here we are completely outside the eighteenth-century demarcations. According to Vizetelly, vines were first planted on the Quinta do Sidrô in the early nineteenth century,[1] when the imposing *palácio* was built by the first Marquês de Soveral, Luís Augusto Pinto de Soveral.[2] Vizetelly also remarks that at the time of his visit (1877) the vines had only recently been attacked by *phylloxera*, with production (one third of it white) down from 150 to 120 pipes, and purchased by Sandeman.[3]

Sidrô continued to belong to the Soveral family, which included Luís de Soveral, Ambassador to the Court of St James and a personal friend of King Edward VII,[4] until it passed to António Correa de Sá Benevides Velasco da Câmara, the first Visconde de Asseca, from whose successors, in 1940, it was rented by Dr Amaro de Oliveira. By 1960 it had passed into the hands of Francisco dos Santos Lopes, from whom it was purchased in 1972 by the Real Companhia Velha.

The *palácio*, which can be seen from the road, has a Moorish look about its white, main façade, with its pointed granite window dressings and castellation. If this is somewhat severe, the other side, which faces you as you enter the quinta, offers a softer, more elegant, nineteenth-century frontage, punctuated by granite pilasters and enlivened by wrought iron balconies. It faces a garden with clipped box hedges and a central fountain, beyond which is a swimming pool.

The *palácio* is built round a central court containing two enormous camellias. The doorway within this court is surmounted by the arms of the Soverals. The interior is in the course of being converted, with considerable lavishness, into a guest house, principally for the use of customers of the Real Companhia Velha.[5]

The old *adega* and *armazém* are in a building next to the public road further down the hill. Its *lagares* are no longer in use, the grapes being vinified at the Quinta das Carvalhas. Nor does the *armazém* contain any wine, for the building has been converted to provide accommodation for quinta workers. A new *adega* is, however, being constructed at the moment.

The planting is either vertical or continuous. Much of the production of the quinta is used for table wine – a white wine is sold under the quinta name – the altitude of the vineyards being rather high for the best quality port.[6] The port which is produced goes into the company's cheaper blends.

Going through São João da Pesqueira we shortly come, on the right, to the road leading to two little villages which are perched above the

Douro — Soutelo do Douro and Nagozelo. From Soutelo tracks lead down to our next two destinations. The first is the Quinta dos Aciprestes of the Real Companhia Velha.

Quinta dos Aciprestes

The Quinta dos Aciprestes is best seen from the opposite side of the Douro, stretching for more than 2 km along the south bank from opposite the Quinta dos Malvedos to beyond the Quinta do Tua. It is immediately identifiable, not only by the six cypress trees which stand like sentinels near the quinta house, but from its undulating, prairie-like character arising from the relative absence of traditional terraces or *patamares*.

Since the 1860s the Quinta dos Aciprestes has been a conglomeration of several quintas. The original quinta — called dos Cyprestes — was founded in the eighteenth century by Dom José de Seabra, one of the ministers of Queen Maria I, and owned by his successors, the Viscondes de Baia. In 1864 it was purchased by Dona Antónia Ferreira and her second husband, Francisco da Silva Torres. The following year, apart from numerous small vineyards, they bought two neighbouring properties to form a large estate, variously referred to as the Casal de Soutelo, and later, amongst the locals, as the Quinta da Viscondessa.[1] These were the Quinta da Boa Vista,[2] purchased from Luís and Dona Adelaide de Sousa Pinto Guedes, and the Quinta dos Negrilhos (also known as Carvalhal). In 1869, the Quinta de Mileu da Cima, purchased from the Visconde de Soveral, was added.[3] All these quintas stand on land which, in the 1758 and 1761 demarcations, had its wine rated at 10,500 *réis*.[4]

Vila Maior describes in detail the costly and radical work undertaken to re-establish the quinta, which at this time was 'for the most part in ruin or very run-down'. Usual methods of regeneration being too slow, an 'almost revolutionary' total reconstruction was embarked on. The improvement was indeed quick. In 1865 the vintage yields were: Aciprestes 4, Boa Vista 22 and Negrilhos 8 pipes; but by 1869, even 'in their present state of transition', the yields were Aciprestes 33, Boa Vista 33 and Negrilhos 11 pipes. Mileu gave 19 pipes. Vila Maior says that the goal aimed at was between 220 and 250 pipes.

The undertaking was immense: apart from making terraces and planting, there was the cost of building two wide roads with interconnecting tracks running the entire length of the estate, and buildings to deal with the increased production.[5]

The estate remained in the hands of a descendant of Dona Antónia until the middle of this century, when it was acquired by Sr Adelino Silva. He also owned the Quinta da Barreira, downstream from Aciprestes (previously in the da Costa Seixas family for countless generations) and this became part of the estate. Then, in the early 1960s, Adelino Silva sold it all to Miguel de Sousa Guedes & Irmão, Lda, incorporated into the Real Companhia Velha in 1965.

In recent years Sr Manuel da Silva Reis, the moving force of the

Real Companhia Velha, has been accomplishing his own 'almost revolutionary' transformation of the quinta. Almost 85 per cent of the vineyards are new plantations. Taking advantage of the fairly gentle gradients of up to 30 per cent, Sr da Silva Reis has embarked upon large-scale vertical planting, now about half the total. There is also a high proportion of continuous planting. 60 per cent of the quinta is mechanized, though there are only a few hectares of *patamares* at Barreira, and not much of the original terracing remains. This gives rise to the open, prairie-like look of the landscape referred to above. Old terraces do remain along the river-bank, but these are planted with olive, almond and orange trees.

The quinta house, built by Dona Antónia and presently occupied by the *caseiro*, has recently been extended. It is noteworthy insofar as the *armazém* and *adega*, although built traditionally one below the other, slope inland, away from the river. The *adega*, *armazém* and *azenha* of Boa Vista, further up-stream, are older. Metal-frame windows indicate relatively recent changes, but the building is now derelict. Indeed, as the grapes are now all taken to the Quinta das Carvalhas for vinification, the *lagares* here and at Aciprestes are unused.

Ferreira at one time marketed a 'Quinta dos Aciprestes' port,[6] but the Real Companhia Velha does not. Three quarters of the wine is made into port, used in the company's premium brands, including the vintage blend.

Somewhat confusingly the quinta is referred to within the company as the Quinta do Tua. Perhaps, in view of its size and history, Sr da Silva Reis might revert to calling it, parallel with Granja, by its 1865 name – the Casal de Soutelo.

Further downstream is the Quinta do Vau of Sandeman & Ca, Lda.

Quinta do Vau

This quinta stands on one side of a re-entrant opposite the eastern extremity of the Quinta da Romaneira and the Castedo railway station, Vau has grown over the years, but particularly since 1980 when its previous owner, Sr Frederico Sarmento, a noted coffee importer, began to acquire several neighbouring properties.

Although omitted from the 1757 demarcation, the margins of this part of the Douro, and, more significantly, the right bank of the little stream (the Ribeiro do Caêdo, which joins the Douro at this point) on which the quinta stands, were rated for wine at 10,500 *réis* in 1758 and 1761. The left bank of the stream was not rated at all.[1] Confusingly, a second Quinta do Vau stands on this side.

The quinta was purchased by Sandeman in 1988 and a big programme of improvement is under way. When I visited Vau in 1989, 17 ha of new *patamares* were being prepared. There is also a small amount of vertical planting. The quinta has a house close to the entrance from Soutelo do Douro, and, down by the river, a modern (I am sorry to say, rather ugly) building which houses both an *adega* and further accommodation. Both are being renovated, and in the meantime the quinta wine is vinified in the company's *adega* at Celeirós.

Sandeman have bought Vau to raise the general quality of wine available from their own vineyards. They are already so pleased with the result that in 1990 they released a single quinta 1988 port, made from their first vintage after acquiring the property.

We return to the main road again, and in a short distance we pass on our left a sign 'Banco Borges & Irmão: Quinta da Soalheira 5.5 km'. As this quinta is in the Rio Torto valley, we shall postpone consideration of it until the appropriate part of this section. It is mentioned now purely for location purposes. Instead, continuing towards Pinhão, we turn right just beyond Ervedosa do Douro to reach the Quinta do Roriz.

Quinta do Roriz

The Quinta do Roriz is deservedly famous. Not only has its wine enjoyed renown since the eighteenth century, when it was amongst the first ever to be exported as a single quinta, but Roriz possesses perhaps the most picturesque quinta buildings of any in the region.

The story of its foundation, as told by Vila Maior, deserves repetition.

> *About the time the demand of English trade for our wines began to encourage the durian viticulture . . . there arrived from England a Scottish gentleman named Robert Archibald who being very much addicted to field sports and used to scouring the hills and glens of Scotland, found the savage wilds and rugged steeps of the Douro very well suited to his tastes. His sporting excursions having carried him to the place of Roriz, it came into his mind to build there a shooting-box . . . This lodge was the beginning of the Quinta do Roriz.*[1]

Archibald's shooting-box was a primitive, free-stone building with a door but no windows, and a conical roof surmounted by a rather lop-sided granite pinnacle. It stood to the east of the present quinta buildings and survived, remarkably enough, in a very dilapidated state, until 1940, when it was demolished to make way for the new Serro de Guarita vineyard.[2] Archibald took a perpetual lease of the surrounding land from its owners, the Tres-Minas da Ordem de Cristo, and apparently started planting.

All this happened at the beginning of the eighteenth century. By the time of the Pombaline demarcations, Roriz was a flourishing quinta and had been inherited by Archibald's son, Diogo, who was clearly an important and respected person in Oporto. To defuse the animosity of the English factors, and to see that fair play was done, Diogo was invited, at the suggestion of the Marquês de Pombal, to accompany the Old Company's deputies as they travelled around the Douro making the 1757 demarcation.[3] In the synopsis of the demarcation

Opposite
38
Quinta de Val Coelho, seen across the Douro with the railway viaduct in the foreground

Overleaf
39
Train crossing the bridge over the Rio Tua where it joins the Douro. The Quinta dos Aciprestes is seen across the Douro

which the deputies were taxed with effecting, Roriz was rated for wine at 15,000 *réis*.[4]

In 1758 this rating was confirmed for the Quinta do Roriz, although surrounding vineyards (which by now apparently existed) were confined to 10,500 *réis*.[5] The following year, however, Diogo petitioned, along with a neighbour, for inclusion in the *feitoria*; both were unsuccessful.[6] The 1758 rating remained unchanged in 1761,[7] to be immediately amended (on the suggestion of the Secretary of State, the Conde de Oeiras) to 19,200 *réis* only days after the details of the demarcation had been confirmed. This concession was a compromise, however, limited to between 60 and 70 pipes per year from the vineyards nearest the quinta houses and the chapel 'because the greater part of the plantations there are of French grapes'.[8]

The Quinta do Roriz was not fully admitted to the *feitoria* until August, 1787.[9] The facts, therefore, do not support Vila Maior's colourful and malicious assertion that the next owner of Roriz, Nicolau Kopke, who took possession following a judicial order against the bankrupt Diogo Archibald, managed to persuade the Marquês de Pombal to allow Roriz into the *feitoria*. He adds, ironically, 'I do not wish to say that, if the Marquês de Pombal had not been Commander of the Tres Minas' – from whom the quinta was leased and – 'to whom the rents were paid, he would not have proceeded in the same way to grant the royal provision to remedy an absurdity and rectify an injustice.'[10]

The Marquês de Pombal was certainly corrupt – he exported wine from his estates at Carcavelos, near Lisbon, as port[11] – but he fell from power with the death of Dom José in 1777, ten years before the date given by Fonseca. In any case, it is likely that, as elsewhere, some way had been found to circumvent the regulations and export the wine, for Vila Maior tells us that although 'the Quinta do Roriz was not included in the demarcation of this area, [it] even then produced the best wines of the Douro and the most esteemed in England'.[12]

The port shipping firm of C N Kopke & Ca, Lda, goes back to 1638 when Cristiano Kopke, the son of the Consul of the Hanseatic towns in Lisbon, settled in Oporto and became a merchant dealing, amongst other things, in wine.[13] When Nicolau took over Roriz, therefore, his firm had been established for more than a century, but the quinta remained the property of the family. The Kopkes had an astonishing propensity for marrying within the family, and when the quinta passed from Nicolau to his son, Cristiano, he was already married to his niece, Leonor Caroline van Zeller, whose father, Henrique Pedro van Zeller, was of Dutch descent. Cristiano was caught up in the War of the Two Brothers[14] and fled to England in 1828. Returning after six years, he was later created Barão de Vilar e Remalde for services to Dom Pedro IV in 1836. After his death, in 1840, the quinta became the property of his wife. Having been born in 1796, she not only outlived her own husband by more than 35 years, but also outlived her only daughter, Dorothea Augusta, and her husband (another cousin), Roberto van Zeller (himself the son of two van Zeller cousins). Thus the quinta was inherited by Leonor's grandson,

Previous page
40
Quinta da Romaneira. This gateway leads into the courtyard of Romaneira Nova

Opposite
41
The Quinta do Cachão

Cristiano van Zeller. The present owners are his grandson, Dr Pedro van Zeller, and his two sons, Pedro and João.

Looking back at Diogo Archibald's time, from various demarcation documents we learn that the quinta was then a league (5 km) in circumference and regularly produced 80 pipes. It already had its handsome chapel, and in 1764 a separate but traditionally arranged *adega* and *armazém* was built – the 'old' *adega*.[15] The modest but charming quinta house, with an *armazém* beneath, is of the same period, and the little cluster of quinta buildings must have looked very much as it does now.

The vineyards, however, were quite different. The 'French grapes', to which the deputies made reference, were reputedly the *pinot noir*, which Robert Archibald had had imported from Burgundy – now known as Tinta Francisca (*not* Tinta Roriz, as one might be pardoned for thinking), and not greatly esteemed nowadays.

Vila Maior, who gives the production at this time as between 50 and 60 pipes (perhaps Diogo had exaggerated to the demarcation commission), says that it only rose above this after the Kopkes had reformed the vineyards and made new plantations. The entire vineyard was laid out, as was very common in the Douro at this time, in *pilheiros*,[16] which survived until the Barão de Massarelos took over the administration of the quinta. He was a cousin of Leonor, the Baroneza de Vilar, and presumably ran the quinta for her after her husband's death in 1840.

The Barão de Massarelos undertook new plantings of some 70 ha. Vila Maior remarks that 'one does not see in this quinta, as in many of our vineyards, a multiplicity of grape varieties with neither order nor selection ... The following preponderate: Tinta Francisca, Alvarilhão and Tinto Cão; but there are also sufficient Touriga, Mourisco, Tinto Carvalho and some Bastardo.' A rather different selection from those in favour today. He adds that 'the proprietors, zealous to preserve the reputation of this quinta's wines, have not altered this original list of varieties, nor allowed the introduction of new varieties which might profoundly change their already established and accepted character.'[17] Vila Maior particularly admired the system of roads which was also installed. 'In this regard there are few properties in the Douro which can compare with Roriz, perhaps none.'[18]

Alas, it was for the successive attentions of *oïdium* and *phylloxera* that he was preparing. The first seems to have taken less toll than elsewhere, and Vila Maior (in 1869) says that, despite rumours to the contrary, he found the vines in 'apparent vigour' and 'not lacking the care and attentive cultivation necessary to their preservation.'[19] But when *phylloxera* struck the result was catastrophic; the entire quinta was virtually wiped out and production sank to 40 *almudes* (just under 2 pipes).[20] After this 'survival' crops of cereal and tobacco were planted, and eventually, as Sellers reports, it was 'all replanted with the American vines'.[21]

Among the improvements made by the Barão de Massarelos were a 'new' *adega* and *armazém*, built in 1852. Unlike the *lagares* in the 'old' *adega*, made of roughly hewed slabs of slate, which Vila Maior thought in poor contrast to the 'nobility of the property', there were granite *lagares* in the 'new' building, which he found smaller but 'very modern'. The 1764 *lagares* were, in fact, removed in 1904-5 and replaced with six 20 pipe and two smaller granite ones. The side of one *lagar* is a single slab of granite 4.5 x 0.75 x 0.22 m. More intriguingly, the smaller *lagares* are equipped with urinals – rather small bowls which overhang the *lagares* with outlets to the exterior of the wall. In the heady atmosphere and the jollity of the vintage one must wonder about the accuracy of the aim of the *lagareiros*! Moreover, after reading Vila Maior, one is surprised to find slate *lagares* in the 'new' *adega*. Did the changes of 1904-5 perhaps consist of switching the *lagares* round and remodelling them?

The 'new' *adega* and *armazém*, with the *caseiro*'s house and some outside stores, complete the existing group of quinta buildings.[22] The 'old' *adega* and *armazém*, with storage in *toneis*, are used today, while the 'new' building remains empty. The chapel is also empty at the moment, but is undergoing restoration. Over the door there is a fine, if heraldically suspect, escutcheon with the arms of Kopke shown alongside those of four families to which the Kopkes were linked by marriage: Schwerein (the wife of Nicolau, the original owner of the quinta); and the other three all English: Whittingham (Nicolau's mother), Moring, and Maynard.

One of the distinguishing features of Roriz is the square terrace which stretches towards the Douro from the house, finishing with a parapet flanked at each corner with a tower-like pavilion. These – one used to be a granary and the other an ox-shed and hay loft – are empty. The view from here used to be a dizzy-making 60 m down to the river before it was dammed, and Dr van Zeller's mother 'had a magnificent bullock-cart, beautifully cushioned, to take one from the boat, up the avenue of cypresses, to the house'.[23] Some of the cypresses remain, but not, alas, the bullock-cart.

Today the vineyards comprise some 50 ha – less, despite new plantings within the last six years, than a century ago. Almost half of the vineyards are planted continuously, with some vertical planting and PDRITM *patamares*, which make about three fifths of the quinta mechanized. More mechanization is envisaged, but not in the immediate future. Tinta Francisca can be found amongst the grape varieties – a mere 3 per cent – which are significantly different from those of last century.

It was C N Kopke & Ca who, of course, purchased the quinta port and built up its reputation in the nineteenth century. Thirteen bottles of what was believed to be the 1834 Quinta do Roriz port were sold by Christie's, the London auctioneers, on 1 December 1983. According to the cellar records it had been purchased by the vendor's forbears in 1839 from Winstanley, the wine merchants, at 50 shillings a dozen (£2.50), and recorked in 1878. This is the earliest extant single quinta port of whose existence I am aware.[24] Roriz port, however, made its London saleroom appearance well over a century before these bottles, with 15 dozen 'Roriz Port 1851' being offered on 31 July 1872, and fetching the extremely high price of 84 shillings (£4.20) a dozen.[25]

Kopke continued to sell the quinta wine during most of last century, even though the firm was bought in 1870 by its London agents, Mason Cattley and Co, owned by the Bohane family. (In 1952 it was purchased by Barros.) A change occurred at the turn of the century, however, when the sherry firm of Gonzalez Byass diversified into port in 1896, and secured a monopoly of the Roriz wine. From 1901 until the mid-1930s their vintage wines were shipped under the Roriz name.[26] So Roriz appeared on the English market at least for over a century as a single quinta wine and appears to have the longest (documented) history of so doing.

When Gonzalez Byass (which has now ceased to exist as an independent port shipper) stopped buying Roriz about twenty years ago, it was bought by Ferreira. From 1990 it has been purchased by Quinta do Noval for a subsidiary company, which trades under the family name, and it is planning, at its next vintage declaration, to launch a single quinta Van Zeller's Quinta do Roriz. It must be said that, given its former reputation, it will be more than a little interesting to see if Roriz can again recapture the pre-eminent position it once undoubtedly had.

6 The Rio Torto valley

At the top of the Rio Torto valley[1] *is the Quinta da Soalheira, located in the previous part of this section between São João da Pesqueira and Ervedosa do Douro.*

Quinta da Soalheira

Few people unconnected with the wine trade, perhaps, have occasion to travel the 5.5 km which lead from the main road to the Quinta da Soalheira.[1] After leaving the main road nothing more is signposted, and secondary tracks lead off confusingly in other directions. The journey quickly becomes rather daunting to all but the most determined. Suddenly the road, which leads to the upper reaches of the Rio Torto, begins a steep descent, twisting and turning down through rocky slopes which, in spring, are a mass of rock-roses and broom. Vertiginous drops give glimpses of the terrace-lined road beneath, so far below that it seems to be impossible that the road one is travelling could descend steeply enough to connect with what one sees.

'Soalheira' means 'the noon-day heat', and in the summer it is wise not to stop the car for a moment lest it should be engulfed by the swirl of choking dust thrown up by the wheels. You have to struggle on, speculating uneasily whether or not you have chosen the proper road; and, eventually, after what seems to be the longest 5.5 km imaginable, you arrive at the quinta not knowing quite what to expect.

Soalheira proves to be a large quinta sitting astride the Rio Torto, which is, at this point, rather narrow but just as twisted as ever. On the left bank wild and tangled woods, useless even for hunting, extend to the summit of the hill, whilst on the right bank there are vineyards on both slopes of a shoulder of land situated in a rightward bend of the river. From here one can look down the Torto valley as far as Lages, with the Casa Redonda at Carvalhas almost on the horizon.

While the approach does not, somehow, suggest that you are about to stumble on an ultra-modern winery, nor does it quite prepare you to find a quinta of such unspoilt enchantment. If you appreciate the sort of remote and timeless tranquillity which soothes the soul and captivates the imagination, then your hot and dusty journey will have been rewarded. In the Quinta da Soalheira you will find one of the real time-warp quintas of the Douro.

Remote though Soalheira is, the indefatigable Vizetelly, despite getting 'lost and benighted' in Ervedosa, managed to pay it a visit. What he says suggests that the quinta was at that time a relatively new one, for which its (un-named) owner had very ambitious plans. It is, he says, 'exceedingly well situated ... outside the extensive circle of vineyards assailed by the *phylloxera*'. Although already 'producing on an average 180 pipes of wine yearly ... the vineyard when completely planted will yield, it is anticipated, from six to seven hundred pipes per annum; and its proprietor, undismayed by the *phylloxera* at the threshold of his quinta, has a band of a couple of hundred men regularly employed every spring in planting additional vines'.[2]

It is clear that these plans were never fully implemented. Had they been, Soalheira would have become one of the largest producing quintas in the Douro. We do not know what happened, but we may guess that the owner's evident optimism that *phylloxera* could be indefinitely kept at bay proved to be unfounded. This may be how Soalheira subsequently came to be acquired for 8 *contos* in 1904 by the Borges brothers, the founders of the bank and the wine company bearing their name.[3]

Needless to say, perhaps, this area was well outside any of the eighteenth-century demarcations. At the moment over half of Soalheira's vineyards are still on traditional terraces, the remainder consisting of *patamares* made first of all between 1973-75 and then through PDRITM.

The quinta buildings are clustered on the divide of the vineyard slopes and overlook the greater part of them. Passing the old *armazém* on your left, you arrive at last on level ground shaded by a vine-covered *ramada*. Above the *armazém* is the *adega*, its *lagares* unused and its *toneis* empty. The grape harvest is now taken to be vinified at the Quinta do Junco. There is also an *azenha*, and, as a kind of *quid pro quo*, olives are brought from Junco to Soalheira to be made into oil.

Beside the steps leading down to the *armazém* there are cascades of flowers and a *tanque* in which carp swim. At this point the *ramada* divides; one branch leads to stores, whilst the other longer branch leads past plots of potatoes and roses to the *caseiro*'s house. A dog is chained so that it cannot chase the guinea-fowl which are pecking on the path. The pigs are in an enclosure next to the house, and a cage with a tame bird hangs by the door.

Next to the house the quinta kitchen, with its corner fireplace, leads into the *azenha*. Beyond the kitchen, the refectory for the workers is dominated by a notice with the 'do's and 'don't's of the house which has been put there by Sr Carlos Silva, the *caseiro*. It bids the workers welcome, cautions them against dirtying the floor, not taking care of the beds, and, above all, causing the *caseiro* any trouble! Changed days: for Vizetelly also reports that he found the running of Soalheira, like Roêda, in the charge of a priest. 'It is considered that a priest is able to exercise far greater influence over the people employed than an overseer taken from their own class ... The rural clergy here have not lost their hold upon the peasantry'.[4]

But the workers are nowhere to be seen; nobody except Sr Silva and his wife and daughter appears to be around. It is the old story; labour is hard to get here, particularly because of the remoteness of the place. The rigours of life on a quinta like Soalheira, particularly in the middle of winter, should not be under-estimated. Yet life is not entirely without its comforts. Although electricity made its appearance only in 1988, a battery television (covered, like the radio and the telephone, with a chintz 'tea-cosy') previously brought *Fawlty Towers* and other British comedies to brighten life in the quinta kitchen. Despite electricity it still does!

The atmosphere of tranquillity and happiness which dominates this quinta, and which clearly surmounts the obvious problems of living in such isolation, seems to owe little to such incongruous modern comforts. It is something to ponder as, in another cloud of dust, you urge your car up the steeply twisted road and back to so-called modern civilization.

Resuming our route at Ervedosa do Douro, we continue down-hill. Just as the Douro, with good views across to Pinhão, comes in sight the road dips to the left into the valley of the Rio Torto – accurately called 'the twisted river'. To our right are slopes belonging to the Quinta das Carvalhas, and to the left we have fine views up the valley. A road to the left, signed to Sarzedinho, takes us across the Rio Torto. If we turn left we reach the Quinta das Lages.

Quinta das Lages

This is one of the largest and most important quintas of the Rio Torto valley. In 1792 its owner, Sylvestre José Vieira Pimenta of Canelas, petitioned for the inclusion of the quinta in the then expanding *feitoria* – it was in an area already rated at 10,500 *réis* in 1761. His case was that the quinta was only a small distance from the Douro (actually about 4 km) and from other quintas, such as Bom Retiro, which were already within the demarcation. The petition also mentions that the quinta has young vines (already yielding abundantly), and this suggests that the quinta had, perhaps, not long been founded.[1]

The quinta remained in the possession of the same family for most of the next century, the owners in 1869 being António Augusto Vieira Pimenta and his brothers.[2] Shortly after this, however, the quinta was in the possession of Francisco Franco of Espinhosa who, in 1886, sold it to Dr Baltazar Augusto Ribeiro, an ancestor of the present owner, for 200,000 *réis*.[3]

The quinta buildings are reached by a road which climbs past eucalyptus trees and small groves of olive and orange trees, then through some red painted gates and under a *ramada*. The old house was replaced in 1963 by a modern structure, which, though small, contains a tiny oratory and has a delightful terrace opening from its living room. Behind the house is a typical farm yard, with a hen-run and woodshed. Here also is the quinta kitchen, and, in an annexe to the main house, the manager's accommodation. The *cardenhos* are in another building, also dating from 1963, situated downhill towards the river. There is a traditional *armazém* arrangement adjacent to the house. The *toneis* date from 1879, and are festooned with *ramos* preserved from previous vintages. The *adega* has granite *lagares*.

Lages incorporates another quinta, the Quinta Nova (about half the size of the original Lages, although both have since been added to) which was purchased by Dr Ribeiro at the turn of the century for 12,000 *réis*. It is situated further upstream and has a fine quinta house, now undergoing renovation for family use. Inside there is another oratory; but not the least of its features is a handsome pavilionesque loo in the garden – also, it is hoped, to be restored. Here, too, though at the moment unused, is another traditional *adega* with five *lagares*.

Lages is a large quinta; the road from one end to the other (the quinta buildings being at its northern extremity) covers almost 6 km, and the quinta extends from the banks of the Rio Torto to the crest of the hill on which it is situated (over which is the valley of the Rio Távora). Apart from some PDRITM *patamares*, the quinta has broad terraces, mostly on the relatively gentle slopes of the Rio Torto. It is planned, however, to convert more of them into *patamares*, and a *mortório* further up the hillside is to be replanted vertically.

Lages, for more than three quarters of a century, has unfailingly sold its wine to Graham, who have traditionally used it as the backbone of their vintage port. Sr Paulo Duarte, the quinta manager, who has himself worked at Lages for fifty years, is very proud of this connection with Graham. It is a relationship of trust, he told me, based on a long-standing, purely oral, contract by which the port is sold without the price having been discussed beforehand. This is by no means a unique arrangement in the Douro valley, but it must be somewhat unusual (and heartening) for the end of the twentieth century.

Returning to the bridge, we go towards Sarzedinho and the Quinta do Retiro Novo, belonging to Wiese & Krohn, Sucrs, Lda.

Quinta do Retiro Novo

The Quinta do Retiro Novo stands at the edge of the village. The red roof of its *armazém* is conspicuous from a distance, but neither this nor the attractive view of the farm house, seen from the village over the quinta's immaculately kept vegetable rows, quite prepares you for the charm of the scene inside the quinta's rather anonymous green gates. Here you find, entirely secluded, a little court around which are ranged the quinta buildings, white-washed and surmounted by red tiled roofs.

The surface of the court consists almost entirely of raw schist — an eloquent reminder of the nature of the local terrain. Facing you is the *caseiro*'s house — in front of it a mimosa with a swing; on its walls four bird cages, one exotic inhabitant giving a splash of yellow to the scene, another (a thrush) piping its song. To your left is the eighteenth-century *casa de patrão*, in front of it a little *ramada*, under which are a stone coat of arms and a small porch. To the right is the *adega*, and from it a door leads to the lower level *armazém*, containing several *toneis*. These, like the *lagares*, have only recently been reconditioned, because for many years no wine was made on the quinta since the grapes were sold directly to a shipper. At the end of 1989, however, the quinta was acquired by Wiese & Krohn.

The quinta has a long history. It was initially called the Quinta do Lapa, presumably because that was then the name of its owner. It was then acquired by Manuel Magalhães and remained in the family until his great-granddaughter, Maria Leonor Magalhães Bacelar, sold it to Wiese & Krohn. The handsome coat of arms on the wall of the quinta house is that of the Carneiro family. This is not the result of Dr Carneiro, one of the owners of the firm, wishing to put a proprietary stamp on the quinta; it was put there some twenty years ago by the previous owner's husband, whose grandmother was a Carneiro.

As is so often the case when a shipper takes on a new quinta, there is much to be done to remedy years of less than ideal maintenance. Dr Carneiro would be the first to agree that Retiro Novo was no exception. The two *cardenhos* were in need of total renovation and electricity and water had yet to be installed in some parts of the quinta.[1] But it was the vineyards which needed most attention.

A mule still works on the terraces, but mechanization is rapidly being introduced. The quinta contains a small re-entrant, and the terraces follow its curve, climbing the hill up to the village from the Rio Torto. Beyond, where the quinta borders the Quinta do Bom Retiro Pequeno, over a hectare of *patamares* has already replaced some olive planted *mortórios*, and a further 6 ha will be planted in 1992. The oldest vines are between the *armazém* and the Rio Torto. The shoulder of the hill is so steep here that, looking across from the top terrace to the Quinta do Cedavim on the opposite bank, one cannot see the river. 'Of course, a point will be reached when the transferring of this vineyard will be inevitable,' Dr Carneiro told me, 'but we want to keep it for as long as possible because here the quality is very high.'

The work that needs to be done will take time, but Wiese & Krohn are confident that in the Quinta do Retiro Novo they have found an asset which will prove its value in the future.

Rejoining the main road we go down to Casais do Douro, where we find the entrance to the quintas of Bom Retiro, belonging to Adriano Ramos-Pinto, Vinhos, SA, and Bom Retiro Pequeno, which is privately owned.

Quinta do Bom Retiro

Anyone who has seen the marvellous series of sexy *art nouveau* posters commissioned by Adriano Ramos-Pinto,[1] the founder of the firm which bears his name, will recognize that he had a certain appreciation of the female form. The quinta lives up to its name as a 'good retreat', although I doubt whether we should believe the stories which have it that he used the quinta as a discreet rendezvous for entertaining beautiful women brought all the way from Paris to Pinhão, without running the Oporto gauntlet![2] On the other hand, Bom Retiro appears to have an unchallenged claim to being the first quinta to have had the fleshly delights of a swimming pool – albeit disguised as a garden pond[3] – so perhaps the vision of flapper nymphs dipping their toes in the water may not be so wide of the mark after all.

The precise origins of the quinta are obscure, but it appears to have had its origin in the beginning of the eighteenth century. Until 1772 it belonged to Luís Beleza de Andrade, Provedor of the Old Company, from whom it passed to João Henrique de Magalhães, an Oporto wine exporter, and remained in his family until the second decade of this century. He it was who managed to have the quinta included in the *feitoria*, having successfully petitioned the crown in 1789.[4] The somewhat odd sketch map which accompanied this petition is used by Ramos-Pinto as a label for the twenty year old quinta tawny which came on to the market in 1985.

The original Quinta do Bom Retiro was larger than it is now, since it was split into two – Bom Retiro Grande and Bom Retiro Pequeno – after having been inherited by two heirs. Bom Retiro Grande, now known simply as Bom Retiro, went to Dr Luís de Magalhães, and Bom Retiro Pequeno to Dona Joaquina Soares Veloso Guimarães.[5] Subsequently, Bom Retiro passed to Luís Cipriano Coelho de Magalhães and his wife, who sold it in 1919 to Adriano Ramos-Pinto.

The right bank of the Rio Torto rises more steeply than the left, which, just before the Quinta da Côrte is reached, widens out into a basin which, being surrounded by hills, is extremely sheltered. Seen from the road which continues from Ervedosa towards Bateiras, on the opposite side of the Rio Torto, the terraces rise steeply from the river and dramatically emphasize its tortuous twists, while the quinta buildings sit on a little plateau immediately above. Beyond them the land climbs more gently up to a crest on which is sited the little village of Valença do Douro. One can also see from the road a distinctive row of twenty-four cypress trees, now more than sixty years old, beside which a dense thicket of the original Douro forest has been preserved, and beyond which extensive vertical planting can be seen.

Indeed, with its varied terrain and methods of planting, Bom Retiro is a quinta which repays study, and for that reason is often visited by students of viticulture. Under the aegis of Sr José António Ramos-Pinto Rosas, until recently the president of the firm, and his nephew Eng° João Nicolau de Almeida, Ramos-Pinto has for many years taken a keen interest in viticultural research and has welcomed experimentation on the quinta by the Centro de Estudos Vitivinícolas do Douro (CEVD). Thus, it was at Bom Retiro that *patamares* were first tried out in the Douro to study the possible mechanization of the vineyards.

Despite the widespread acceptance of *patamares* both by the CEVD and by many other farmers, Ramos-Pinto, at any rate, have never been convinced of their success. They have, instead, favoured vertical planting as a solution with, on balance, more advantages than disadvantages, and Bom Retiro was, apart from an earlier and unsuccessful experiment at the Quinta das Murças, the first Douro quinta to have vertical planting.[6] Despite Ramos-Pinto's pride in its mechanization, its surviving walled terraces are to be retained for historical reasons, and aesthetically they are most attractive.

Ramos-Pinto were also closely involved in experiments to determine the best grape varieties and independently arrived at the final list of five varieties blessed by the CEVD and exclusively used in PDRITM.[7]

Vinification in pump-over tanks has replaced all but one of the original *lagares*, which has been retained for experimental purposes only. In the best years part of the production goes into the vintage blend; in other years it goes to other blends and, of course, to aging for the quinta's twenty year old tawny.

Last century a single quinta vintage wine was produced, and the quinta name was registered as an English trade mark prior to 1873.[8] It also appeared in an early Christie's auction in London, on 12 March 1888: 1 dozen Cockburn's Bom Retiro, bottled November 1849, sold for 155 shillings (£7.75), and on 9 May 1888, 40 dozen Bom Retiro 1861, bottled 1864 by Eddison, sold for 70 shillings (£3.50) a dozen.[9]

Apart from the twenty year old tawny already mentioned, a vintage character wine from the Quinta da Urtiga is sold under this name. The Quinta da Urtiga, with a derelict farmhouse, abandoned at the time of *phylloxera*, was incorporated into Bom Retiro in 1933.

The Bom Retiro quinta house, originally of traditional design incorporating *adega* and *armazém*, is a typical provincial farm-house of the eighteenth century, but now modernized. There is no chapel. In 1919 the front part was remodelled and a most attractive verandah added. Bathed in the scent of the surrounding flowers, and with a beautiful view up the Rio Torto valley, meals are served here in warm weather. In front are the semi-formal gardens with the swimming pool, while, leading away from the house in the direction of Sarzedinho, is the *avenida*. At 1.5 km long, it is one of the few almost level quinta roads of this length in the Douro. Lined with mature palm-trees which later give way to the cypresses mentioned above, it offers an agreeable walk. It is one of the traditions of the quinta that, after dinner, the diners stroll along the *avenida* in the cool of the evening, enjoying the balmy air, and, if they are lucky, the song of the nightingales. In such moments the blessed stillness of Bom Retiro, unsullied by the sound either of train or car, makes its name very apt.

Quinta do Bom Retiro Pequeno

Bom Retiro Pequeno is also an important quinta, although its early history is, of course, shared with Bom Retiro. It has belonged to the Serôdio family since 1935, and its wine has for many years been a major component in Warre's ports, making it one of the most valued of the Rio Torto quintas to the Symingtons.

Although smaller than Bom Retiro in terms of total land area, it is in fact slightly bigger in terms of vineyards. Its buildings, adjacent to those of Bom Retiro, include an old traditional *armazém*, next to which there is a small house. The wine is still made in *lagares*.

From Casais we continue towards Pinhão, passing the Quinta de Santa Bárbara of the CEVD, to rejoin the Douro at Bateiras. On the other side of the bridge, on the left, a road leads towards the Quinta do Côrte, situated between the quintas do Bom Retiro Pequeno and Seixo.

Quinta da Côrte

The Quinta da Côrte – previously das Côrtes – is amongst the most traditional quintas to be found in the Douro and is conspicuous for the monumental regularity of its terraces. An exact date cannot be given to the quinta, but from its situation, it presumably dates back to the early- or mid-eighteenth century. It is a family concern, registered under the ownership of Pacheco & Irmãos Lda. They have run the quinta since almost the beginning of the century, having inherited it from the ancestors of the Cirne family, who, with the Pachecos, are joint owners of the company. There is now a close liaison with Delaforce, Sons & Ca, who are part of Croft.

The quinta buildings are perched about two thirds of the way up the hill and are reached by a rather narrow and precipitous road which winds through the terraces. Dating from the nineteenth century, and renovated about 1947, the quinta house is a low-lying, rectangular building without any special architectural interest. Adjoining this is the farmer's house, with a good traditional farm kitchen.

Across a yard and at a lower level are the *adega* and *armazém*, built one above the other in the usual Douro way. The *adega* has both *lagares* and autovinifiers, which were installed in 1966. The latter are normally used, though the former are also used when there is an excess of production. The wine is stored in the *armazém* over the winter.

As mentioned earlier the entire vineyard, recessed into a curve in the hillside, is traditionally terraced, and its massive walls are kept in meticulous repair. The impressive terraces vary in depth, but tend to have from four to eight rows of vines on each, and, as one would expect in such a quinta, the planting is mixed. There have been no vast new replantation schemes, although regular gradual renewal has been taking place for a number of years. The tradition of mixed planting is continued, the vines having, over-all, the extremely high average age of about fifty years.

There is no mechanization of any sort on the quinta, which is entirely worked by hand according to traditional methods. Sr António Augusto Teixeira, the farm manager, has worked at the quinta for thirty years. To him the quinta is unproblematical: he says he finds that it has neither any special virtues nor any special drawbacks. Certainly it appears to enjoy a good position and exposure, though when I visited it in April 1989 very high winds were creating some anxiety for the safety of the young vine shoots. Vintaging normally starts three or four days after Roêda, and Croft use their measurements of the sugar content of the grapes at Côrte as a general marker for the vintage.

Fifty years ago the quinta's production was purchased by Cockburn, but now it is bought by Delaforce who have for a long time used it as a major component of their declared vintages. What has brought the quinta into more recent prominence, however, is the long-term marketing agreement reached between Pacheco & Irmãos and Delaforce in 1979 to sell Côrte as a single quinta port; 1978 was the first vintage to appear, now followed by several others. Delaforce are delighted with its success so far.

Aesthetically pleasing though the montage of Côrte's splendid terraces undoubtedly is, and however problem-free it happily may now be to Sr Teixeira, Côrte is precisely the kind of quinta which seems most vulnerable to the labour problems looming so large in the future. Sooner or later the owners will have to take a decision about what to do to safeguard that future, and it will certainly not be an easy decision to take. Nevertheless, in the last analysis it is the production of fine port which gives everything else its rationale, so the advent of the bulldozers may become inevitable.

The Douro Superior

The Douro Superior is the third and, in terms of area, the largest of the sub-divisions of the port-producing area. It starts from the Cachão de Valeira and goes up river to Barca d'Alva, a distance of 35 km. Indeed, for a further 27 km beyond Barca d'Alva the river itself forms the eastern border of the area. Likewise of irregular shape, the area is bounded by the Rio Tua at Vilarinho das Azenhas in the north west and extends to Escalhão in the south east, giving the whole a depth of about 45 km.

Covering 110,000 ha, the Douro Superior is almost two and a half times larger than the Baixo Corgo, and almost half of the demarcated area. Yet, with 4,785 ha of vineyards, only 4.4 per cent of it is planted, making its production very small in comparison with the other two divisions. This is partly a reflection of the wholly unsuitable terrain of most of the area, partly a reflection of what, as one moves eastwards from the Cachão, is an increasingly inhospitable climate, and partly a result of history, the area having been so inaccessible for so long.

Nevertheless, it is becoming less inaccessible now, and increasingly shippers are beginning to discover the attractions of having quintas in the Douro Superior. In 1989, a shipper told me: 'Within four years the price of buying a quinta has increased four times. In 1985 one was talking about 500,000 *escudos* [£2,400] per pipe of production as the purchase price. Of course there might well have been additional costs for renovating the place and putting it into proper order. Now one is thinking of a cost more in line with 2,000,000 *escudos* [£8,000] per pipe.' So why buy an expensive and run-down quinta, probably un-mechanized, when one can start from scratch and mechanize at considerably lower cost?

Some shippers are sceptical of the quality which can be produced once you move too far east of the Cachão.[1] Those, however, who have established vineyards in what the others regard as 'suspect' areas say that the quality is very high. It is interesting, therefore, to see how enthusiastic Vila Maior was a hundred and twenty years ago about areas like Moncorvo and Vila Flor, where two shippers have now established themselves.

> The actual production of wine in all these concelhos is still far from what one day it is going to be, when our commercial links have attained that spread which they must achieve through . . . the incessant progress of civilization. . . . A great part of the more or less steep slopes which form the sides of the mountains and ranges surrounding the basin of Vilariça, or of the valleys and ridges which run towards it, as also in the concelhos of Moncorvo, Vila Flor and Alfândega da Fé, are unarguably suited to the

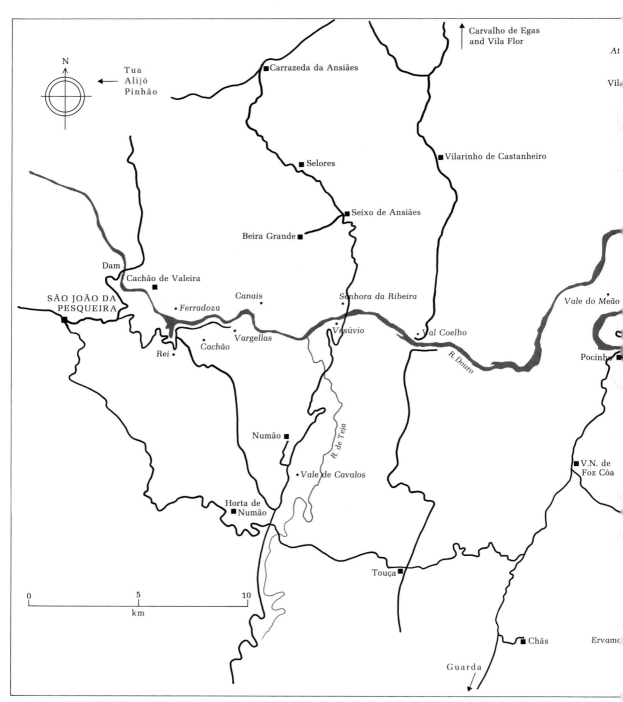

The Douro Superior

culture of the vine, and none of the others will be able to rival it when its products can be easily transported away, and when it does not lack the supports to labour which it requires, and intelligence and know-how for their effective management.[2]

I think it is likely that we shall find more shippers moving into these areas in the future.

Most of the quintas considered in this section are close to the river, and all but one belong to shippers. From São João da Pesqueira we take the road south of the Douro to Pocinho, cross the river, and return by way of Torre de Moncorvo and Vila Flor.

From São João da Pesqueira we pass the entrance to the Quinta do Sidrô, but, instead of turning left towards Valeira, we continue straight on downhill to the east of São Salvador do Mundo to the Quinta do Cachão, which belongs to the Sociedade Agrícola e Comercial dos Vinhos Messias, SA.

Quinta do Cachão

Despite its position so close to the Cachão de Valeira, the Quinta do Cachão was not amongst the first to be founded after the river became navigable. It was planted in 1845 by the Barão de Seixo,[1] and later acquired by Afonso Cabral. In the 1860s it was producing 70 – 80 pipes a year,[2] but with the onset of *phylloxera* this dropped to 15 pipes.[3] It was then inherited by his son Afonso do Vale Pereira Cabral, a noted engineer and viticulturist, just before his marriage in 1881.[4]

He took the quinta in hand and appears to have nursed it very successfully through the crisis. The Visconde Vilarinho de São Romão, writing in 1896, singled out the quinta for special mention.

> *An extremely noteworthy fact, worth citing because it is such a rare example in the whole region, is the large area [in the quinta] planted with* nacional *varieties, clearly sustained and preserved in full growth and vigorous production by treatment with insecticides and careful cultivation. Treatment with carbon disulphide for more than forty years has once more confirmed its great efficacy . . . in completely resisting and safely surviving the invasion of* phylloxera.[5]

It is interesting that ungrafted vines were being successfully cultivated so late in the century.

Afonso do Vale Pereira Cabral died in 1946, and when Messias purchased the quinta in 1956 it was in a very run-down state. Starting in 1958, Messias has undertaken a complete renovation of the quinta, with almost half of the vineyards on *patamares*. The majority of the vineyards are on the slopes of a hill surmounted by a small chapel dedicated to Santa Bárbara, which looks across to the chapels on São Salvador do Mundo and the entrance to the Cachão gorge. The climb

Vila Flor and Bragança

Laranjeiras

Mogadouro

Torre de Moncorvo

lho Melhor

Leda

Almendra

is worthwhile, not just for the view, but because from there you can see the well-tended broad terraces and the extent of the quinta, which cannot be properly appreciated from the road below. Beneath is a small inlet created from a re-entrant by the damming of the river – causing, incidentally, the loss of 12,000 of the quinta's vines. At the head of this re-entrant is the small Quinta do Rei, purchased from Gonzalez Byass in 1958 and now incorporated in Cachão, and this occupies part of the slopes on the opposite side of the re-entrant.[6]

In effect, the Quinta do Rei is now the heart of the entire quinta. Its house has been modernised to provide for the comfortable reception of guests, and the *adega* has been extended. The original Cachão buildings are also in use. The house, built as recently as 1910, was remodelled in 1982 to accommodate the farm manager and *caseiro* on the first floor, with *cardenhos* below. There is also a modernised *azenha*.

The *armazém* is one of the most imposing in the Douro. Reminiscent inside of an old English barn, its rafters are supported on huge stone brackets and tied in the middle. Its location has always been advantageous: originally it was close to the river; then, when the railway arrived, it was immediately next to that; and now that the railway has been diverted because of the damming of the river, the old track has conveniently been made into a road.

Built on the traditional two levels, its *lagares* were replaced with additional storage when the Quinta do Rei was renovated. From the old *adega* two doors lead to a gallery overlooking the *armazém*, where one of the *toneis* bears the construction date of the *armazém* – 1853.

The quinta production is used mainly for vintage and *colheitas*, and a single quinta vintage is released from time to time.

Between the Quinta do Rei and the armazém *of the Quinta do Cachão a little road on the right takes us through the tiny village of Vale da Figueira to the Quinta de Vargellas, belonging to Taylor, Fladgate & Yeatman, Vinhos, SA.*

Quinta de Vargellas

There were originally three quintas at Vargelas: Vargelas da Cima, Vargelas do Meio, and Vargelas de Baixo (also known as the Quinta de Golegã) – Upper, Middle and Lower Vargelas. The name of the district, *Vargelas*, has no specific meaning.

Today they form a single property owned by Taylor, who purchased them between 1893 and 1896 – and who prefer, incidentally, the old spelling with two 'l's.[1] For clarity, however, it is simpler to deal with the previous history of the three parts separately.

Vargelas da Cima (also called do Vale, and the most easterly of the three) belonged originally to Pedro Gomes da Silva, who sold it in 1831 to Dona Antónia's uncle, António Bernardo Ferreira. It was inherited by his son (of the same name). On his death in 1844 a trust was formed, of which his wife (Dona Antónia) and children were beneficiaries. When his daughter married in 1860 (becoming the

Opposite
42
The roofs of Gouvães looking across the Pinhão valley towards Casal de Loivos

Overleaf
43
Quinta de Santa Bárbara, at the mouth of the Rio Torto. This is the experimental station of the CEVD

Condessa de Azambuja), the trust settled her inheritance upon her. This included Vargelas da Cima, which she immediately leased back to her mother.

Like the wine of Vargelas de Baixo, as we shall presently see, that of the Ferreira quinta was well established on the English market in the first half of the nineteenth century. In a letter dated 27 April 1836, António Bernardo Ferreira writes: 'The wine of Vargelas is fantastic and must merit such a reputation to all who know about wine'.[2] On 20 September 1848, Dona Antónia noted that 'the wines of Vesúvio and Vargelas are to go to Sandeman, as in past years'. That the wine was exported under the quinta name is clear from a letter to Dona Antónia from her agent, José da Silva Azevedo, dated 27 December 1850. In this he says that he is waiting for wine to come from the Douro to be sold through Franklin, adding that 'I have ordered a brand saying *Vargellas*, following your orders to put the name on the pipes being sent to Franklin'.

According to Vila Maior, the quinta was modelled on Vesúvio, and he says that in the mid-1870s it was yielding '70 to 80 pipes of excellent wine . . . for exportation'.[3] In fact it was yielding considerably less, as will later appear.

Vargelas do Meio (between the other two) belonged in 1831 to Sebastião António Gomes, and in that year he rented it for six years to António Bernardo Ferreira. When Gomes died in 1833, half of both the quinta and the house went to his second wife, Dona Teotónia de Eça e Carvalho, and the other half to his daughter Jacinta Antónia Gomes. The lease to the Ferreiras was extended, and they built a *cardenho* in 1838. Later, in 1852, Jacinta inherited the quinta upon the death of her stepmother. Dona Antónia must have asked about buying it from her, for Jacinta wrote to Dona Antónia's agent on 28 August to say that she intended to keep the farm, although she was prepared to rent it for a further year, after which she would discuss its future. A covering note from Azevedo to Dona Antónia explains that her main interest was in the house which, apparently, served all three quintas. In the event she must have decided not to sell, and quite possibly did not renew the lease beyond 1854, for Vila Maior states that in 1865 the quinta's owner was Dona Jacinta de Carvalho Pinto, adding that 'they tell me it is becoming badly looked after'.[4] In 1876 he states that it was producing '50 pipes of wine for exportation'.[5]

For a time, therefore, these two quintas were run in tandem by the Ferreiras. Production figures for 'Vargelas' appear from time to time in the Ferreira *Arquivo Histórico*, but only once, in 1831, for the three quintas separately:

Vargelas da Cima – 40 pipes
Vargelas de Meio – 45 pipes
Vargelas de Baixo – 25 pipes

Thereafter, it is not clear whether the production figure applies only to the Ferreira quinta, Vargelas da Cima, or includes (at least until 1853–4) Vargelas de Meio. The figures for 1831 tend to suggest the latter.[6] After surprising highs of 126 and 124 pipes in 1841 and 1849, production never again exceeded double figures. The average for the eight recorded years of the decade up to 1875 was only 38.75 pipes – as against Vila Maior's reported '70 to 80 pipes'. *Phylloxera*, which was detected at Vargelas in 1878, brought production down from 3 pipes in 1886 to nothing in 1893, and less than a pipe in the two succeeding years.

The third quinta, Vargelas de Baixo (the most westerly, also called the Quinta do Brito), also has an interesting history.[8] Its first known owner was António Bernardo de Brito e Cunha, who was born in Matosinhos in 1781.[9]

It is unclear how he came by the quinta, but it is remarkable that, so soon after the opening up of the Douro Superior to the wine trade, he had promoted the Vargelas wine with such success that, by 1822, it was already established under the quinta name on the British market.

At a time when smuggling into the *feitoria* area was rife, it is perhaps not surprising that he managed to market his wine directly to London without selling it through the local agents. In view of the fact that he was Controller of the Royal Estates in Oporto and a former Deputy of the Old Company, it was not advisable for him to be seen to be directly engaged in commerce. From 1819, therefore, he used his friend João Pereira Viana de Lima, a Lisbon merchant, as a 'front' man; and from 1825 until 1829 he sold through a newly established firm called Viana & van Zeller.[10]

The firm to which the Vargelas wine was exported was Warre Brothers (not to be confused with Warre & Ca of Oporto), and a series of thirty-seven letters between 1822 and 1825, all addressed to João Pereira Viana de Lima, bears testimony to the reputation of the wine in London. Two quotations relating to the 1822 vintage must suffice.

> 16th April, 1823: *It is true that the quality of the wine has been greatly talked about and also tasted by many people and everybody agreed the quality was excellent. One of our customers, a very difficult but knowledgeable one and with a good nose . . . took a pipe to sample it and then came back and bought the remaining . . . He would have bought even more had we got it.*

> 1st October, 1823: *The good name of Vargellas wines continues, in spite of the problems of the London market and low reputation of the 1822 wines . . . your wines were preferred, probably due to the fame Vargellas Wines got.*

António Bernardo was not only a skilful salesman and a prominent figure in the life of Oporto, but a man whose liberal sympathies, in the political kaleidoscope of the times, led him to support Pedro in the War of the Two Brothers.[11] As a result of the temporary victory of Miguel, he was hanged in Oporto in 1829. All his goods were sequestrated, and on 30 August 1830, an advertisement appeared in the *Correio do Porto* announcing that 'on 3rd September, around 11 a.m . . . the Quinta de Vargelas, which belonged to the condemned António Bernardo de Brito e Cunha, will be offered for rental'.

It appears that if the quinta was indeed rented then it was to António's widow, Dona Teresa Benedicta, because in 1830 she was in need of someone to administer it for her. She asked António Bernardo Ferreira, out of consideration for the friendship between the two families, and because of the proximity of the Ferreira quintas, to oversee it for her in the absence of her two sons. Both in their early twenties, they had gone the day before their father's execution to England, where they were helped by the Warres and the Sandemans (one of whom was their brother-in-law), and where, oddly enough, they became familiar with the wine their father had exported before his death.

António Bernardo Ferreira, who accepted the job, later claimed that he found the quinta 'in a state of total ruin, because, besides being very badly planted, it was full of brambles, docks, etc., which in a short time had destroyed the whole production'. In 1831, he said, the quinta had produced only 8 or 9 pipes; in 1833 16 pipes; and he hoped that in 1834 it might produce 20 pipes. It is to be noted that the 8 or 9 pipes for 1831 does not square with the 25 pipes recorded in the Ferreira papers.

In the meantime, Dona Teresa Benedicta's two sons returned to Portugal in 1832 with an invasion army led by Pedro, the brother whom their father had supported, and who was at last able to establish himself as king in 1834. With this further political change they were once more able to involve themselves in Vargelas, although formal restitution was not made until 1839. João Eduardo, who looked after the quinta on behalf of his mother until his early death in 1849, began by complaining (perhaps with some reason, given the above discrepancy) to António Bernardo Ferreira about what he considered to have been the under-production of the quinta during his exile. Despite this, however, matters were patched up and António Bernardo Ferreira continued to administer the quinta. On 10 February 1852, we find Azevedo writing to Dona Antónia to say that António Bernardo Brito e Cunha (the eldest son of Dona Teresa Benedicta, who from 1851 had been looking after his mother's interests) thinks that the administrator at Vesúvio ought to run all three farms, taking his orders directly from him. Dona Antónia agreed.

Dona Teresa Benedicta continued to own the quinta until her death in 1869, after which her ten heirs owned it jointly. António Bernardo carried on overseeing the quinta on their behalf, but he eventually became an absentee landlord, and by the 1880s he was living in Lisbon. With the onslaught of *phylloxera* the production of the quinta dropped from 17 pipes in 1877 – itself a low figure, considering that *phylloxera* had not yet arrived – to 3 pipes in 1883. Not only were there no profits to divide amongst the owners, but worse, the running costs were not even covered and, naturally enough, they lost all interest in the property.

Then, in 1884, a miracle happened. The extension of the railway to Barca d'Alva meant that part of the quinta had to be expropriated. But, better than that, Domingos Burguets, the general contractor of the railway, offered to acquire the entire property. Here, at last, was a heaven-sent opportunity to wash their hands of the whole wretched business. The fact that they accepted 1,500 milréis for the whole quinta, as compared with 300 milréis official compensation for the 1.546 ha needed for the railway, shows how keen they were to disembarrass themselves. The sale was concluded on 14 July 1886.

Burguets and his colleague Martins had already acquired Vargelas do Meio in May, 1883, and it was from them that Taylor purchased Vargelas de Baixo and do Meio on 19 April 1893. The acquisition of the quinta more or less as it stands today was completed three years later when, on the death of Dona Antónia, the Countess of Ajambuja unburdened herself of the unproductive Vargelas da Cima.

One can guess at the state in which the Vargelas quintas must have been by 1893. Charles Sellers, reporting the purchase in 1899, tellingly remarks that Vargellas was 'once famed for its fine wines'.[12] Taylor may have been following the fashion for British shippers to acquire a Douro property; or they may have been looking for a replacement for Roêda, which effectively passed out of their hands in 1875.[13] The new owners set to with a will. New terraces were built and 60,000 vines on grafted americano root stock were planted. That number has grown and is still growing steadily. By 1962 it had more than doubled to 132,616,[14] and by 1989 it had nearly trebled at 165,000. Production has grown commensurately, from 70 to 80 pipes in 1911[15] to 225 pipes at present.

There are two roads into the quinta now, but by far the most spectacular approach is from the higher one. As you turn in at the gate the view looking over the Douro towards the Quinta dos Canais, with its huge waterfall of Síbio, is specially grand. Shortly you see the entire quinta spread like a scallop shell below you, with steep sides but shallow in the middle. The red roofs of the quinta buildings are also some distance below, in the centre and clustered near the river. The road snakes down through patamares, weaving from side to side across the middle of the quinta until you encounter a sign saying 'Casa', the quinta house being further up the hill than the other buildings.

The idiosyncratic house is like no other in the Douro. In recent years it has been in an almost perpetual state of change, so it is difficult to be certain that today's description will tally with tomorrow's reality. Shortly after its purchase Charles Skeffington built a bungalow similar to that at Bomfim, and this is now the bedroom wing. The front part of the house, with its spacious and elegant sitting and dining rooms, dates from the late 1960s, and the neo-Georgian pedimented colonnade which greets the visitor, from 1989. Along the side of the house nearest the river is a pergola-covered terrace, below which there is a swimming pool, so recent that the author has not yet seen it. The total effect of this not quite English, not quite Portuguese, but extremely comfortable house, is difficult to convey succinctly. The style, both inside and out, is reminiscent of Clough Williams-Ellis: in fact it is largely due to Gillyanne Robertson, the wife of Alastair Robertson, the managing director of Taylor.

The cluster of buildings down towards the railway station

includes the *adega* and *armazém*, of which more later, and, on the up-stream side, a building in an Hispanic style, completed only in 1989, which turns out to be quite the most luxurious *cardenhos* and *refectório* to be found in the Douro. Behind this a narrow street runs between cottages and farm buildings towards the house and to what surely must be unique in the Douro, if not in Portugal – a pig garden. This unusual project had just been started by Gillyanne Robertson (whose designing talents are by no means confined to the house) when I visited the quinta, so I have not yet heard how well the pigs have appreciated this amenity.

The *adega* and *armazém* complex is modern, but built in the traditional manner against the slope of the hill. The *lagares* and *armazém* were completed in 1976, but the new *adega*, where the grapes bought from neighbouring farmers are vinified, was built only in 1985. The quinta wine is made in the *lagares*. The vintage at Vargellas is the occasion for a large party, and house guests climb into the *lagares* and help with the treading – as is testified by blow-ups of witty drawings of quinta life by Willie Rushton which hang on the walls of the *adega*. Between vintages, as in most quintas, the *lagares* are put to good use as storage space – in this case for onions and a sailing boat.

The modern *adega* contains temperature-controlled pump-over tanks which have a greater diameter than usual. Special pumps which, instead of spraying the must over the cap, let it fall slowly on to it in a much gentler action (thus getting the maximum colour extraction with the minimum of pumping) were installed in 1989. About 1,000 pipes are produced in this *adega* each year.

It is, however, the vineyards which are of most interest. The original, walled terraces are mainly on the down-stream side of the quinta, curving round to face the house. Here the vines are in some cases fifty years old or more, and the quality if not the quantity of the yield is very high. For that reason Taylor are in no hurry to alter things and, despite labour problems, have decided to keep these terraces indefinitely.

It is interesting that Frank Yeatman's original plantings just after the purchase of the property were basically of the five grape varieties which currently receive official approval from the CEVD. Predominant amongst these, and still making up a quarter of the total vines was Touriga Francesa, which is thought to account for the wine's characteristic smell of violets. Moreover, in vineyards made in 1927 and 1935, single grape varieties were planted in rows (an approach towards the modern concept of block planting), with their names on painted plaques attached to the terraces. Experimental vinifications of some single varieties were made as far back as 1937, but it is not clear what conclusions were drawn from them.

The rest of the vineyards are mainly on *patamares*, Vargellas being one of the first quintas to have them in 1973, but there is a small amount of vertical planting (up to 30 degrees only). Taylor were able to purchase some land to the west of the quinta in 1988, which has enabled them to make a new road into the quinta (connecting with the Ferradoza road which passes the Quinta do Cachão), and provides further opportunities for vertical planting.

The quinta wine has formed part of Taylor's vintage blend since 1908, and there are bottles of single quinta Vargellas in Taylor's cellars dating back to the 1910 vintage. Although there have been bottlings of the single quinta wine over the years, until 1958 this was more for the convenience of special customers than a conscious marketing effort.[16] Since 1958, however, Taylor have offered Quinta de Vargellas in a wide variety of non-declared years, and it must be reckoned not only one of the best-known, but one of the most established of the single quinta ports.

We return to São João da Pesqueira and take the road for Vila Nova de Foz Côa. Just after Horta de Numão we turn left at the sign for 'Estação de Vesúvio', and near Numão we reach the Quinta de Vale de Cavalos, belonging to Manoel D Poças Júnior, Vinhos, SA.

Quinta de Vale de Cavalos

This quinta is on undulating land between the main road and the valley of the Rio Teja, in an area in which there has already been some vineyard development and whose attraction is that its gradients are gentle and completely mechanizable. The quinta was formed gradually by Sr Januário Alonso, some parts having been planted as experimental fields in about 1968 by the CEVD, and was acquired in 1988 by Poças. It incorporates the separate Quinta da Ribeira Teja, which is situated further down the Rio Teja.

Apart from tractor sheds there are no buildings, but an *adega* is projected. There is a mixture of *patamares*, continuous planting (with rows of up to 500 metres long), and, near the river, some vertical planting is planned. When complete the quinta will be worked by only three men.

Poças are enthusiastic about Vale de Cavalos not only because of its mechanization and high quality grapes, but because when it is in full production it will supply close to 18 per cent of the firm's needs.

Now we continue down the road towards the Douro. It is a grimly desolate scene, with a massive granitic mountain on our left. In front of us the road rises again to a neck of land across the valley. At its summit we enter the Quinta do Vesúvio, which belongs to the Symingtons.

Quinta do Vesúvio

'Epic' and 'colossal' were amongst the hyperboles used for the Quinta do Vesúvio by writers in the nineteenth century, for whom Vesúvio was the ultimate quinta. Some approached it almost with awe: 'Imagine, if you can, a vineyard containing within its walls seven hills and thirty valleys!'[1] For Vila Maior it was a *folie de grandeur*: 'The first impression received on viewing this extensive property . . . is well nigh of wonder,' he said, '[but] this quinta was laid out in a princely style, without judgment or calculation, more to satisfy the caprices of wealth than to procure a fitting return of the capital invested.'[2]

The quinta, which was originally called the Quinta das Figueiras,[3] has a history going at least as far back as 1565.[4] By the beginning of the nineteenth century the quinta, which until then had grown corn crops, belonged to the Conde de Lapa, and in 1823[5] he leased it in perpetuity to António Bernardo Ferreira, the uncle and father-in-law of Dona Antónia Ferreira.

In the following twelve years António Bernardo set about creating this legendary quinta, constructing terraces and roads, building – and, of course, planting, planting, planting. In 1835, just as the house was completed, he died, and Vesúvio was inherited by his son (of the same name) who had been married to Dona Antónia for just three months. After her husband's death she increased its size still further with the purchase, in 1850, of more land (called the Quinta Nova) and, in 1872-3, land to the east of the property on the Monte de Espinho.[6] At that stage, according to Vila Maior, the quinta, which was walled, had a circumference of 12 km.[7] Such enormous size appears to have bred, as later at the Quinta do Vale do Meão, wild speculations about production. Vila Maior says he was told it had 'formerly' reached 600 pipes[8] and Monteiro even speaks of 1,200 pipes; but, sadly, it was always far from that. In 1838 production was 561 pipes, a figure unequalled again that century. After 1850 it only twice exceeded 300 pipes (by a small margin) and in 1891 it sank to a mere 20 pipes.[9] Well might Vila Maior complain that 'having cost many hundreds of contos de réis and notwithstanding the regular manner in which it is kept and managed, if we attend only to its present income, we cannot estimate its value at more than 100 contos of réis, so wastefully has money been lavished upon it'[10] – and Vila Maior actually thought that, at that time, annual production was averaging 300 pipes! In short, he thought that Vesúvio was something of a white elephant.

Vesúvio, during Dona Antónia's reign, achieved a reputation for lavish hospitality. Sellers memorably describes a 'breakfast' of chicken, duck, and sucking pig – 'the table groaned under a heavy load of dainty food, most perfectly cooked' – at which 'even the toothsome Scotch was not forgotten, not even Schweppe'.[11] More seriously, apart from an abortive scheme for rearing silkworms, under Dona Antónia there appear to have been aspects in the wine management of the quinta which are often thought to be twentieth century in origin. For one thing, although the wine was generally made with a mixture of grape varieties,[12] some, namely Bastardo, Sousão, Mourisco and Moscatel, were 'vinified separately . . . if it is possible, with even more perfection and scruple for cleanliness [than the ordinary wines], to maintain the reputation which they have already largely established in the trade'.[13] More surprisingly, close examination of a photograph of Vesúvio (after the advent of the railway) reveals that the vines between the house and the river are planted vertically.[14]

Given the vastness of Vesúvio, it is difficult to give an accurate, let alone understandable, general description. From the opposite bank of the Douro one sees two large mountains within the curve of the river: to the left (eastwards) is the vast Monte de São Martinho, inferior parts of which – the Monte do Olival and the Monte do Espinho – are part of the quinta; to the right (westwards) is the Monte do Raio with two inferior hillocks within the quinta – the Monte de Boa Vista and Picanceira – beyond which is the Rio Teja, the boundary of the quinta. Between these mountains there is a low col, in front of which a basin, the Vale da Mina, inclines towards the Douro.

The road from Numão winds down the Vale da Mina towards the Vesúvio railway station and the quinta house, strategically placed in the centre of things. Built to face up-river, its eclectic architectural style, with overhanging eaves decorated with elaborate frets, immediately suggests an Alpine chalet. Only the luxuriant palm tree growing in the forecourt reminds us that we are in warmer climes. Of considerable size, with twenty-three bedrooms, the house also contains the quinta office and, to its rear, a passage leading to the chapel. Built facing the river, the chapel has an elaborate façade modelled on traditional Portuguese church baroque.

A short distance down-stream are the traditional *adega* and *armazém* and, in a separate building, the old *azenha*. These were rightly the special wonders of the quinta. The *adega*, 58.9 m long, had eight 25 pipe capacity *lagares*, each worked by seventy men.[15] Completed in 1827, it was, for its time, astonishingly large,[16] and António Bernardo Ferreira basked in the glory. He wrote to his agent in Oporto: 'All the English who were here greatly praised my warehouse . . . adding to this that they did not find a second cellar in the Douro to be compared to mine, which made them believe in the passion I have for good wines.'[17]

It was his son, however, who built the even more sensational *azenha*, with an hydraulic mill powered by water brought in a narrow canal over 1 km long from the distant Rio Teja. Olive oil was already an important part of the quinta's production, and was to become more so when António Bernard Ferreira, the grandson of the founder, planted a further 10,000 olive trees in the wake of *phylloxera*.[18] Alas, when I visited the *azenha* in 1988 it was derelict, with a hole in its roof, and water was spilling unchecked from the end of the aqueduct. Olives were no longer even collected at Vesúvio: it was too difficult, needed too much labour, and gave no profit.

Yet again the problem of man-power raises its head. It is instructive to make a comparison of how this huge quinta was manned in 1865 and in 1988 – making due allowance for the fact that in 1865, according to Vila Maior's calculations, there were 140 ha of vineyards,[19] while in 1988 there were only 85. In 1865 the quinta was divided into three separate administrative zones with separate *cardenhos*: in 1988, while these divisions had in some respects survived, for day to day purposes the quinta was treated as a single unit. Of the *cardenhos* – seven in all – only one was in use, the others having become sheep shelters.[20]

Opposite, above
47
Quinta de la Rosa. The house is on the left, and its large *armazém* displaying the quinta name is on the right, nearest the river

Opposite, below
48
Quinta das Carvalhas, reflected in the mirror-like surface of the Douro, seen from Quinta da Roêda. Before the damming of the river there was a noisy rapid between Carvalhas and Roêda

Overleaf
49
Roofscape at Quinta do Noval

1865	1988
Permanent staff:	
1 administrator (and technical director)	1 *caseiro* (in charge of administration and wages)
1 book-keeper (in charge of food-stuffs and stores)	1 *caseiro* (in charge of field-work and workers)
1 *feitor* (also cooper) supervising *armazéms*, *adegas*, and security and maintenance of stores and equipment	
1 blacksmith and 1 assistant	
2 bullock cart drivers	1 tractor driver
1 farm hand	7 non-resident workers
1 cook and 1 or 2 assistants	1 cook (*caseiro's wife*)
	1 housekeeper/cook (*the other caseiro's* wife)
Non-permanent staff:	
Depending on work to be done 3 up to 20 *feitors*	
Up to 200 workers, organized in 3 squads (one per zone), generally of 40 men, but of 20–25 men for pruning.	30-40 (mainly women) for grafting. 30-40 for pruning (who stay in the *cardenhos*).
At the vintage:	
80–125 women (in 4 or 5 squads of 20–25	70 men and women. Some treading was done in the *lagares* after picking. Must pumped over instead of using *macacos*.
2 boys (to empty *cestos* into *gigos*)	
70 men for each *lagar*.	

Vesúvio, unfortunately, was one of the quintas to suffer from the damming of the river, and in 1973 lost many of its best vineyards when the water level rose by at least 10 m.

The quinta remained in the hands of the family (latterly with eighteen owners), and the wine was sold to Ferreira, until 1989, when the property was purchased by the Symingtons. Clearly this will be a turning point in its history, for the Symingtons are probably, of all shippers, best in a position to tame the beast. They have already begun to make enormous changes, the principal one being the creation of a further 50 ha of vineyards, bringing the total closer to what it was a century ago.

More excitingly, the quinta is not tied to any single company owned by the Symingtons, who plan to run and market the quinta independently, along the lines of a Bordeaux château. This means that eventually a single quinta Vesúvio port will re-appear – for Dona Antónia sold her wine mostly to English merchants, and Vesúvio was available as a single vintage in the nineteenth century. However,

Opposite, above
50
Douro vineyards at the beginning of autumn

Opposite, below
51
Vertical block planting at Quinta do Seixo. The different colours show the different vine varieties

having recently started to market their other single quintas in non-declared years, in the traditional British manner, the Symingtons have already announced their intention of breaking the mould and offering Vesúvio also in declared years. Their aim is to make something quite special and unique out of the quinta, restoring it to, as the grudging Vila Maior was forced to admit, 'a large and magnificent wine-producing establishment, notable amongst the most notable of the country'.[21]

Returning to the main road we continue towards Vila Nova de Foz Côa. Just short of it we join the Foz Côa – Guarda road and, turning right, head south until we come to the road to Chãs (on our left). A 7-km track leads from Chãs to the Quinta da Ervamoira, which belongs to Adriano Ramos-Pinto, Vinhos, SA.

Quinta da Ervamoira

In the Quinta da Ervamoira Ramos-Pinto have not only their newest quinta, but one of the most recently founded of the quintas considered in this book. With considerable foresight, as the need for mechanization to cope with growing labour shortages began to dawn in the early 1970s, the firm sought to establish a new quinta which, so far as it was possible, satisfied two major considerations: the climatic conditions would be optimum for the growing of first-class port grapes and the terrain would be suitable for maximum mechanization. Sr José António Rosas, then the president of the company, pored over military maps, studying the contours until he discovered what seemed to be a near-ideal site on the left bank of the Rio Côa, about 7 km from its confluence with the Douro.

This proved to be the Quinta de Santa Maria, which had belonged for many generations to the Botto family. It was at this time, as it always had been, planted with cereal crops. An additional advantage therefore was that, never having had vines before, its soil was not exhausted.

Unfortunately for Sr Rosas, Santa Maria's owners, two sisters, had no wish to sell the quinta. Nor, after their death, had their sixteen heirs, until the uncertainties of the Revolution made them change their minds. The purchase of the quinta was thus made in 1974, and in the same year the firm, having decided to diversify into table wines, purchased the nearby Quinta dos Bons Ares. This quinta, whose soil and altitude are unsuitable for growing port grapes, has a very modern vinification centre which was completed in 1989, where both the Bons Ares table wines and the Santa Maria port are made.

Ramos-Pinto claim that Santa Maria was the first vineyard in the Douro to be block planted with just the five grape varieties approved by the CEVD. Moreover, it is probably the only vineyard to have 100 per cent vertical planting. With its gentle slopes Santa Maria proved an ideal site to plant in this way and even PDRITM was persuaded to waive its usual requirement for *patamares*. It is interesting, in this regard, to note that Santa Maria yields 55 hl of must per ha, as compared with Bom Retiro's 41 – even bearing in mind that the latter's plantations are older.

Experimentation continues. In conjunction with ADVID and with the blessing of the CEVD, a pilot irrigation scheme is being assessed:[1] but, because of the gentle slopes of the terrain, water cannon have been found effective in fine mist spraying of the vines.

Not just because it is one of the most easterly port quintas, nor because of its long approach road, the quinta seems to have one of the most remote and peaceful situations of any I know. Coming over the crest of a hill, just where its boundary is situated, one sees the quinta spread before one like a vast, rather secluded, amphitheatre sloping gently down to the Rio Côa, with a back-drop of stark and rocky hills beyond.

Occupying an almost central position, the square, rustic quinta house is rather rudely constructed of large granite blocks without, of course, any *adega* or *armazém*. It has been in existence for about 150 years and is built from stone salvaged from a chapel which used to stand within the quinta boundaries. Traces of the ruins are still visible. This chapel was situated, as the quinta is today, within the confines of two *freguesias*, Chãs and Muxagata. Inside the chapel there used to be a seventeenth-century statue of Nossa Senhora de Socorro and when the two *freguesias* heard that the chapel was about to be demolished they both laid claim to the statue. It proved impossible to find grounds on which to decide the matter, so it was agreed to hold an official race to the chapel between the two parishes. Chãs won, and the statue can still be seen in the church of the town of that name.

Shortly after their purchase of the quinta, Ramos-Pinto found, to their disappointment, that the name 'Quinta de Santa Maria' had already been registered by Cockburn,[2] and so it would not be possible for them to sell the quinta port under its own name. As they were puzzling what to do, Suzanne Chantal, the French historical novelist who has specialized in writing about Portugal, published a novel called *Ervamoira* – the name of a small white flower indigenous to the Douro. It is the purely fictional saga of a family of port producers whose quinta is called Ervamoira, starting with the (real-life) stampede of civilians crossing a pontoon bridge linking Oporto and Vila Nova de Gaia in 1806, and continuing until the 1930s. What was most amazing was the way in which the description of Ervamoira's situation seemed to correspond with that of Santa Maria. Sr Rosas immediately wrote to Mme Chantal and asked her permission to re-name his new quinta 'Ervamoira'. Not only did Mme Chantal readily agree, she came to the 'christening' ceremony, at which the local priest officiated, using the forms of service for blessing crops, and thus became the quinta's 'godmother'! The 'Quinta da Ervamoira' is therefore now the registered trading name of the quinta, though its name remains Santa Maria.

Ramos-Pinto are expecting great things from Ervamoira. Already they produce on their own quintas 60 per cent of all their port requirements – vastly more than any other shipper – and by 1993 they estimate that they will be entirely self-sufficient. Since 1985 a ten year old tawny has been sold under the quinta label. Planting continues, as does the acquisition of neighbouring land. Since not all the land on the quinta is suitable for cultivation, Ramos-Pinto have combined with their neighbours to establish a 400 ha hunting reserve. Like Bons Ares, the quinta also has archaeological remains which are in the course of excavation. They appear to consist of a small Roman settlement, possibly a military post overlooking the Rio Côa, although there are traces of both earlier and later occupation.

Ervamoira seems certain to earn a place in the history of port as the first vineyard to have been completely vertically block-planted and designed to be as totally mechanized as any Douro vineyard probably ever can be. It may seem odd, therefore, to end by reporting that, unbeknown to Ramos-Pinto at the time of purchase, a plan exists to flood the Côa valley as part of the Douro hydroelectric scheme, which, if carried out, would submerge virtually three quarters of the quinta. For the time being, however, it seems unlikely that this will happen because money is short and imported electricity from Spain is cheap. It would be a sad end to a brave and potentially immensely successful venture if such a thing ever came to pass.

From Chãs we head back north to Vila Nova de Foz Côa, and just short of the town we turn left towards Figueira de Castelo Rodrigo. At the sign for the 'Estação de Almendra' we turn left for the Quinta da Leda, which belongs to A A Ferreira, SA.

Quinta da Leda

The landscape here is notable for its large number of dovecots, all of which appear to be in the middle of nowhere. Our road twists down a hill, and at the bottom you come to a small church. If you take the track immediately to the left you eventually, and somewhat unexpectedly (for there is nothing else about the landscape to lead you to suppose that you are in wine country) find yourself driving through vineyards. As you surmount the last rise you enter the quinta and find yourself, again unexpectedly, on a fine granite block road.

The Quinta da Leda is set on the north bank of a small river, the Ribeiro Seco, in a basin surrounded by small hills with almond tree plantations. In the distance there are more vineyards.[1] Most of the quinta, which was started by Ferreira in 1979, is on *patamares*, with a little vertical and continuous planting. It is easy to see how young it is from the large chunks of slate in the vineyard, and at times it almost looks as if it had been intended to be a rockery. One is also immediately struck by the cleanliness and tidiness of everything. The effects of mechanization are clear.

The quinta, which now utilizes all its available space, is block planted. In addition, a small experimental field has been established. The only building stands in the centre – a small utilitarian hut with an adjacent rustic summerhouse – and there is no *adega*. The produce is taken to be vinified at the Quinta do Vale do Meão, some 40 km distant. At the moment the wine is used for standard blends, but

Ferreira anticipate that when the vines reach full maturity the wine will have sufficient quality to go into their vintage blend.

Returning the way we came, we now go through Vila Nova de Foz Côa and head north to Pocinho. A road from the railway station crosses the track and leads us past the Quinta do Reguengo to the Quinta do Vale do Meão.

Quinta do Vale do Meão

'Vast and grandiose' were the words which Afonso Cabral chose to describe the Quinta do Vale do Meão (or, as it was then known, the Quinta do Monte Meão). It was in many ways the culmination of Dona Antónia Ferreira's achievements, only completed at the time of her death in 1896. Today the quinta's main fame is as the home of Barca Velha, arguably the best red Douro table wine. Nevertheless, it still produces an appreciable quantity of port, and is a quinta of considerable historical interest.

Claro de Fonseca, Dona Antónia Ferreira's agent in Régua, wrote sceptically to her second husband, Francisco Torres, on 3 May 1877: 'From what you say I understand that you are going to have your way in the conquest of Monte Meão. Perhaps this conquest will give you some pleasure, for it will certainly give no profit.' Fifty-three parcels of what had previously been common land, ordered to be sold off by the government, were purchased at auction from the *câmara* of Foz Côa between April 1877 and July 1879. Within a year Francisco Torres was dead, leaving Dona Antónia, widowed a second time, to supervise the entire Ferreira empire. The land, meanwhile, was leased to a Dr Cavalheiro until 1886.

Work on establishing the quinta started in 1887, and by the following year 800 men were being employed in construction work and planting. The first plantation of *americano* vines on any of Dona Antónia's properties followed in 1889. By 1892 the quinta was already producing 82 pipes. By 1892, also, enough of the basic services had been established for work to start on the chapel (where the first mass was said in 1894) and on the house, which was finished in 1895. A year later Dona Antónia herself was dead.[1]

The cost was immense. According to Afonso Cabral the purchase price of 14,000,000 *réis* was derisory compared to the reputed 300,000,000 *réis* spent in construction work and planting.[2] But, according to Sellers, by the end of the century over 900,000 vines had been planted and 'it is possible in an average year to produce about 2,000 pipes of good wine'.[3] This is an absurd figure, given that the actual production for 1896 was 389 pipes.

The domestic buildings are just inside the main gate of the quinta, where the quinta house is flanked on the nearer side by the chapel, and by the manager's house on the other. With an interior similar in many ways to that of Vesúvio, but on a much smaller scale, the house retains its *fin de siècle* furnishings, If Dona Antónia were to walk through the door she would not feel the least out of place. The adjoining chapel, a lofty building with a gallery, is pure Victorian baroque. The irregular spots on its walls are said to be splashings of port, sprinkled in thanksgiving for good harvests.

The house looks across the quinta's gently sloping vineyards towards the river (which, incidently, cannot be seen from here), but to have the best view of them it is worth climbing to the little chapel dedicated in 1895 to Nossa Senhora do Monte, built by Dona António to honour a wish of her agent, Claro de Fonseca. It sits beyond the house in a commanding position halfway up Monte Meão. From here, where the air is heavy with the scent of wild rosemary, you can see down to where the river turns at the mouth of the broad Vilariça valley, and across to a new road north to by-pass Torre de Moncorvo, which has been built along the north bank of the Douro. Immediately below there are some new *patamares*, whilst above everything is wild and mountainous, the haunt of goats.

Many of Dona António's *cardenhos* and *adegas* are now empty, but not the impressive Barca Velha *armazém*, completed in 1895. Entering through its green doors, one is amazed at its size – 61 m long. Its roof is a tied beam construction, and its continuous surrounding gallery is reached by a central flight of metal steps which lead, in turn, to the *adega*. This, the largest *casa dos lagares* in the Douro, contains seven 30-pipe capacity *lagares*, under each of which there is a cavity with a door. The idea, though I cannot believe it would have worked well, was that during fermentation the temperature of the *lagar* could be reduced by opening the door, or, conversely, raised by lighting a fire under it. Alas, the *lagares* were last used in 1980 and the wine is now made using modern equipment which, with stainless steel storage tanks, has now largely ousted the old wooden *cubas* from the *armazém*.

The quinta is still in the possession of Dona António's descendants, the Olazabal family: Francisco de Olazabal is president of Ferreira, and the company buys the port which goes towards their premium blends.

Now we cross the Douro and continue north through Torre de Moncorvo. Just as we come to the Rio Sabór, on our right we find the Quinta das Laranjeiras, belonging to Sandeman & Ca, Lda.

Quinta das Laranjeiras

This old quinta, on gentle slopes on the left bank of the Rio Sabór, was acquired by Sandeman in 1981. The buildings are largely derelict, and it still awaits full development. Apart from a small part which is continuously planted, and an experimental vineyard in which different types of planting are being compared, all the planting is vertical. The produce is taken for vinification to nearby Pocinho, where Sandeman have a large *adega*, and the wine is used in the firm's blends.

Continuing north in the direction of Bragança we come along the east side of the Vilariça valley and look for the turning on the left to Vila

Flor. At the bridge a track leads to the Quinta do Atayde, belonging to Cockburn, Smithes & Ca, Lda.

Quinta do Atayde

The Quinta do Atayde, though mentioned briefly by Vila Maior, has never been famous. Dating back to at least the seventeenth century, at 130 ha it is now the largest of several neighbouring quintas – Canada, Tourão and do Tenreiro are the others – which, with a vineyard at Assares (35 ha), form the important 200 ha Vilariça development started in the mid-1970s by Cockburn.

Cockburn, when two competitors were scared off, resolutely continued to look for land here during the troubled times of 1974, realizing that, being almost flat as well as having basically schistous soil, it showed immense promise as a site for fully mechanized vineyards. It is not, however, ideal. Average rainfall is only 440 mm per annum, just enough for growing vines, and temperatures can reach as much as 53 degrees Centigrade. Moreover, as there are no vinification facilities, the harvest has to be taken to the Quinta do Tua, just over an hour away. Picking is done as early in the day as possible, and so far problems of oxidization have been avoided. The company's future plans include the building of an *adega* within three years.

Vilariça is a very long-term project which has been planned in phases. It has been directed from the beginning by Eng° Miguel Corte Real Gomes, an authority on vine diseases. First to be established, on an anonymous site quite separate from the rest of the project, was a virus-free vine nursery using hybrids of *vinifera* and *rupestris* from Montpellier University. Here hybrids have been developed to suit differing soil conditions, and virus-free graft material has been supplied for use in PDRITM, as well as to other farmers in exchange for preferential buying rights.

The vineyards are block planted almost entirely with red varieties, and records are scrupulously kept to monitor a large number of factors, including affinities between grape varieties and root stock, clonal selection, and the vinification qualities of different grape varieties. The wine made from the harvest here, averaging some 800 pipes, goes to the firm's premium quality wines, mainly Cockburn's Special Reserve.

When I saw it, the old quinta house at Atayde was only a shell, but since then it has been taken down and reconstructed, stone by stone, using company labour. When completed, it will be Cockburn's fourth Douro house, destined at least partly to be used for public relations purposes. Beside it are an old chapel and reconditioned dependencies providing an office, a tractor shed, and employee housing.

Vilariça is testimony to Cockburn's commitment to the highest viticultural standards, and it is widely recognized in the Douro that they are amongst the leaders in this field.

From Vila Flor we go towards Carrazeda de Ansiães. Just after Carvalho de Egas a turning on the left takes us, by way of Vilarinho de Castanheiro, to the Quinta de Val Coelho, which also belongs to Cockburn, Smithes & Ca, Lda.

Quinta de Val Coelho

'Rabbit Valley' may sound a charming name, but rabbits are by no means the vine grower's best friends, being partial to the tender leaves of young vine-stock. As always, however, the name of a quinta is usually an indication of its situation, and the Quinta de Val Coelho is no exception. In the visitors' book for the Quinta do Tua (another of Cockburn's properties) one finds under the date 4 February 1937: 'The rabbits have not done any damage at V Coelho' – with the clear implication that, since it would not otherwise have been worth remarking, normally they did.

Although Val Coelho is now the name by which the quinta is generally known, it appears that it may be of comparatively recent (exasperated) origin. The original name was undoubtedly Quinta do Lobazim de Baixo. This is the name on a map of the property at the Quinta do Tua drawn for Cockburn in 1893, and it is also shown thus on a printed map at Tua dated 1932, yet in the Tua visitors' books, which start from 1935, it is invariably called Val Coelho. It would appear, therefore, that at some stage prior to 1935 Val Coelho became a private nickname within the company, and one which has now stuck. Oddly enough, for I have never seen it remarked on elsewhere, the quinta, like Tua, has also been known in some quarters as the Quinta dos Ingleses.[1]

As mentioned above, the quinta was already in Cockburn's possession in 1893, but precisely when it was bought is not known. It is an isolated property, far up the Douro on its right bank and not quite a kilometre downstream, and across from the railway station at Freixo de Numão.

The early history of the quinta is sketchy. Vila Maior mentions the Quinta de Lobazim [da Cima] in 1876 (together with the upstream Quinta da Telhada – see below).[2] It is a property of considerable antiquity and size whose land completely surrounds Val Coelho, and of which Val Coelho may therefore originally have formed a part. It is mainly planted with olives and almonds, and has belonged to the Castro family for sixteen generations – and before that to the Gomes family, into which the Castros married.[3]

Monteiro also alludes briefly to the Quinta de Lobazim's 'truly British buildings and plantations',[4] though the significance of this observation escapes me. Indeed, apart from the quinta house, which is charmingly and traditionally Portuguese, the absence of buildings at Val Coelho is one of its most obvious characteristics. The quinta house stands just above the river and beside the little stream which comes down the valley. At a higher level, dominating the quinta house, is the comparatively modern (post-Monteiro) *caseiro*'s house, which we learn from the Tua visitors' book was built in 1937.

Val Coelho, being remoter, has always been a more private house than Tua. Apart from being used at the time of the vintage, it has

Opposite
52
The gateway to the house and garden at Quinta da Eira Velha

Overleaf
53
A bulldozer demolishes old walled terraces to make way for *patamares*. Note the steepness of the slope (by no means unusual) and the rockiness of the schistous terrain

been (and still is) a place of haven for the directors and their families, if only for a day. It was also visited, as reported in the Introduction, by John Gibbons.

At Val Coelho shooting parties – and not just of rabbits – were common, and, as Gerald Cobb points out, the partners took advantage as often as possible of the opportunity 'to return from Freixo to Tua by boat, and thereby pick up some interesting rock pigeon shooting on the way in the [Cachão] gorge'.[5]

The quinta house, built sideways into the hill-side, was constructed, according to Sr Floriano Malheiro, the manager at Tua, by his grandfather. This rather supports the view that Val Coelho, as a quinta, is of comparatively recent origin. The house has the usual (but disused) *armazém* underneath, the upright of its door being marked with the levels of the floods of 1906 and 1962. It was here, according to the entry in the Tua visitors' book for 6 October 1953, that John Smithes, a famous spitter of wine, achieved his legendary feat of extinguishing a lighted cigarette at a range of 14 feet (4.5 m) – 'see inscription on wall of Quinta Val Coelho (excursions every Sunday)'. Alas, the inscription has now disappeared.

Passing the *armazém*, the track leads up to a small paved terrace in front of the house. Here, under the shade of a cherry tree, you can sit in utter tranquillity and gaze down on to the stream and watch the myriad of golden carp which sun themselves just under the surface of the water.

The house has great charm, its bedrooms featuring (as in all the Cockburn houses) mosquito nets. Previously, however, its privations were even greater than at Tua, for there was no bathroom in the house: one went across the yard to a two-seater loo.[6]

Val Coelho now incorporates the Quintas of Cadima, Pescoça and Telhada – all situated within the 3 km immediately up-river from Val Coelho. Formerly there was a small winery at Cadima with *lagares* and an *armazém*, and this was used in the 1970s to make wine from the grapes which Cockburn bought from local farmers. This winery is no longer used, and all the grapes are now taken to Tua for vinification. The Quinta da Telhada, which Cockburn acquired in 1980, was only planted in 1986 and has not, therefore, reached the stage of giving a significant crop. These developments, however, again show Cockburn's forward-looking policy of establishing viable conjunctions of vineyards in prime grape-producing areas.

We return the way we have come, taking a short-cut to Carrazeda de Ansiães (on the left, north of Vilarinho de Castanheiro) which joins the main road again at Mogo de Ansiães. From Carrazeda de Ansiães a road leads back down to the river through Selores and Seixo de Ansiães.

Quinta da Senhora da Ribeira

The Quinta da Senhora da Ribeira sits facing the Quinta do Vesúvio across the Douro. Deriving its name from the little chapel between the quinta house and the river, this was the second quinta to be acquired by George Warre (in 1889).

Although Zimbro was originally the centre of Silva & Cosens's Douro operations it was soon supplanted by Senhora da Ribeira as a family retreat – it had a better situation (no railway behind the house) and magnificent shooting – just as, later on, it was itself overtaken by Bomfim.

Disappointingly the visitors' book has few references to the quinta, but the reader has already had a glimpse of Senhora da Ribeira just before the Second World War in the Introduction.[1] In fact, it is far from being the 'great mansion' to which Gibbons refers: it was, and is, rather modest both in size and character. Paul Symington, writing to the author, gives us a better idea of what it was like:

> It was incredibly remote in those days and the family would arrive on the Vesúvio side (by train or car) and then cross by boat to Senhora da Ribeira. My great uncles, John and Ron, were particularly fond of this Quinta and used it for shooting parties. As I am sure you know, the 'Twins' were famous in the North of Portugal for their love of shooting. An extension was built to the house just after the war specially for shooting parties. [They] were a big event in the yearly calendar[2] . . . The house and lodge is virtually unchanged since we sold it in 1952 (same reason as Zimbro).[3] The house is full of gun racks, walking sticks, photos, etc., dating from our ownership. S & C is still written over all the vats in the lodge.

Although too young to remember these days, he admits that it still tugs at his heartstrings when he sees these vats.

A brief entry for 21 May 1952 in the Zimbro visitors' book records the sale. 'Went to S.R. to conclude the sale of Quinta da Senhora da Ribeira to Mr António Trigo Moutinho . . . It's been a most sad occasion but we leave the happiest memories and many good and faithful friends there.'

The Moutinhos are a family which has long been established in the area. Happily the link between the quinta and Silva & Cosens has not disappeared. Having continued to make the wine after 1952, the Symingtons were disappointed when the contract went to another shipper. However, in 1988 the connection was restored and it is once more an important part of Dow's vintage and other premium blends.

Going back to Seixo de Ansiães, we turn left for Beira Grande to visit another Cockburn quinta – the Quinta dos Canais.

Quinta dos Canais

This vast property sits on the right bank of the Douro facing the Quinta de Vargellas. Its most striking natural feature, visible from Vargellas and from Ferradoza except in the dry summer months, is the Falls of Síbio. This is a huge waterfall which cascades across an immense expanse of granite on the summit of a mountain at the western extremity of the estate. Last century a prodigious engineering feat was accomplished by bringing water from the falls in a succession of canals, some blasted out of the living rock, others built up, stretching for well over a kilometre across the face of the mountain. These provide a water supply for the quinta's enormous area of olive trees, and it is, of course, from these canals that the quinta derives its name.

This is a quinta which I visited while boating on the river. One lands close to the white house of the Quinta do Bartol, Canais's southern neighbour. From the landing stage there is quite a climb to be negotiated to reach the quinta buildings, but the path is bordered by a rushing brook, and, uniquely in my experience of Douro quintas, everywhere one is conscious of the cooling sound of splashing rivulets and streams. Water appears to be springing up and gurgling all over the place. Although my visit was in May, and the Falls of Sîbio were already prematurely dry through lack of winter rain, the supply of water seemed to be inexhaustible. If for no other reason, this would give Canais a memorable individuality.

The quinta incorporates six old quintas, known last century as the quintas of Canais, for the most part purchased forty or fifty years ago. The biggest of these is the Quinta do Sîbio (designated as the Quinta de Forneiras in Forrester's map), which at that time produced from 80–100 pipes.[1] This was purchased at the beginning of the century by Francisco Manoel da Costa, who was then the owner of Canais. According to Manuel Monteiro, Sr da Costa was a celebrated capitalist whose enthusiasm for Canais went almost to the point of fanaticism. This was just as well, for Canais is within the *concelho* of Carrazeda de Ansiães, which had been very badly afflicted by *oïdium* last century, and when he purchased the quinta from its previous owner, the Condessa de Taboeira, it was in a deplorable state.

Notwithstanding, Sr da Costa poured a fortune into the rehabilitation of the property. 'Dozens and dozens of *contos* were swallowed up and continue to be so, guaranteeing bread almost yearly to between one and two hundred workers'.[2] The result of this prodigious expense was around 100 pipes of wine, most of it then bought by Sandeman.

In 1942 Canais was purchased by Eng° Ramiro da Costa Cabral Nunes de Sobral. The terrain of Canais lends itself to the hunting parties which are so much a feature of life in the region, and Canais was, I am told, reckoned the best shoot in the Douro. Gerald Cobb recalled that 'a typical Douro partridge shoot, at which I have had the good fortune to be a guest, is given annually by Snr Eng Ramiro Sobral at his Quinta das [sic] Canais. The Snr Engineiro [sic], as he is always called, is a superlative host and his weekend sport is organised on a lavish scale, both in the field and at the table. It has in the past had a particularly international flavour . . . '[3]

Jeremy Bull recalls another example of Eng° Sobral's lavishness – a celebration lunch given at Canais in the summer of 1946 to mark Cockburn's first visit to the quinta after the war. Jeremy, aged about fourteen, and Anthony Cobb (the son of Peter) were fortunate enough to be included in the party. The lunch was modelled on a celebrated dinner given at the Factory House in 1911,[4] with eleven dishes, eleven wines and eleven ports – although, on this occasion, there were twelve. Halfway through lunch the young Jeremy and Anthony disappeared from the table to be sick in the garden.

But with Eng° Sobral's advancing years, the famous shooting parties became a thing of the past and, when I visited the house in the spring of 1989, I found it tinged with a degree of melancholia, a sense of better times gone by, which runs counter to Monteiro's enthusiastic hyperbole: 'The noble house, the heraldic *solar* with its chapel, has an amazing atmosphere, not only because of the sumptuousness which fills it but from the plenitude which surrounds it'.[5]

As you wend your way up the path from the river you pass, near the top and on the left, the building which houses the olive press. With its marvellous water supply, Canais (unlike many other large quintas in the area) still has a large production of olive oil. Almost immediately afterwards you arrive at a group of buildings more or less on the same level, which include the *cardenhos* and the *caseiro's* house. Over to the right, on the very edge of the property, is the quinta house with its *lagares* and *armazéms*.

The modest quinta house (hardly a *solar*) is set on a terrace backing on to Bartol, and is approached through a gate which opens into an orange grove. A central pergola leads through the orchard to the house, where it divides and runs along the façade in both directions. At this level there are two *armazéms*. The first, which occupies the entire space under the house, is cobwebby and cool, filled with old oak *toneis*. Against the river side of the house, and without the shelter of a building on top, there is a second *armazém*, smaller and warmer than the first, where the wine matures more quickly. In past years the new vintage would remain at the quinta until May or June of the following year, but now it is moved out immediately it has been made.

A flight of stairs at the end of the pergola furthest from the river leads up to the level of the house, which is approached by way of a central courtyard. Inside one encounters traditional, scrubbed, wooden floors, wood-boarded wainscotting and good plain country furniture. The kitchen is particularly fine, with its old stone sinks, chopping boards and array of traditional pots and pans.

One side of the little courtyard is formed by the *adega*, which is adjacent to the living quarters. The wine is still made in the *lagares*, although with the aid of a *movi-mosto* machine, which pumps the must out of the *lagar* and sprays it over the *manta* (the cap of skins and pips). Some wine makers maintain that this method has the disadvantages of over-exposing the must to the air and of being uneven in its pumping action, but I was assured that at Canais such difficulties have not been experienced, and that it has proved an efficient method of producing high quality port.

The quinta, most of whose southern boundary follows an 'S' made by the Douro, has the quintas de Telheira and do Carvalho for western neighbours, the Quinta do Bartol on the south east, and the

Quinta do Comparado on the east. The original terraces of Canais are extremely old, with some vines thought to date back over a century, but in recent years much of the quinta has been converted to *patamares*, with a small bit of continuous planting.

For over fifty years the quinta wine has been purchased by Cockburn, for whom it has formed the backbone of their vintage blend. In this respect, therefore, Canais has been more important to them than any of their own quintas. It was not too much of a surprise, therefore, that when Eng° Sobral decided in 1989 to sell Canais Cockburn snapped it up. What is now certain is that the atmosphere of torpor over the quinta will quickly disappear. More mechanization is already planned, and the house will doubtless again be famed for its hospitality.

Appendices

Appendix I

Quintas owned by port shippers

J H Andresen, Sucrs, Lda
No quinta

Barros, Almeida & Ca – Vinhos, SA
Quinta Dona Matilde
Quinta de São Luiz

Sociedade dos Vinhos Borges & Irmão, SA
No quinta. The quintas associated with this firm, and which
belong to the Banco Borges & Irmão, are: Quinta da Casa Nova;
Quinta do Junco; and Quinta da Soalheira.

J W Burmester & Ca, Lda
No quinta

A A Cálem & Filho, Lda
Quinta da Foz (incorporating Quinta do Sagrado, Quinta de
Santo António, Quinta da Sangra and Quinta do Vedial)

Churchill Graham, Lda
No quinta. This firm sells a single Quinta da Água Alta.

Cockburn, Smithes & Ca, Lda
Quinta do Atayde
Quinta dos Canais
Quinta de Santa Maria
Quinta do Tua
Quinta de Val Coelho

Croft & Ca, Lda
Quinta da Roêda

Delaforce Sons & Ca, Vinhos, Lda
No quinta. This firm sells a single Quinta da Côrte.

A A Ferreira, SA
Quinta do Caêdo. This Rio Torto quinta was purchased in 1990,
too late to have a separate entry. Details are, however, included
in Appendix IV.
Quinta da Leda
Quinta do Porto
Quinta do Seixo

Fonseca Guimaraens – Vinhos, SA
Quinta do Cruzeiro
Quinta do Panascal
Quinta de Santo António

Forrester & Ca, Lda
Quinta da Boa Vista

W & J Graham & Co

Quinta dos Malvedos

Gran Cruz Porto – Sociedade Comercial de Vinhos, SA

No quinta. This firm resolutely failed to reply to my enquiries. According to Chantal Lecouty, Gran Cruz has recently purchased 500 virgin ha at Almendra, and four quintas are in the course of being planted: 'Granja (80 ha), Rapada Grande (50 ha), Rapade Petita [sic](50 ha) and Torão (40 ha)'. See Lecouty, p 136.

Sociedade Agrícola e Comercial dos Vinhos Messias, SA

Quinta do Cachão (incorporating Quinta do Rei)

Quinta do Sossego na Ribeira do Rodo. This quinta, with a storage capacity of 500,000 litres, is situated in Régua.

Niepoort – Vinhos, SA

Quinta de Nápoles

Osborne (Vinhos de Portugal) & Ca, Lda

No quinta

Produtores Associados dos Vinhos Progresso do Douro, Lda

No quinta

Manoel D Poças Junior – Vinhos, SA

Quinta das Quartas

Quinta de Santa Bárbara

Quinta de Vale de Cavalos

Quinta do Convento de São Pedro das Águias, Lda

Quinta do Convento de São Pedro das Águias (incorporating Quinta do Paço and Quinta Monte Redondo)

Quinta do Noval – Vinhos, SA

Quinta do Noval (incorporating Quinta das Canadas and Quinta do Silval)

Quinta da Barca, situated in Soutelo (28.6 ha, of which 20 are being replanted)

Adriano Ramos-Pinto – Vinhos, SA

Quinta da Ervamoira

Quinta do Bom Retiro (incorporating Quinta da Urtiga)

Quinta de São Domingos

Companhia Geral da Agricultura das Vinhas do Alto Douro, SA (The Real Companhia Velha)

Quinta dos Aciprestes (incorporating Quinta da Boavista, Quinta de Mileu, Quinta dos Negrilhos)

Quinta Casal de Granja

Quinta do Carvalhal

Quinta das Carvalhas

Quinta de Ferradoza, situated at Vale de Figueira (approx 250 ha, of which 3 are planted)

Quinta Nova

Quinta do Sidrô

Real Companhia Vinícola do Norte de Portugal, SA

Quinta do Corval

Quinta do Síbio

Romariz – Vinhos, SA

No quinta

Rozés, Lda

No quinta

Sandeman & Ca, SA

Quinta das Laranjeiras

Quinta do Vau. Sandeman also has the leasehold of two other quintas: Quinta de Vale de Mendiz (12.3 ha, 7.65 of which are planted) – this quinta has four splendid granite *lagares*, two of which, uniquely as far as I know, are completely round; Quinta do Passadouro, also in Vale de Mendiz (11 ha, 2.88 of which are planted).

C da Silva – Vinhos, SA

Quinta de Avidagos

Silva & Cosens, Ltd

Quinta do Bomfim

Smith Woodhouse & Ca, Lda

No quinta. This firm, belonging to the Symingtons, has a lease of Quinta do Vale de Dona Maria, in the Rio Torto (25 ha, 15 of which are planted).

Taylor, Fladgate & Yeatman – Vinhos, SA

Quinta da Terra Feita

Quinta de Vargellas

Warre & Ca, SA

Quinta da Cavadinha

Quinta de Santa Madalena, situated in the Rio Torto (8 ha, 7.5 of which are planted).

Wiese & Krohn, Sucrs, Lda

Quinta do Retiro Novo

Appendix II

Glossary of Portuguese terms

Adega	A building containing *lagares* or fermentation tanks in which wine is made.
Água pé	A diluted wine made from the last pressings mixed with water. A refreshing drink for vineyard workers and the *roga*.
Aguardente	Brandy. The white spirit used for fortification.
Alambique	Spirit still, used in the Douro for making *bagaceira*.
Aloirado	The Portuguese word sometimes used for 'tawny'.
Andar nobre	The floor with the principal rooms of a large house – cf. *piano nobile*.
Armazém	A building used for the storage of wine, generally called a 'lodge' in Gaia and in the Douro.
Artistas	Employees on the quinta with special skills or responsibilities.
Azenha	The building which houses an olive press.
Azulejos	Painted tiles, so called because they were traditionally blue (*azul*) on a white ground.
Bacalhau	Dried salt cod – the Portuguese national dish.
Baga	Elderberry juice, used illegally (most commonly in the eighteenth century) to add colour to port.
Bagaceira	A marc distilled from *bagaço*.
Bagaço	The pressed skins, seeds and stalks of the grapes.
Baixo	Low – hence *de baixo*, lower.
Balão (Balões)	Balloon – external concrete storage vat.
Balseiro	Upstanding wooden vat.
Barco rabelo	Traditional Douro boat, gondola-shaped with a sail and a long paddle for steering, used until this century for transporting casks of port down-river to Vila Nova de Gaia.
Branco	White – as in *vinho branco* and *porto branco*.
Cadastro	Register of vineyards, graded 'A' to 'H' on

basis of points awarded for variables connected with land (26 per cent), vine (30 per cent) and climate (44 per cent).

Câmara — Town Council.

Cardenho — Building used as a segregated dormitory for quinta workers both during the year and at the harvest.

Casa — A house or building such as a *casa dos lagares*. See *adega*.

Caseiro — The farmer or *quinta* manager who lives on the *quinta*.

Casta — Grape variety.

Cesto de vindima — Harvesting basket.

Cima — Top – hence *da cima*, upper.

Colheita — Vintage. Used, more particularly, to refer to aged tawnies made from a single vintage.

Comissário — Agent.

Concelho — An administrative division of the country, subordinate to a *distrito*, which contains *freguesias*.

Conto — 1000 *escudos*.

Corte — The Portuguese word for 'cut', used to describe the initial crushing of the grapes. Originally done by the treaders in the *lagar*, this is now done mechanically.

Costa — Bank, or shore.

Cuba — Vat. Upstanding large wooden storage container, sometimes made of concrete.

Cuba de fermentação — Fermentation tank, made either of concrete, stainless steel, or resin painted steel.

Cuba de cimento — Concrete vat used for storage.

Distrito — An administrative division of the country, subordinate to a *província*, which contains *concelhos*.

Dorna — (Also *dornacho*.) Small tank in front of a *lagar* used for adding spirit as the must is drawn off.

Enxertador — The 'grafter' – a specialised job carried out by workers who travel around the Douro.

Feitor — Factor or manager. Often used interchangeably with *caseiro*, but sometimes to mean his deputy.

Freguesia — Small administrative division of the country, roughly equivalent to 'parish' and subordinate to a *concelho*.

Gallegos — The itinerant Spanish (Gallician) workmen who laboured in the vineyards last century.

Geo — A traditional narrow vineyard terrace.

Gigo — Large harvesting basket, holding about 60 kg, used to take grapes from the

	vineyards to the *adega* (or intermediate transport).
Inox	Stainless steel.
Lagar	A stone (generally granite, occasionally slate) or concrete tank, of a variable capacity up to about 25 pipes, used for treading grapes.
Lagareiros	The treaders in *lagares*.
Lote	A 'lot' – a parcel of wine, either blended or not, kept separate for a special reason.
Macaco	The Portuguese word for 'monkey' – in wine terms, a nobbly paddle used to push the *manta* into the must in order to maximize contact with the skins.
Manta	The 'cap' of grape skins and seeds which rises to the top of fermenting grape juice.
Miradouro	A vantage-point for admiring scenery.
Mortórios	'Mortuaries'! – the name given to vine terraces either abandoned or planted with olive trees after the *phylloxera* plague.
Mosto	Must – the fermenting grape juice prior to fortification or to becoming wine.
Obras	Work (generally construction or building) in progress. A word much beloved of the British shippers!
Patrão	The boss. The owner of a *quinta*.
Patamar	A vineyard terrace, and, more specifically, one with slightly sloping shoulders and no retaining wall, made by bull-dozing along the contours of a hillside. Used in this book only in the sense of a bull-dozed terrace.
Pé	A 'foot' – often used to refer to an individual vine.
Pilheiro	Antique method of growing vines planted in holes in terrace walls, so that the terrace could be used for growing crops such as maize.
Pipa	A 'pipe' is a cask of variable capacity containing wine. The Douro measurement, which is used exclusively in this book, is 550 litres; a Vila Nova de Gaia lodge pipe for storage normally contains 620 litres; and a pipe for shipping or export measures 534.24 litres.
Podador	A workman who prunes vines.
Pombal	Dovecot.
Porto	(a) the Portuguese name for Oporto; (b) the Portuguese name for port wine, also used in the USA.

Pousada	Inn.
Prédio	Estate.
Ramada	Overhead trellis on which grapes are grown.
Ramo	A branch. Traditionally, a decorated branch is presented to the *patrão's* wife by the *roga* at the end of the vintage.
Refectório	Canteen.
Réi	One thousandth of an *escudo*: hence 1 *milréi* equals 1 *escudo*.
Remontagem	System of vinifying wine by pumping over within a fermentation vessel such as a cylinder.
Ribeiro	A rivulet – hence *ribeirinho*, a brook.
Rio	A river.
Roga	Team of workers, often from far distant villages, who assist in the grape harvest and, where *lagares* are in use, in treading the wine.
Rogador	The team leader or foreman of a *roga*.
Socalco	A walled terrace, generally used to refer to traditional broad vineyard terraces.
Solar	Traditional manorial house.
Tinta	Dye – hence *vinho tinto*, red wine.
Tonel (Toneis)	A large wooden cask, of a variable capacity from about 20 to 60 pipes, for storing wine.
Turismo de habitação	A government sponsored scheme to provide bed and breakfast or self-catering accommodation in private houses or derelict buildings which have been restored for this purpose.
Uva	Grape.
Videira	A vine.
Vindima	The vintage.
Vinha	A vineyard.
Vinhedo	A vineyard.
Vinho	Wine.

Appendix III

Visiting the Douro region and Port Quintas

Tourism in the past

Charles Sellers reports on travelling in the Douro at the turn of the century:

> 'Good wine makes a soft bed' is a true Portuguese proverb. Had it not been for this excellent creature comfort the beds in the Alto Douro, with all their offensive pests, would have been absolutely unbearable. The pillowslip was one mass of cunningly devised embroidery; the sheets were also fringed with a similar abundance of this now costly work, but the pillows were stuffed with sawdust, and the mattresses with straw . . . Carpet there was none, but the ceilings were generally festooned with coloured fly-catchers, so old and dirty, however, that it made one ill to look at them. Soap was almost unknown; and the luxury of a bath had not dawned on the mind of the Portuguese lower classes. But of course they are much improved now, as, by travelling beyond their own frontiers, they have adopted very many salutary innovations. Once, at an hotel at Regoa, the chambermaid brought me a hair brush and a tooth brush, remarking that they were only used by their richer guests.[1]

Happily Portugal of ninety years later is quite unlike that pictured here, but the need for more and better hotels has been recognized for a long time. E H Cockburn, writing in 1935, said: 'You would hardly be safe in expecting to find a range of first class Hotels in the Douro District, so that if any of you ever visit there, you would be wise to make friends with a shipper and get him to put you up at one of his Quintas.'[2] And, at the First National Congress of Tourism the year after, J C Valente Perfeito made the following point. 'Port by itself, and through the region of the Douro where it is produced, is destined to play a role of prime importance in the tourist industry in Portugal. To achieve such an objective it is indispensable to promote the construction of hotels in the Douro.'[3]

Tourism today

It is only now that these words are being heeded and, at present, for the visitor to the port region the hotel facilities are scarcely adequate, though infinitely improved on those reported above. Accommodation in the area includes a *pousada* (i.e. government controlled inn) at Alijó, two at Amarante, a handful of hotels in Lamego, two in Régua, and a couple of modest guest houses in Pinhão. Hotel accommodation further afield, as at Vila Real, is inconveniently distant for the traveller who wishes to spend his time near the Douro.

An alternative, and one which offers the opportunity of staying on a quinta, is the growing provision of *turismo de habitação*. Akin to bed-and-breakfast in some areas of Portugal, particularly in the Minho, in the Douro this tends to consist of small houses and cottages which may be rented by the week. Some of this accommodation is provided by private enterprise, but some is the result of a government financed scheme which aims to provide an extra 250 beds for tourists through the rehabilitation of the many old and derelict properties in the region.

Both the Quinta da Foz and the Quinta de la Rosa have detached cottages which may be rented, and other quintas are already converting surplus buildings for the same purpose, such as Ramos-Pinto at their Quinta dos Bons Ares. The Quinta do Sidrô has been made into a luxurious rural hotel (more particularly for clients of its owners) and will shortly open. So it is already possible for the port enthusiast to stay on a quinta while exploring the area, and these opportunities are steadily growing.

Main roads in the area, although rather winding and sometimes narrow, usually have good surfaces except in remote areas. In general, the communications linking the Douro are being swiftly improved. Access from Spain is good, both to Miranda do Douro and to Vilar Formoso, from which a modern expressway connects, via Viseu, with the Lisbon to Oporto motorway. The latter, at the time of writing, has not yet been completed, but is scheduled to be fully open by the mid 1990s. Another expressway, again not quite completed, connects Oporto with Bragança by way of Vila Real, and thence to Miranda do Douro. The port area is thus easily accessible from both north and south.

By far the best way of seeing the Douro valley is from the railway, which opened at the end of last century, connecting Oporto with Barca d'Alva and Spain, but which now only operates as far east as Pocinho. It remains close to the river at all times and thereby enables the tourist to see parts of the Douro and quintas which are otherwise either extremely difficult or quite impossible to visit. Moreover, the branch line from Tua to Mirandela, which is under threat of closure because of a scheme to dam part of the Rio Tua, is fast becoming a star tourist attraction, and there are hopes that the hydroelectric scheme may be managed in such a way as to preserve it.

The river itself provides other tourist facilities. In the summer there are periodic combined train and steamer excursions covering the entire river from Oporto to Barca d'Alva. It is also possible to explore the lower reaches of the river on day excursions from Oporto.

The future

The future of the river and the future of the region are inextricably bound together. Inaccessible for so long, but an area rich in what it can offer the discriminating tourist, the Douro region is ripe for development. The government, keen to provide a counterpoise to the Algarve and to prevent the region from being denuded of population by further migration of the work force, has finally started to act. A committee on the development of tourist facilities in the region has been set up, and funds have been made available for the development of tourist facilities.

Apart from the improvement of accommodation, there are plans to encourage tourists to investigate not only the wine aspects of the region, but also its historic (archaeological) and natural (geological and botanical) resources. Many parts of the region provide excellent hunting and shooting. The river has, of course, a big role to play in all this. The dams have been built with locks which, when completed in the early 1990s, will allow for relatively large barges and tourist steamers to climb at least as far as Pocinho. Moreover, with the lake-like width of the river, the scope for developing canoeing, water-skiing and other aquatic sports is already being exploited.

This picture of developing tourism is not one which Douro traditionalists necessarily relish, but it is generally accepted that touristic development of some sort is essential to the future prosperity of the region.

Visiting the quintas

Although E H Cockburn, quoted above, recommends the would-be quinta visitor to try to get himself invited to stay at a quinta by a friendly shipper, I regretfully have to stress that in almost all cases quintas, whether those of shippers or others, simply do not have the facilities and are not equipped for entertaining the general public. They are working farms, and most of them are not even geared to allowing day-time visits, let alone putting people up overnight. The shippers, in any case, concentrate their public relations operations in Vila Nova de Gaia, where many have elaborate arrangements for receiving individual tourists, showing them their lodges, and enabling them to taste their ports.

Please bear in mind that the road directions given in the main text are *indicative* only. If you drive off the main road and down a track you will end up trespassing on private property as an unwelcome guest. If you simply *have* to visit a quinta the following points should be borne in mind:

1) Casual visits are absolutely out (except in a few cases *specifically indicated*) and you are more likely to be received if you write asking for an appointment well in advance of the date you have in mind.

2) Group visits, properly organized under the umbrella of, for example, a wine club, are more likely to be accepted than individual requests. In both cases your chances are greatly increased if you can persuade a shipper's overseas agent to give you a letter of introduction and recommendation. On the other hand, one or two of the private quintas who wish to publicize their names, and the wines which they are bringing to the market, may give you a warmer welcome than a

shipper, to whom visits from the general public, rather than the trade, cause a disproportionate expenditure of time and resources.

3)   If you are fortunate enough to be accepted as a visitor please make sure that you arrive on time. Looking at a map in Portugal can sometimes give no indication of the time it will actually take to cover comparatively short distances. From Oporto to Pinhão, for example, normally takes at least three hours by car whichever route you choose. On to that you should add a generous supplement, leaving a margin for slow roads to your ultimate destination, unforeseen delays, and even for losing your way. Conscious of these problems, quinta owners often volunteer to take their guests to the Douro from Oporto. If you are going by yourself, it is a wise precaution to ask your host for an estimate of the time you should allow for travelling.

Despite what has been written above, there are exceptions to this general advice. In Appendix IV, under the heading *Visitors*, the entry for each quinta indicates clearly the policy of its owner. In some cases, it will be seen, visitors are more welcome than in others. For example, the Quinta da Foz at Pinhão now has a guide and welcomes casual visitors. The Quinta de São Domingos at Régua has a visitors' centre with tasting facilities.

Opposite
57
Quinta dos Frades, in the Cima Corgo

Overleaf, left
58
The Valeira Dam, showing the entrance to the Cachão de Valeira, which marks the start of the Douro Superior

Overleaf, right
59
The entrance to Quinta do Vale do Meão. Dated wrought iron gates are a feature of all Dona Antónia Ferreira's important quintas

Following page
60
Patamares at the Quinta de Vargellas. Note the sloping shoulders without built-up stone walls

Appendix IV

Quinta statistical data

In this appendix an attempt has been made to present comparatively some of the basic statistics of the main quintas dealt with in the book. The information given in the tables reflects the position in July 1991, and has been supplied by the owners of the quintas themselves. Unfortunately not all of them have been able (or, in a very few cases, willing) to provide precise information under all of the headings, and where no information has been supplied this is indicated by *NIS*. The quintas are listed in alphabetical order.

   The following notes are intended to elucidate the individual headings used in the tables:

Altitude

In metres above sea level. Note that the heights of the river level between the various dams are approximately: Between Carrapatelo and Régua: 47 m. Between Régua and Valeira: 74 m. Between Valeira and Pocinho: 105 m.

Predominant aspect(s)

Where the configuration of the terrain makes it unrealistic to give just one aspect as the main one, others have been indicated in order of predominance: e.g. S : SSW.

Vine varieties

Where possible the percentage of each vine variety has been given. Where, as is common in old vineyards, the planting is *promiscuous* (i.e. higgledy-piggledy) this is indicated by the term *mixed plantings*, usually with some indication of which varieties are predominant.

Average age of vines

The symbols '<' and '>' have been used to indicate 'greater than' or 'less than' and '±' to indicate 'more or less'. Thus:
25< years means '25 years or more'
10> years means '10 years or less'
±45 years means 'more or less than 45 years'
5/15 years means 'between 5 and 15 years'

Cadastro grade(s)

Very few quintas are exclusively of a single grade. Only the predominant grades are given here. Much of the information included in this appendix is, of course, used in determining the cadastro grade of a quinta.

PDRITM

This indicates whether the quinta participated in the World Bank Scheme to finance new plantings, and, if so, how many hectares were planted.

Vineyard layout   The percentages indicated under each heading, given the wide variety to be found in the Douro, can only be an approximation. Thus 'Walled terraces' includes both narrow (1 or 2 rows) and broad (up to 10 rows) terraces, and 'Continuous planting' neglects the occasional low wall where the over-all configuration of the planting is continuous.

Average yield of port   The figure given here is the average of port – i.e. fortified must – which has been produced recently. It is expressed in Douro pipes of 550 litres. Two things should, however, be borne in mind.
(1) New plantations do not get their *benefício* until three years after the vines have been grafted. The production of quintas with new plantations may, therefore, rise dramatically in the near future.
(2) Only quintas with a Cadastro rating of A or B normally get a *benefício* for their entire production: if they are rated C or lower some of the wine they make must be sold as table wine. (In years when there is a serious overall shortfall in production (like 1989, for example) this rule is relaxed to ensure that there is no shortage of stocks in future.) The yield of port, therefore, for quintas with ratings of C or lower is normally only a proportion of their total wine production.

Winemaking facilities   Unless otherwise indicated in a note, the wine is made on the quinta.

Wine utilization   Where it is indicated that a privately owned quinta sells to a shipper, it should be remembered that such arrangements can change. In some cases a private proprietor may bottle his own wine (or part of it) and sell the rest to a shipper. In the case of a shipper's own quinta, if the wine is normally earmarked for one or more of the shipper's own products, this has been indicated.
N.B. 'Vintage' indicates a shipper's vintage blend, of which the quinta's port will normally form a component. This should be distinguished from 'single quinta', which indicates that the production, or a proportion of it, is sold as a port *exclusively* from the quinta.

Single quinta port   This may be a single quinta vintage, a single quinta *colheita*, a single quinta LBV, or a single quinta tawny ruby or white port.

Recent vintages   The vintage years given here are those of the single quinta vintages only. They do *not* refer to shippers' declared vintage blends.

Visitors   Please refer to the section dealing with quinta visiting in Appendix III. It cannot be stressed enough that with very few exceptions Douro quintas are not organized to receive unscheduled individual visitors.

Name of Quinta	Quinta dos Aciprestes	Quinta da Água Alta
Full postal address	Soutelo do Douro,	Gouvinhas,
	5130 São João da Pesqueira	5100 Sabrosa
Concelho (council)	São João da Pesqueira	Sabrosa
Freguesia (parish)	Soutelo do Douro	Covas do Douro
Registered owner	Real Companhia Velha	Sr António Borges de Sousa
Year acquired	1972	Before 1580
Total area (ha)	300	Approx. 90
Altitude (m), min–max	110–340	150–250
Predominant aspect(s)	NE	SE, SW
Area of vines (ha)	120	40
Number of vines	300,000	130,000
Vine varieties	Tinta Barroca (28%)	*Old plantings* (65%)
	Touriga Francesa (28%)	Tinta Roriz (Predominant)
	Tint Roriz (22%)	Tinta Barroca
	Touriga Nacional (3%)	Touriga Francesa
	Tinta Amarela (3%)	Tinto Cão
	Mourisco Tinto (3%)	*New Plantings* (35%)
	Rufete ⎫	Tinta Barroca (12%)
	Tinta Francisca ⎪	Tinta Roriz (7%)
	Códega ⎬ (8%)	Touriga Francesa (7%)
	Rabigato ⎪	Touriga Nacional (7%)
	Gouveio ⎭	Tinto Cão (2%)
	Others (5%)	
Average age of vines	30% – 25< years	Old plantings – 50/60 years
	70% – 5> years	New Plantings – 10 years
Cadastro grade(s)	A	A
PDRITM (ha)	No	10
Vineyard layout		
Walled terraces		66%
Bulldozed terraces	5%	44%
Vertical planting	45%	
Continuous planting	50%	
Average yield of port	204 pipes	100 pipes
Red	95%	100%
White	5%	
Winemaking facilities	*	
Lagares	6 (not in use)	4 (in use) + 2 (standby)
Pumpover tanks		
Autovinifiers		
Other		
Wine utilization	Premium blends	Sold to shippers, mainly Churchill-Graham for vintage, single quinta, crusted or 'finest vintage character'
Single quinta port	None (but one planned for future)**	Yes (Churchill-Graham)
Recent vintages		83, 87
Visitors	Trade, wine writers by appointment only	No
Other information	*Wine vinified at *Quinta das Carvalhas* **A tawny and a 10 year old tawny are sold in France under the name *Quinta da Boavista* (one of the quintas which forms part of the property)	Other quintas belonging to the Borges de Sousa family from which Churchill-Graham buys port are *Quinta do Fojo*, *Quinta da Manuela* and *Quinta de Roncão Pequeno*

Name of Quinta	Quinta da Amêda	Quinta do Atayde
Full postal address	São Mamede de Riba Tua, 5070 Alijó	5360 Vila Flor
Concelho (council)	Alijó	Vila Flor
Freguesia (parish)	São Mamede de Riba Tua	Vila Flor
Registered owner	Manuel Carlos Agrellos, Herdeiros	Cockburn Smithes & Ca, Lda
Year acquired	Before 1800	1980
Total area (ha)	25	200
Altitude (m), min–max	90–250	150–250
Predominant aspect(s)	E, S	S, E, W
Area of vines (ha)	12*	150
Number of vines	45,000*	550,000
Vine varieties	Touriga Nacional (30%)	Touriga Nacional (% NIS)
	Touriga Francesa (22%)	Tinta Roriz
	Tinta Barroca (22%)	Tinta Barroca
	Tinta Roriz (22%)	Touriga Francesa
	Tinto Cão (4%)	Tinto Cão
		Mourisco
		Malvasia Fina
		Rabigato
		Codega
Average age of vines	4 years	6 years
Cadastro grade(s)	A	A
PDRITM (ha)	8	No
Vineyard layout		
Walled terraces		
Bulldozed terraces	95%	10%
Vertical planting	5%	
Continuous planting		90%
Average yield of port	Not yet in production**	960 pipes
Red	100%	95%
White		5%
Winemaking facilities	***	None*
Lagares		
Pumpover tanks		
Autovinifiers		
Other		
Wine utilization	Eventually for a single quinta port	'Special Reserve' and other premium blends
Single quinta port	No (but one is projected)	None
Recent vintages		
Visitors	Trade and wine press by appointment only	Trade and wine writers by appointment only
Other information	*8 further ha with 32,000 vines to be planted in 1991	*Wine vinified at Quinta do Tua. A new adega is planned for 1994
	**Projected 72 pipes in 1991, rising to projected 120 pipes in 1998	
	***An adega is yet to be built	

Name of Quinta	Quinta de Avidagos	Quinta da Boa Vista
Full postal address	Alvações do Corgo,	Chanceleiros,
	5050 Peso da Régua	5085 Pinhão
Concelho (council)	Peso da Régua	Sabrosa
Freguesia (parish)	Alvações do Corgo	Chanceleiros
Registered owner	C da Silva Vinhos, SA	Forrester & Ca, Lda (86%)
		Seminário do Sagrado Coração de
		Jesus (14%)
Year acquired	1971	1979
Total area (ha)	20	98
Altitude (m), min–max	110–160	80–290
Predominant aspect(s)	W	S, W
Area of vines (ha)	15	50
Number of vines	120,000	173,000
Vine varieties	Tinta Francesa (30%)	Tinta Barroca (20%)
	Tinta Roriz (20%)	Tinta Amarela (18%)
	Malvasia Fina (20%)	Touriga Nacional (15%)
	Tinta Barroca (10%)	Malvasia Preta (15%)
	Viosinho (10%)	Tinta Roriz (7%)
	Malvasia Corada (5%)	Rufete (5%)
	Fernão Pires (5%)	Touriga Francesa (3%)
		Others (17%)
Average age of vines	50% – 10> years	50% – 20< years
	30% – 10/30 years	
	20% – 30< years	
Cadastro grade(s)	B	A
PDRITM (ha)	No	4
Vineyard layout		
Walled terraces	50%	60%
Bulldozed terraces		40%
Vertical planting		
Continuous planting	50%	
Average yield of port	200 pipes	240 pipes
Red	90%	88%
White	10%	12%
Winemaking facilities		
Lagares	4 (in use)	6 (not in use)
Pumpover tanks	22 (concrete)	4 (stainless steel)
Autovinifiers	15	
Other		
Wine utilization	Vintage, LBV or aged tawny	Vintage, LBV, and premium blends
Single quinta port	Ruby, LBV and vintage	Yes – both vintage and LBV
Recent vintages	82, 85, 87	75, 77, 80, 82, 83, 85, 87
Visitors	Trade and journalists only	Trade, wine writers by appointment
Other information		

Name of Quinta	Quinta do Bomfin	Quinta do Bom Retiro*
Full postal address	5085 Pinhão	Casais do Douro, 5130 São João da Pesqueira
Concelho (council)	Alijó	Tabuaço
Freguesia (parish)	Pinhão	Valença do Douro
Registered owner	Silva & Cosens, Ltd	Adriano Ramos-Pinto Vinhos, SA
Year acquired	1890	1919
Total area (ha)	59	101
Altitude (m), min−max	80−130	100−400
Predominant aspect(s)	S	S, E
Area of vines (ha)	35	60
Number of vines	164,142	234,000
Vine varieties	Touriga Francesa (28%)	*Old plantings*
	Tinta Roriz (12%)	Mixed (37%)
	Tinta Barroca (11%)	*New plantings*
	Touriga Nacional (10%)	Touriga Francesa (17%)
	Old mixed vines (39%)	Tinta Roriz (17%)
		Tinta Barroca (15%)
		Touriga Nacional (13%)
		Tinto Cão (1%)
Average age of vines	41% − 30< years	Old plantings − 50 years
	46% − 6> years	New plantings − 4/20 years
Cadastro grade(s)	A	A
PDRITM (ha)	10	No
Vineyard layout		
Walled terraces	50%	17%
Bulldozed terraces	46%	19%
Vertical planting	4%	21%
Continuous planting		43%
Average yield of port	143 pipes	400 pipes
Red	100%	100%
White		
Winemaking facilities		
Lagares	2 (not in use)	1 (in experimental use)
Pumpover tanks		13 (concrete), 16 (stainless steel)
Autovinifiers	11 (stainless steel), 20 (concrete)	
Other		
Wine utilization	Vintage (Dow*), single quinta, LBV and aged tawnies	Vintage, blends, single quinta and other tawnies
Single quinta port	Yes	Yes − 20 year old tawny: also a *Quinta da Urtiga* − vintage character
Recent vintages	78, 79 (82, 84, 86, 87, 88 not yet released)	
Visitors	By appointment only	Groups and viticultural students only
Other information	*'Dow' is the name under which Silva & Cosens, Ltd, which belongs to Symingtons, sell their port	*The data given here *include* the *Quinta da Urtiga* (15 ha, of which 10 are planted)

Name of Quinta	**Quinta do Bom Retiro Pequeno**	**Quinta do Cachão**[*]
Full postal address	Casais do Douro,	Ferradoza,
	5130 São João da Pesqueira	5130 São João da Pesqueira
Concelho (council)	Tabuaço	São João da Pesqueira
Freguesia (parish)	Valença do Douro	Vale de Figueira
Registered owner	Sociedade Agrícola do Bom Retiro	Sociedade Agrícola e Comercial dos
	Pequeno	Vinhos Messias, SA
Year acquired	1935	1956
Total area (ha)	73	170
Altitude (m), min–max	180–280	105–250
Predominant aspect(s)	E	S
Area of vines (ha)	63	80
Number of vines	163,000	200,000
Vine varieties	Tinta Barroca (10%)	*Old plantings* (56%)
	Tinta Roriz (10%)	Touriga Francesa (16%)
	Tinta Amarela (10%)	Tinta Roriz (16%)
	Touriga Francesa (10%)	Tinta Barroca (10%)
	Touriga Nacional (10%)	Tinta Nacional (4.5%)
	Mourisco (10%)	Periquita (4.5%)
	Malvasia Preta (10%)	Other reds (5%)
	Tinta Francisca (10%)	*New plantings* (44%)
	Donzelinho (10%)	Touriga Francesa (18%)
	Rufete (4%)	Tinta Roriz (18%)
	Tinto Cão (3%)	Tinto Cão (4%)
	Rabigato (3%)	Tinta Nacional (4%)
Average age of vines	10% – 4 > years	Old plantings – 15 years
	35% – 4/25 years	New plantings – 3 years
	55% – 25 < years	
Cadastro grade(s)	A	A
PDRITM (ha)	8	17
Vineyard layout		
Walled terraces	40%	56.25%
Bulldozed terraces	31.5%	43.75%
Vertical planting		
Continuous planting	28%	
Average yield of port	200 pipes	262 pipes
Red	100%	100%
White		
Winemaking facilities		
Lagares	5 (in use)	1 (not in use)
Pumpover tanks		7 (stainless steel)
Autovinifiers		8 (concrete)
Other		
Wine utilization	Sold to Warre: used for vintage,	Vintage, *colheitas*, LBV and aged
	premium blends, and aged tawnies	tawnies
Single quinta port	None	Yes
Recent vintages	76, 82, 84, 85	
Visitors	Trade and wine writers only, by	Welcomed (by appointment)
	appointment with Warre's public	
	relations officer	
Other information		[*]The *Quinta do Rei* (2 ha planted)
		forms part of the *Quinto do Cachão*

Name of Quinta	Quinta do Caêdo	Quinta dos Canais
Full postal address	5130 Ervedosa do Douro	Beira Grande,
		5140 Carrazeda de Ansiães
Concelho (council)	São João da Pesqueira	Carrazeda de Ansiães
Freguesia (parish)	Ervedosa	Beira Grande
Registered owner	A A Ferreira, SA	Cockburn Smithes & Ca, Lda
Year acquired	1990	1989
Total area (ha)	30	Approx. 300
Altitude (m), min–max	140–260	110–540
Predominant aspect(s)	W, S	S, SW
Area of vines (ha)	15	50
Number of vines	53,000	170,000*
Vine varieties	Touriga Francesa (60%)	Tinta Roriz (% NIS)
	Tinta Roriz (20%)	Tinta Barroca
	Tinta Amarela (10%)	Touriga Nacional
	Other reds (10%)	Tinta da Barca
		Touriga Francesa
Average age of vines	60 years	8.82% – 1 year
		20.59% – 2 years
		11.77% – 6/25 years
		58.82% – 25< years
Cadastro grade(s)	A	A
PDRITM (ha)		10
Vineyard layout		
Walled terraces	60%	40%
Bulldozed terraces		45%
Vertical planting	30%	
Continuous planting	10%	15%
Average yield of port	50 pipes	100 pipes
Red	100%	100%
White		
Winemaking facilities		
Lagares	4 (not in use)	5 (n use)
Pumpover tanks		
Autovinifiers		
Other		
Wine utilization	Vintage and premium quality blends	Vintage and premium blends
Single quinta port	None	None
Recent vintages		
Visitors	No	Not at present
Other information	Crop vinified at Quinta do Seixo	*It is hoped that a further 150,000
		vines will be planted by 1995

Name of Quinta	Quinta do Carvalhal	Quinta das Carvalhas
Full postal address	Santa Eugénia, 5070 Alijó	5085 Pinhão
Concelho (council)	Alijó	São João da Pesqueira
Freguesia (parish)	Pegarinhos	Casais do Douro
Registered owner	Real Companhia Velha	Real Companhia Velha
Year acquired	c. 1890	1956
Total area (ha)	Approx. 100	Approx. 600
Altitude (m), min–max	365–495	80–375
Predominant aspect(s)	NNW	NNE, SSE
Area of vines (ha)	15	150
Number of vines	53,420	573,643
Vine varieties	Códega (25%)	Touriga Francesa (22%)
	Gouveio (20%)	Tinta Roriz (20%)
	Malvasia Fina (17%)	Tinta Barroca (15%)
	Praça (15%)	Tinta Amarela (8%)
	Formosa (5%)	Rufete (5%)
	Rabigato (5%)	Malvasia Preta (5%)
	Moscatel Galego (3%)	Tinta Francisca (4%)
	Others, including some reds (10%)	Mourisco Tinto ⎤
		Touriga Nacional ⎥
		Tinta da Barca ⎥ (8%)
		Periquita ⎥
		Bastardo ⎥
		Moreto ⎦
		Others, including some whites (10%)
Average age of vines	25 < years	90% – ±25 years
Cadastro grade(s)	D, E	A
PDRITM (ha)	No	10
Vineyard layout		
Walled terraces	100%	80%
Bulldozed terraces		
Vertical planting		20%
Continuous planting		
Average yield of port	50 pipes	662 pipes
Red	5%	95%
White	95%	5%
Winemaking facilities	*	*
Lagares	1 (not in use)	3 (not in use)
Pumpover tanks		
Autovinifiers		14 (concrete)
Other		
Wine utilization	Lower quality blends	Premium blends
Single quinta port	None	No (but one is planned for future)*
Recent vintages		
Visitors	No	Trade, wine writers by appointment only: but tourist reception facilities at present under construction
Other information	*Wine vinified at *Quinta de Casal de Granja*	*The quinta name is used on a tawny brand, and a tawny brand is sold in France under the name *Quinta da Cruz* (a quinta which forms part of the property

Name of Quinta	Quinta Casal de Celeirós	Quinta Casal de Granja
Full postal address	Celeirós do Douro, 5060 Sabrosa	Granja, 5070 Alijó
Concelho (council)	Sabrosa	Alijó
Freguesia (parish)	Celeirós do Douro	Granja
Registered owner	Sociedade Agrícola Quinta do Casal e do Confradeiro, Lda	Real Companhia Velha
Year acquired	1991	1972
Total area (ha)	15	250
Altitude (m), min–max	± 500	520–640
Predominant aspect(s)	NNW, ENE	ESE
Area of vines (ha)	15	140
Number of vines	79,000	618,000
Vine varieties	Touriga Francesa (20%)	Touriga Francesa (20%)
	Tinta Barroca (12%)	Tinta Barroca (20%)
	Tinta da Barca (10%)	Tinta Roriz (10%)
	Tinta Roriz (8%)	Moscatel Galego (14%)
	Sousão (3%)	Malvasia Rei (8%)
	Malvasia Fina (10%)	Malvasia Fina (5%)
	Malvasia Rei (10%)	Donzelinho (5%)
	Gouveio (5%)	Códega (4%)
	Others (22%)	Chasselás (3%)
		Other reds and whites (10%)
Average age of vines	54% – 25< years	60% – 25< years
	46% – 12 years	40% – 15 years
Cadastro grade(s)	C	C, D, E, F
PDRITM (ha)	No	No
Vineyard layout		
Walled terraces		
Bulldozed terraces		
Vertical planting		
Continuous planting	100%	100%
Average yield of port	108 pipes	600 pipes*
Red	70%	40%
White	30%	60%
Winemaking facilities	*	*
Lagares	4 (in derelict adega)	3 (not in use)
Pumpover tanks		
Autovinifiers		24 (stainless steel); 8 (concrete)
Other		
Wine utilization		White ports and lower quality blends
Single quinta port	None	None**
Recent vintages		
Visitors	By appointment only	Trade, wine writers by appointment only
Other information	*The company will, for the time being, sell its grapes to shippers	*Actual amount varies widely from year to year. Occasionally total production of 1,300 pipes receives port benefício
		**Table wines produced here are sold under the name 'Grandjo' and 'Porca de Murça'

Name of Quinta	**Quinta da Casa Nova**	**Quinta da Cavadinha**
Full postal address	5085 Pinhão	Provezende, 5085 Pinhão
Concelho (council)	Sabrosa	Sabrosa
Freguesia (parish)	Gouvães do Douro	Provenzende
Registered owner	Banco Borges & Irmão	Warre & Ca, SA
Year acquired	1926	1980
Total area (ha)	59	41
Altitude (m), min–max	190–400	120–350
Predominant aspect(s)	E	SE
Area of vines (ha)	24	29
Number of vines	84,300	138,945
Vine varieties	Red (74%)	Touriga Francesa (58%)
	Mourisco (15%)	Tinta Roriz (6%)
	Touriga Francesa (12%)	Tinta Barroca (2%)
	Touriga Nacional (10%)	Touriga Nacional (2%)
	Tinta da Barca (10%)	Old mixed vines (32%)
	Tinta Barroca (8%)	
	Tinta Roriz (7%)	
	Tinto Cão (6%)	
	Others (6%)	
	White (26%)	
	Malvasia (8%)	
	Fernão Pires (6%)	
	Codega (6%)	
	Others (6%)	
Average age of vines	Old plantings – 55 years	80% – 30< years
	New Plantings – Part 10 years, part 5 years	20% – 7 years
Cadastro grade(s)	B	A
PDRITM (ha)	No	No
Vineyard layout		
Walled terraces	66.7%	90%
Bulldozed terraces	25%	10%
Vertical planting		
Continuous planting	8.3%	
Average yield of port	107 pipes	178 pipes
Red	90%	100%
White	10%	
Winemaking facilities	*	
Lagares	3 (last used in 1974)	3 (not in use)
Pumpover tanks		
Autovinifiers		
Other		4 (stainless steel) temperature controlled, 23 pipe tanks with both pump-over and autovinification capacities
Wine utilization	Sold to Sociedade dos Vinhos Borges & Irmão	Vintage, single quinta, LBV and aged tawnies
Single quinta port	No	Yes
Recent vintages		78, 79, 82 (84, 86, 87, 88 not yet released)
Visitors	Strictly by appointment	By appointment only
Other information	*Wine is vinified at *Quinta do Junco*	

Name of Quinta	Quinta do Convento de São Pedro das Águias*	Quinta da Côrte
Full postal address	5120 Tabuaço	Valença do Douro, 5120 Tabuaço
Concelho (council)	Tabuaço	Tabuaço
Freguesia (parish)	Távora	Valença do Douro
Registered owner	Quinta do Convento de São Pedro das Águias, Lda	Pacheco & Irmãos, Lda
Year acquired	1986	NIS
Total area (ha)	212	40
Altitude (m), min−max	250−400	100−250
Predominant aspect(s)	E, W	N, S
Area of vines (ha)	130	35
Number of vines	243,500	160,000
Vine varieties	*Old plantings (50%)* Tinta Roriz (10%) Touriga Francesa (6.6%) Touriga Nacional (3.5%) Tinto Cão (2.5%) Mourisco (1.5%) Other reds and whites (including Malvasia Fina) (26%) *New Plantings (50%)* Tinta Roriz (16%) Tinta Barroca (16%) Touriga Nacional (9%) Touriga Francesa (9%)	Touriga Francesa (35%) Tinta Roriz (20%) Tinta Amarela (20%) Rufete (15%) Tinto Cão (5%) Others (10%)
Average age of vines	90% − 15/20 years 10% − 2 years	Old plantings − 70 years New plantings − 14 years
Cadastro grade(s)	B, C	A
PDRITM (ha)	No	No
Vineyard layout		
Walled terraces	3.5%	100%
Bulldozed terraces	76.5%	
Vertical planting		
Continuous planting	20%	
Average yield of port	115 pipes**	180 pipes
Red	75%	100%
White	25%	
Winemaking facilities		
Lagares	4 (to be used in future)***	2 (used only for excess production)
Pumpover tanks		
Autovinifiers		4
Other		
Wine utilization	Presently being matured for quinta products	Sold to Delaforce: vintage, single quinta and aged tawnies
Single quinta port	No (but planned for the future)****	Yes
Recent vintages		78, 80, 84, 87
Visitors	Trade only	By appointment through Delaforce & Sons
Other information	*Including *Quintas do Paço* (30 ha planted) and *Monte Redondo* (42 ha planted) **Rising to 475 pipes by 1995 ***Wine presently vinified at *Quinta da Avaleira* ****10 and 20 year old tawnies, etc, not made at quinta are sold under all three quinta names	

Name of Quinta	Quinta do Corval	Quinta da Costa*
Full postal address	5085 Pinhão	Galafura, 5050 Peso da Régua
Concelho (council)	Alijó	Peso da Régua
Freguesia (parish)	Pinhão	Galafura
Registered owner	Real Companhia Vinícola do Norte de Portugal	Aida Coimbra Aires de Matos & Filhos, Lda
Year acquired	1921	Before 1785
Total area (ha)	4	12
Altitude (m), min–max	100–160	200–360
Predominant aspect(s)	SSW	W
Area of vines (ha)	3.5	12
Number of vines	12,125	35,000
Vine varieties	Tinta Roriz (35%)	Mixed plantings (% NIS)
	Tinta Carvalha (15%)	Touriga Francesa (predominant)
	Touriga Francesa (10%)	Tinta Roriz
	Tinta Barroca (10%)	Tinta Amarela
	Mourisco Tinto (10%)	Tinta Barroca
	Tinta Bairrada (5%)	
	Malvasia Preta (3%)	
	Tinta Aguiar (2%)	
	Other reds (10%)	
Average age of vines	25 < years	Old plantings – ±70 years
		New plantings – 11 years
Cadastro grade(s)	A	B
PDRITM (ha)	No	No
Vineyard layout		
Walled terraces		83.4%
Bulldozed terraces		16.5%
Vertical planting		
Continuous planting	100%	
Average yield of port	19 pipes	43 pipes
Red	100%	100%
White		
Winemaking facilities		**
Lagares		1 (remains in ruined adega dated 1575)
Pumpover tanks		
Autovinifiers	18 (concrete)	
Other		
Wine utilization	Premium blends	Part sold to shippers; part kept for company's own wines
Single quinta port	None*	No
Recent vintages		
Visitors	Trade, wine press by appointment only	By appointment only
Other information	*The quinta name is used for ruby and tawny brands	*This is also the name of the Aires e Matos estate of 60.7 ha, containing the Quintas do Vermelho, Velal, Cruz and Barroca, and other vineyards. There is a total of 54 ha planted with 254,270 vines producing 250 pipes annually, of which 150 are port
		**Wine is vinified at company's adega, with 6 (concrete) autovinifiers in Galafura

Name of Quinta	Quinta da Costa de Baixo*	Quinta do Côtto*
Full postal address	Gouvinhas,	Citadelhe,
	5060 Sabrosa	5050 Peso da Régua
Concelho (council)	Sabrosa	Mesão Frio
Freguesia (parish)	Gouvinhas	Citadelhe
Registered owner	Sr Dr José Afonso Moreno Bulas Cruz	Montez-Champalimaud Lda
	Sra Maria Gabriel Moreno Bulas Cruz	
Year acquired	1951	Prior to 1300
Total area (ha)	52	116
Altitude (m), min–max	75–450	100–430
Predominant aspect(s)	S	S, SW
Area of vines (ha)	28	52
Number of vines	120,000	225,000
Vine varieties	*Old mixed plantings (65%)*	Tinta Roriz (35%)
	Tinta Roriz (26%)	Touriga Francesa (20%)
	Touriga Francesa (13%)	Touriga Nacional (20%)
	Tinta Barroca (9.75%)	Bastardo (10%)
	Tinta Amarela (6.5%)	Other reds (15%)
	Tinta da Barca (6.5%)	
	Others (3.25%)	
	PDRITM (35%)	
	Tinto Cão (10.5%)	
	Tinta Barroca (10.5%)	
	Tinta Roriz (10.5%)	
	Touriga Nacional (3.5%)	
Average age of vines	Old plantings – 50< years	30 years
	New Plantings – 6 years	
Cadastro grade(s)	A	C
PDRITM (ha)	10	No
Vineyard layout		
Walled terraces	53.6%	
Bulldozed terraces	46.4%	30%
Vertical planting		2%
Continuous planting		68%
Average yield of port	78 pipes	235 pipes
Red	97.5%	100%
White	2.5%	
Winemaking facilities		
Lagares	4 (in use)	Removed (last used 1964)
Pumpover tanks		
Autovinifiers		8
Other		
Wine utilization	Some sold to shippers (grapes as well as wine) – remainder for single quinta port	Sold to shippers unless reserved for single quinta port
Single quinta port	Yes – tawny (without indication of age)	Yes
Recent vintages		82**
Visitors	Not at present	
Other information	*Data include *Quinta da Foz Ceira* (12 ha, of which 6 ha are planted)	*The balance of production not made into port is made into red and white douro table wine, notably 'Grande Escolha' red.
		**The only vintage produced so far

Name of Quinta	Quinta do Crasto	Quinta do Cruzeiro
Full postal address	Gouvinhas,	Vale de Mendiz,
	5060 Sabrosa	5070 Alijó
Concelho (council)	Sabrosa	Alijó
Freguesia (parish)	Gouvinhas	Vale de Mendiz
Registered owner	Sociedade Agrícola da Quinta do Crasto	Fonseca-Guimaraens Vinhos, SA
Year acquired	1910	1973
Total area (ha)	140	15
Altitude (m), min−max	75−500	130−200
Predominant aspect(s)	S, E	W
Area of vines (ha)	42	10
Number of vines	183,000	43,745
Vine varieties	*Old plantings (43%)*	Tinta Roriz (29%)
	Tinta Amarela (10.8%)	Touriga Francesa (29%)
	Tinta Roriz (6.4%)	Touriga Barroca (21%)
	Touriga Francesa (6.4%)	Touriga Nacional (9%)
	Touriga Nacional (4.2%)	Tinta Amarela (4%)
	Mourisco (4.3%)	Tinto Cão (1%)
	Moscatel Hamburgo (4.3%)	Others (7%)
	Sousão (2.2%)	
	Others (4.2%)	
	New Plantings (57%)	
	Touriga Francesa (17.1%)	
	Tinta Roriz (11.4%)	
	Touriga Nacional (11.4%)	
	Tinta Barroca (11.4%)	
	Tinto Cão (5.7%)	
Average age of vines	Old plantings − 40 years	85% − 18 years
	New Plantings − 5 years	15% − 50 years
Cadastro grade(s)	A	A
PDRITM (ha)	24	No
Vineyard layout		
Walled terraces	33%	30%
Bulldozed terraces	57%	65%
Vertical planting	10%	5%
Continuous planting		
Average yield of port	110 pipes*	64 pipes
Red	100%	100%
White		
Winemaking facilities		
Lagares	6 (in use)	5 (in use)
Pumpover tanks		
Autovinifiers		
Other		
Wine utilization	Mainly matured for quinta wines: remainder sold to shippers	Fonseca (or Guimaraens) vintage, 'Bin 27' or aged tawnies
Single quinta port	Yes	No
Recent vintages	78, 82, 85, 87	
Visitors	Strictly by appointment	Only by letter of introduction
Other information	*Rising to 320 pipes when the 24 ha of new plantings come on stream	

Name of Quinta	Quinta Dona Matilde (do Enxodreiro)	Quinta da Eira Velha
Full postal address	Bagaúste, 5050 Peso da Régua	5085 Pinhão
Concelho (council)	Régua	Sabrosa
Freguesia (parish)	Poiares	Gouvães
Registered owner	Sociedade Agrícola de Bagaúste	Messrs Richard and Peter Newman
Year acquired	1927	1938
Total area (ha)	120	47
Altitude (m), min–max	110–190	130–200
Predominant aspect(s)	SW	S, SE
Area of vines (ha)	26	25
Number of vines	145,000	134,250
Vine varieties	Tinta Amarela ⎫ Tinta Barroca ⎬ (55%) Tinta Roriz ⎭ Tinta da Barca ⎫ Mourisco ⎬ (25%) Other reds ⎭ Malvazia Fina ⎫ Fernão Pires ⎬ (20%) Other whites) ⎭	*Old plantings (85%)* Tinta Barroca (23%) Tinta Amarela (23%) Touriga Francesa (17%) Tinta Roriz (8.5%) Rufete (8.5%) Others (5%) *New plantings (15%)* Tinta Barroca (3%) Tinto Cão (1.5%) Touriga Francesa (3%) Tinta Roriz (4.5%) Touriga Nacional (3%)
Average age of vines	40 years	25/30 years New plantings – 3 years Some old plantings 100< years
Cadastro grade(s)	B	A
PDRITM (ha)	No	7
Vineyard layout		
Walled terraces	25%	85%
Bulldozed terraces	75%	15%
Vertical planting		
Continuous planting		
Average yield of port	240 pipes	120 pipes
Red	80%	97%
White	20%	3%
Winemaking facctilities	*	
Lagares	4 (last used 1985)	5 (in use)
Pumpover tanks		
Autovinifiers		
Other		
Wine utilization	Mostly aged for tawny	Single quinta, or sold to Cockburns who use it mainly for 'Special Reserve'
Single quinta port	None**	Yes
Recent vintages		78, 82 (87 not yet released)
Visitors	Trade only	Private visitors only
Other information	*Wine is vinified at *Quinta de São Luiz* **Quinta name is used for a tawny brand	

Opposite
61
Quinta da Boa Vista. Notice the massive terraces on this side of the quinta buildings, built by the Barão de Forrester's sons and amongst the most imposing in the Douro

Overleaf
62
Quinta da Soalheira. The *caseiro*, Sr Carlos Silva and his wife

Name of Quinta	Quinta da Ervamoira (Santa Maria)	Quinta do Estanho
Full postal address	Chãs, 5150 Vila Nova de Foz Côa	Cheires, 5070 Alijó
Concelho (council)	Vila Nova de Foz Côa	Alijó
Freguesia (parish)	Chãs/Muxagata	Sanfins do Douro
Registered owner	Adriano Ramos-Pinto Vinhos, SA	Jaime Acácio Queiroz Cardoso
Year acquired	1974	1975
Total area (ha)	200	7.5
Altitude (m), min–max	120–300	270–360
Predominant aspect(s)	E	W
Area of vines (ha)	75	7
Number of vines	450,000	33,671
Vine varieties	Touriga Nacional (25%) Tinta Roriz (26%) Tinta Barroca (26%) Touriga Francesa (20%) Others (3%)	Touriga Francesa (40%) Tinta Roriz (15%) Tinta Barroca (15%) Tinta da Barca (10%) Tinta Carvalha (10%) Others (10%)
Average age of vines	7 years	25 years
Cadastro grade(s)	A	C
PDRITM (ha)	9	No
Vineyard layout		
Walled terraces		70%
Bulldozed terraces		
Vertical planting	100%	
Continuous planting		30%
Average yield of port	360 pipes	78 pipes*
Red	100%	98%
White		2%
Winemaking factilities	None*	**
Lagares		2 (in ruined adega)
Pumpover tanks		
Autovinifiers		
Other		
Wine utilization	Vintage, single quinta, tawnies and other wines	Part sold to shippers, part used for quinta products
Single quinta port	Yes – 10 year old tawny	Yes – 10 and 20 year old tawny; old white
Recent vintages		
Visitors	Trade, journalists, viticultural students	No
Other information	*Wine vinified at Quinta dos Bons Ares	*Rising, with full production, to 98 pipes **Wine is vinified at adega in Cheires

Previous page
63
Quinta do Vale do Meão; the kitchen. The array of pots and pans is typical of a traditional quinta kitchen

Opposite
64
Broad and narrow terraces on the Rio Torto. Those on the right belong to the Quinta da Côrte

Name of Quinta	Quinta da Foz*	Quinta do Infantado
Full postal address	5085 Pinhão	Covas do Douro, 5085 Pinhão
Concelho (council)	Sabrosa	Sabrosa
Freguesia (parish)	Gouvães	Covas do Douro
Registered owner	A A Cálem & Filho, Lda	Herdeiros do João Lopes Roseira
Year acquired	1885	NIS
Total area (ha)	90	85
Altitude (m), min–max	100–430	180–650
Predominant aspect(s)	E, SW	S, SW
Area of vines (ha)	49.5	55
Number of vines	190,000	200,000*
Vine varieties	*Old plantings (47.4%)*	Touriga Francesa (20%)
	Touriga Francesa (11.9%)	Tinta Roriz (15%)
	Tinta Barroca (9.5%)	Touriga Nacional (10%)
	Tinta Roriz (9.3%)	Tinta Barroca (10%)
	Tinta Francisca (6%)	Tinto Cão (5%)
	Touriga Nacional (4.7%)	Other reds (30%)
	Other reds (6%)	Whites (10%)
	New Plantings (52.6%)	
	Tinta Roriz (21%)	
	Touriga Nacional (10.6%)	
	Touriga Francesa (10.5%)	
	Tinta Barroca (10.5%)	
Average age of vines	15 years	Old plantings – 35 years
		New plantings – 5 years
Cadastro grade(s)	A	A
PDRITM (ha)	20	20
Vineyard layout		
Walled terraces	47.4%	5.5%
Bulldozed terraces	52.6%	54.5%
Vertical planting		7.25%
Continuous planting		32.75%
Average yield of port	180 pipes**	180 pipes**
Red	100%	90%
White		10%
Winemaking facilities		
Lagares	4 (in use)	5 (in use)
Pumpover tanks		
Autovinifiers		
Other		
Wine utilization	Vintage, single quinta, LBV, *colheitas* and aged tawnies	Normally used entirely for quinta products
Single quinta port	Yes	Yes – vintage, LBV, *colheita* (77), 20 year old tawny, ruby and white
Recent vintages	82, 84, 86, 87	78, 81, 82, 83
Visitors	Groups and individuals by application	By telephone appointment (one week's notice) either 054-72477 or 02-884495
Other information	*Data given include the *Quintas do Sagrado* (29 ha, 9.5 ha planted), *do Vedial* (32 ha, 20 planted) and *de Santo Antonio* (10 ha, 8 ha planted) **Rising to 340 pipes by 1995	*Of which 70,000 are not yet producing **Rising to 300 pipes by 1993

Name of Quinta	**Quinta do Junco**	**Quinta das Lages**
Full postal address	5085 Pinhão	Sarzedinho,
		5130 São João da Pesqueira
Concelho (council)	Sabrosa	São João da Pesqueira
Freguesia (parish)	São Cristovão/Provezende	Sarzedinho
Registered owner	Banco Borges & Irmão	Eng° Alvaro Baltazar Moureira da
		Fonseca
Year acquired	1906	1886
Total area (ha)	80.86	180
Altitude (m), min–max	200–500	110–425
Predominant aspect(s)	S	NW, W
Area of vines (ha)	46	80
Number of vines	180,500	197,000
Vine varieties	*Red* (84%)	Touriga Francesa (20%)
	Touriga Francesa (20%)	Rufete (20%)
	Touriga Nacional (17%)	Tinta Roriz (20%)
	Mourisco (10%)	Tinta Barroca (7%)
	Tinta Roriz (10%)	Touriga Nacional (5%)
	Tinta da Barca (12%)	Tinta Francisca (3%)
	Tinta Barroca (8%)	Other reds (25%)
	Tinto Cão (5%)	
	Others (2%)	
	White (16%)	
	Malvasia (7%)	
	Fernão Pires (7%)	
	Others (2%)	
Average age of vines	Old plantings – 60 years	50% – 25< years
	New plantings – part 16 years, part 5	25% – 10/25 years
	years	25% – 10> years
Cadastro grade(s)	A	A
PDRITM (ha)	No	10
Vineyard layout		
Walled terraces	70%	87.5%
Bulldozed terraces	26%	12.5%
Vertical planting		
Continuous planting	4%	
Average yield of port	230 pipes	200 pipes
Red	92%	100%
White	8%	
Winemaking facilities		
Lagares	(Removed – last used in 1964)	6 (in use)
Pumpover tanks		
Autovinifiers	8 (concrete)	
Other		
Wine utilization	Sold to Sociedade dos Vinhos Borges	Sold to W & J Graham & Co, used for
	& Irmão	vintage and premium brands
Single quinta port	Yes – a *colheita* (79, 85)	None
Recent vintages		
Visitors	Strictly by appointment	No
Other information		

Name of Quinta	**Quinta das Laranjeiras**	**Quinta da Leda**
Full postal address	5160 Moncorvo	5150 Almendra
Concelho (council)	Moncorvo	Vila Nova de Foz Côa
Freguesia (parish)	Moncorvo	Almendra
Registered owner	Sandeman & Ca, SA	A A Ferreira, SA/SVP Constantino Lda
Year acquired	1981	1979
Total area (ha)	210	55
Altitude (m), min−max	115−135	150−300
Predominant aspect(s)	W	S
Area of vines (ha)	14	37
Number of vines	49,000	120,000
Vine varieties	Touriga Francesa (40%)	Touriga Francesa (35%)
	Touriga Nacional (20%)	Tinta Barroca (30%)
	Tinta Barroca (20%)	Tinta Roriz (30%)
	Tinta Roriz (15%)	Others (5%)
	Tinto Cão (5%)	
Average age of vines	Old plantings − 20 years	8 years
	New plantings − 3 years	
Cadastro grade(s)	B	B
PDRITM (ha)	10	10
Vineyard layout	14.5% (experimental)*	
Walled terraces		
Bulldozed terraces		65%
Vertical planting	78.5%	15%
Continuous planting	7%	20%
Average yield of port	83 pipes	93 pipes
Red	100%	100%
White		
Winemaking facilities	**	None*
Lagares	Ruined	
Pumpover tanks		
Autovinifiers		
Other		
Wine utilization	Used for Sandeman's ports	Port blends − eventually for vintage
Single quinta port	None	None
Recent vintages		
Visitors	By appointment only	No
Other information	*Includes broad and narrow terraces and vertical planting	*Wine vinified at *Quinta do Vale do Meão*
	**Wine is vinified at Sandeman's Pocinho *adega*	

Name of Quinta	Quinta dos Malvedos	Quinta do Monsul
Full postal address	São Mamede de Riba Tua, 5070 Alijó	5051 Peso da Régua
Concelho (council)	Alijó	Lamego
Freguesia (parish)	São Mamede de Riba Tua	Cambres
Registered owner	W & J Graham & Co	NIS
Year acquired	1890	1469
Total area (ha)	146	22
Altitude (m), min–max	80–280	NIS
Predominant aspect(s)	SSW	NIS
Area of vines (ha)	88	10
Number of vines	273,000	NIS
Vine varieties	Tinta Roriz (25%)	Red varieties (30%)
	Touriga Francesa (20%)	White varieties (70%)
	Tinta Barroca (15%)	
	Touriga Nacional (10%)	
	Tinta Amarela (6%)	
	Other reds (24%)	
Average age of vines	7% – 25< years	NIS
	93% – 10> years	
Cadastro grade(s)	A	NIS
PDRITM (ha)	10	No
Vineyard layout		
Walled terraces	7%	
Bulldozed terraces	90%	
Vertical planting	3%	
Continuous planting		100%
Average yield of port	124 pipes*	NIS
Red	100%	
White		
Winemaking facilities	**	
Lagares	4 (no longer used)	5 (last used in 1985)
Pumpover tanks		
Autovinifiers		
Other		
Wine utilization	Vintage, single quinta, LBV and aged tawny	Grapes sold to Taylor
Single quinta port	None (but see main text for fuller explanation)	None
Recent vintages		
Visitors	By appointment only	No
Other information	*Rising to 350 pipes by 1992–93 **Until the new winery is ready the wine will be vinified at *Quinta da Cavadinha*	The above information is based on an interview with a representative of the owners, who, despite repeated requests, failed to provide further details

Name of Quinta	**Quinta dos Murças**	**Quinta de Nápoles***
Full postal address	Covelinhas, 5050 Peso da Régua	5120 Tabuaço
Concelho (council)	Régua	Armamar
Freguesia (parish)	Covelinhas	Vila Seca
Registered owner	Murças Lda	Niepoort (Vinhos), SA
Year acquired	1940	1988
Total area (ha)	138	52.5
Altitude (m), min–max	80–307	75–400
Predominant aspect(s)	S	E, N
Area of vines (ha)	60	15 (+14 ha of *patamares* and 1 ha of vertical planting in preparation)
Number of vines	300,000	45,000
Vine varieties	*Mixed old plantings (50%)* (in which Tinta Amarela and Tinta Francisca predominate, and which include some white varieties) Touriga Francesa (17%) Tinta Roriz (17%) Tinta Barroca (8%) Touriga Nacional (8%)	*Old mixed plantings* Mourisco (predominant) Touriga Francesa Tinta Roriz Bastardo Tinta Amarela *New plantings* Touriga Nacional (30%) Tinta Roriz (20%) Tinta Amarela (15%) Touriga Francesa (10%) Other varieties (25%)
Average age of vines	Old plantings – 35< years 80% of new Plantings – 12< years	Old plantings – 50% – 35 years 50% – 15 years
Cadastro grade(s)	B	A
PDRITM (ha)	9	No
Vineyard layout		
Walled terraces	20%	50%
Bulldozed terraces		50%
Vertical planting	80%	
Continuous planting		
Average yield of port	525 pipes	24 pipes
Red	100%	98%
White		2%
Winemaking facilities		
Lagares	8 (last used 1956)	3 (last used in 1968)
Pumpover tanks		4 (stainless steel)
Autovinifiers	10 (concrete)	
Other		
Wine utilization	85% sold to shippers: remainder matured for single quinta port	Not yet decided
Single quinta port	Yes – at present only an LBV	None
Recent vintages	86 (87, 88, 89, 90 to be released)	
Visitors	No	Trade, wine writers by appointment only
Other information		*Data include *Quinta do Carril* (10.5 ha, of which 5 ha are planted)

Name of Quinta	Quinta Nova	Quinta do Noval*
Full postal address	Covas do Douro,	Vale de Mendiz,
	5085 Pinhão	5050 Pinhão
Concelho (council)	Sabrosa	Alijó
Freguesia (parish)	Covas do Douro	Vale de Mendiz
Registered owner	Real Companhia Velha	Quinta do Noval Vinhos, SA
Year acquired	1987	1894**
Total area (ha)	120	168.6
Altitude (m), min–max	80–350	100–410
Predominant aspect(s)	S, SW	SW
Area of vines (ha)	35	106.5
Number of vines	155,000	213,352
Vine varieties	Touriga Francesa (NIS %)	Old mixed plantings (91%)
	Tinta Roriz	Touriga Nacional
	Mourisco Tinto	Tinta Barroca
	Tinta Amarela	Touriga Francesa
	Tinta da Barca	Tinta Roriz
	Alicante Boucket	Mourisco
	Grande Noir	Sousão
	Malvasia Preta	New plantings (7%)
	Tinta Carvalha	Touriga Nacional
		Tinta Barroca
		Touriga Francesa
		Tinta Roriz
		Ungrafted plantings (2%)
		Tinta Roriz (10%)
		Sousão (15%)
		Touriga Francesa (41%)
		Touriga Nacional (4%)
		Others (including Tinto Câo) (30%)
Average age of vines	20% – 25< years	Old plantings – 25< years
	80% – 10> years	New plantings – 10 years
		Ungrafted plantings – 30< years
Cadastro grade(s)	A	A
PDRITM (ha)	10	7
Vineyard layout		
Walled terraces		64% (69% narrow and 31% broad terraces)
Bulldozed terraces	28.6%	35%
Vertical planting		1%
Continuous planting	71.4%	
Average yield of port	115 pipes	435 pipes
Red	95%	96%
White	5%	4%
Winemaking facilities		
Lagares		5 (in use for quinta harvest)
Pumpover tanks		1 (stainless steel)
Autovinifiers	9 (concrete)	10 (stainless steel)
Other		
Wine utilization	Premium blends	Vintage, towards 'Noval LB', or aged tawny
Single quinta port	None	Yes
Recent vintages		75, 78, 82, 85, 87
		Nacional: 75, 78, 80, 82, 85, 87
Visitors	Trade, wine writers by appointment only	Trade, journalists and wine enthusiasts strictly by appointment
Other information		*Data are for the entire property which now comprises the original Quinta do Noval (120 ha, of which 67 ha are planted), Quinta do Silval (16.6 ha, of which 9.5 are planted), and Quinta das Canadas (32 ha, of which 28 ha are planted)
		**The date is uncertain: see p. 100

Name of Quinta	Quinta da Pacheca	Quinta do Panascal
Full postal address	Apartado 3, 5051 Peso da Régua	Valença do Douro, 5120 Tabuaço
Concelho (council)	Lamego	Tabuaço
Freguesia (parish)	Cambres	Valença do Douro
Registered owner	Sr Eduardo Serpa Pimentel	Fonseca-Guimaraes Vinhos, SA
Year acquired	1903	1978
Total area (ha)	34	42
Altitude (m), min–max	70–110	80–350
Predominant aspect(s)	Flat area. No exposure predominates	SSW
Area of vines (ha)	34	30
Number of vines	131,000	114,110
Vine varieties	*Old plantings* Mixed (23.5%) *New plantings* (76.5%) Tinta Roriz (11.5%) Touriga Francesa (11.5%) Tinta Barroca (11.5%) Touriga Nacional } Tinto Cão } (11.5%) Malvasia Fina } Códega } Verdelho } (30.5%) Cercial }	*Old plantings* (28.2%) Tinta Amarela (8.5%) Tinta Roriz (5.9%) Touriga Francesa (4.5%) Tinta Barroca (2%) Touriga Nacional (2%) Others (5.3%) *New plantings* (71.8%) Tinta Roriz (25.1%) Touriga Francesa (22.3%) Touriga Nacional (12.9%) Tinta Barroca (6.5%) Tinto Cão (2.2%) Other reds (2.8%)
Average age of vines	Old plantings – 50 years New plantings – 15 years	Old plantings – 20 years New plantings – 5 years
Cadastro grade(s)	C, D	A
PDRITM (ha)	6	17
Vineyard layout		
Walled terraces		17%
Bulldozed terraces		56%
Vertical planting	1.5%	6%
Continuous planting	98.5%	21%
Average yield of port	192 pipes	169 pipes*
Red	68%	100%
White	32%	
Winemaking facilities		
Lagares	7 (in use)	5 (not used between 1978 and 1991)
Pumpover tanks		
Autovinifiers		
Other	10 (stainless steel) for white table wines	
Wine utilization	Port (40% of total production) is sold to Cockburn: table wine is estate bottled	Vintage, single quinta, 'Bin 27' or aged tawnies
Single quinta port	None	Yes
Recent vintages		77, 78, 83
Visitors	Trade and groups strictly by appointment	Visitors welcome by appointment
Other information		*Reaching over 200 pipes by 1992, when new plantations come on stream

Opposite, above
65
The house of Quinta do Bartol, which is opposite Quinta de Vargellas and next to Quinta dos Canais

Opposite, below
66
The imposing gateway of Quinta do Cruzeiro

Overleaf
67
Quinta do Síbio. A marvellously well-preserved traditionally terraced quinta, hardly changed since pre-phylloxera times.

In the distance on the right (across the Ribeira da Póvoa) is Quinta de Roncão da Cima, and in the far distance (across the Douro) Quinta do Ventozelo

Name of Quinta	**Quinta do Porto**	**Quinta das Quartas**
Full postal address	Covas do Douro, 5050 Pinhão	5050, Peso da Régua
Concelho (council)	Sabrosa	Peso da Régua
Freguesia (parish)	Covas do Douro	Fontelas
Registered owner	A A Ferreira, SA	Sociedade Vinícola Terras de Valdigem Lda
Year acquired	1863	1923
Total area (ha)	36	10
Altitude (m), min–max	80–250	145–165
Predominant aspect(s)	S	S
Area of vines (ha)	24	6
Number of vines	92,000	21,670
Vine varieties	Touriga Francesa (40%) Tinta Barroca (30%) Tinta Roriz (20%) Others (10%)	Touriga Francesa (30%) Tinta Barroca (10%) Tinta Amarela (10%) Tinta Roriz (5%) Malvasia Rei (30%) Malvasia Fina (15%) Other reds and whites (10%)
Average age of vines	25 years	25 < years
Cadastro grade(s)	A	C, D
PDRITM (ha)	No	No
Vineyard layout		
Walled terraces	40%	100%
Bulldozed terraces	60%	
Vertical planting		
Continuous planting		
Average yield of port	95 pipes	44 pipes
Red	100%	70%
White		30%
Winemaking facilities	*	
Lagares	4 (used for small percentage of crop)	3 (in use)
Pumpover tanks		1
Autovinifiers		
Other		
Wine utilization	Almost all reserved for quinta wine	Used in blends
Single quinta port	Yes – 10 year old tawny blend	No
Recent vintages		
Visitors	By appointment with Ferreira's public relations manager	Trade, wine writers and groups by appointment only
Other information	*Most of crop is vinified at *Quinta do Seixo*	

Opposite, above
68
Quinta de Santa
Maria. Pipes stacked
high in the cask hall
of the *armazém*. Note
the chocks (for
stabilizing the pipes)
at the bottom right
corner of the
photograph

Opposite, below
69
The entrance to the
visitors' reception
centre at Quinta de
São Domingos. Note
the old beam press
with its massive stone
weight and crew, and
the poster, which is
typical of those used
by Ramos-Pinto

Name of Quinta	Quinta do Retiro Novo	Quinta da Roêda
Full postal address	Sarzedinho, 5130 São João da Pesqueira	5085 Pinhão
Concelho (council)	São João da Pesqueira	Alijó
Freguesia (parish)	Sarzedinho	Pinhão
Registered owner	Wiese & Krohn, Sucrs, Lda	Croft & Ca, Lda
Year acquired	1989	1875
Total area (ha)	26	113
Altitude (m), min–max	125–215	100–250
Predominant aspect(s)	N, NW	SW
Area of vines (ha)	Approx. 10	70
Number of vines	54,000*	334,000
Vine varieties	Touriga Francesa (25%)	Old plantings (33%)
	Rufete (17%)	Tinta Barroca (4.72%)
	Touriga Nacional (15%)	Touriga Francesa (4.62%)
	Tinta Barroca (13%)	Tinta Roriz (4.26%)
	Tinta Roriz (11%)	Tinta da Barca (3.96%)
	Tinta Francisca (9%)	Tinta Amarela (3.12%)
	Tinto Cão (6%)	Tinto Cão (2.31%)
	Others (4%)	Touriga Nacional (1.12%)
		Others (8.89%)
		New Plantings (67%)
		Touriga Francesa (11.86%)
		Touriga Nacional (11.06%)
		Tinta Barroca (10.79%)
		Tinta Roriz (9.98%)
		Tinto Cão (6.77%)
		Tinta da Barca (5.7%)
		Tinta Amarela (2.75%)
		Others (8.09%)
Average age of vines	57% – 25< years	Old plantings – 60/70 years
	24% – from 6 to 24 years	New plantings – 9 years
	19% – 6> years	
Cadastro grade(s)	A	A
PDRITM (ha)	No	No
Vineyard layout		
Walled terraces	30%	33%
Bulldozed terraces	70%**	66%
Vertical planting		1%
Continuous planting		
Average yield of port	60 pipes	430 pipes
Red	100%	100%
White		
Winemaking facilities		
Lagares	5 (in use)	1 (last used 1963)*
Pumpover tanks	2 (stainless steel)	28 (concrete) 6 (painted metal)
Autovinifiers		
Other		
Wine utilization	Vintage, colheita and premium wines	Vintage, single quinta, LBV, aged tawnies and other quality wines
Single quinta port	None	Yes
Recent vintages		67, 70, 78, 80, 83, 87
Visitors	No facilities except for occasional clients	Special visitors by prior arrangement
Other information	*A further 20,000 vines will be planted in 1992	*Except for making comparative experiments
	**Including 6 ha of patamares already prepared for planting in 1992	

Name of Quinta	Quinta da Romaneira	Quinta de Roriz
Full postal address	Cotas, 5070 Alijó	Ervedoza do Douro, 5130 São João da Prequeira
Concelho (council)	Alijó	São João da Pesqueira
Freguesia (parish)	Cotas/Castedo	Ervedosa do Douro
Registered owner	Sociedade Agrícola da Romaneira, SA and Sociedade Agrícola de São Martinho, SA*	Dr Pedro van Zeller, Srs Pedro and João van Zeller
Year acquired	1967	c. 1775
Total area (ha)	420	150
Altitude (m), min–max	75–525	80–200
Predominant aspect(s)	W	W, N
Area of vines (ha)	87*	50
Number of vines	335,000	172,905
Vine varieties	Old plantings (70%) Mixed red and whites New plantings (30%) Touriga Nacional (7.5%) Touriga Francesa (7.5%) Tinta Roriz (7.5%) Tinto Cão (7.5%)	Tinta Roriz (22%) Touriga Nacional (18%) Tinta Barroca (15%) Touriga Francesa (12%) Mourisco Tinto (12%) Tinta da Barca (10%) Tinta Francisca (3%) Cornifesto (3%) Others (15%)
Average age of vines	Oldest plantings – 60/80 years New plantings – 73% 5 years 27% 1 year	58% <6 years – average 25 years 42% >6 years –average 4 years
Cadastro grade(s)	88% – A, 12% C	A
PDRITM (ha)	17	17
Vineyard layout		
Walled terraces	28%	14%
Bulldozed terraces	34%	28%
Vertical planting	6%	12%
Continuous planting	32%	46%
Average yield of port	280 pipes	120 pipes
Red	98%	100%
White	2%	
Winemaking facilities		4 (in use)
Lagares	4 (ruined in Quinta da Carrapata)	
Pumpover tanks		
Autovinifiers	4 with pumpover facilities	
Other		
Wine utilization	For quinta products	Sold to Van Zellers & Ca, Vinhos, Lda
Single quinta port	Quinta da Romaneira vintage, LBV, colheita (67, 70), tawny, ruby and white Quinta da Pulga ruby and tawny (from 1990)	One is projected for next vintage declaration
Recent vintages	82, 84, 85, 87	
Visitors	Trade and wine writers by appointment only	Strictly by appointment
Other information	*40 ha (of which 7 ha are planted) are registered in the name of the second society	

Name of Quinta	**Quinta de la Rosa***	**Quinta de Santa Bárbara**
Full postal address	5085 Pinhão	5050 Peso da Régua
Concelho (council)	Sabrosa	Lamego
Freguesia (parish)	Gouvães	Valdigem
Registered owner	Dourosa Investments Ltd	Sociedade Vinícola Terras de Valdigem, Lda
Year acquired	1906	1980
Total area (ha)	160	16
Altitude (m), min−max	90−260	90−175
Predominant aspect(s)	E, S	W, NW
Area of vines (ha)	Approx. 41	Approx. 14
Number of vines	195,000	85,000
Vine varieties	*Old plantings* (50%)	Tinta Roriz (25%)
	In order of predominance:	Tinta Barroca (20%)
	Tinto Cão	Touriga Francesa (10%)
	Tinta Roriz	Tinta Amarela (10%)
	Touriga Nacional	Mourisco (5%)
	Tinta Barroca	Malvasia Rei (15%)
	Bastardo	Malvasia Fina (5%)
	Touriga Francesa	Other reds and whites (10%)
	Malvasia Preta	
	Mourisco	
	Tinta Amarela	
	Sousão	
	Tinta Carvalha	
	Grande Noir	
	Calmete	
	Malvasia Fina	
	Códega	
	New plantings (50%)	
	Tinta Barroca (12.5%)	
	Touriga Francesa (12.5%)	
	Tinta Roriz (12.5%)	
	Touriga Nacional (12.5%)	
Average age of vines	Old plantings − 80 years	70% − 40< years
	New plantings − 6 years	30% − 10> years
Cadastro grade(s)	A, B	B, C
PDRITM (ha)	20	No
Vineyard layout		
Walled terraces	50%	16%
Bulldozed terraces	50%	
Vertical planting		4%
Continuous planting		80%
Average yield of port	115 pipes**	130 pipes
Red	97%	50%
White	3%	50%
Winemaking facilities	***	*
Lagares	8 (3 in use; 5 modified but not now in use)	4 (not in use)
Pumpover tanks		
Autovinifiers	4	
Other		
Wine utilization	For quinta products	Quinta wine, or used in blends
Single quinta port	Yes − see text for details	Yes − A *colheita* (80)
Recent vintages	88	
Visitors	By prior telephone arrangement: in Portugal 054-72254: in England 0296-748989	Not at present
Other information	*Data given include *Quinta das Lamelas*	*Wine vinified at *Quinta das Quartas*
	**Expected to yield 200 pipes by 1995	
	***8 combined autovinifier and pump-over tanks, as at *Quinta da Cavadinha*, shortly to be installed	

Name of Quinta	Quinta de Santa Júlia de Loureiro	Quinta de Santa Maria
Full postal address	Loureiro, 5050 Peso da Régua	Godim, 5050 Peso da Régua
Concelho (council)	Régua	Régua
Freguesia (parish)	São Pedro de Loureiro	Godim
Registered owner	Sr Eduardo da Costa Seixas	Cockburn Smithes & Ca, Lda
Year acquired	1981	1973
Total area (ha)	Approx. 60	6.5
Altitude (m), min–max	200–410	100–120
Predominant aspect(s)	E, S	E, S
Area of vines (ha)	Approx. 30	5
Number of vines	110,000	15,000
Vine varieties	Malvasia Fina (40%)	Touriga Nacional (33%)
	Codega (10%)	Tinta Roriz (20%)
	Malvasia Corada (8%)	Tinta Barroca (17%)
	Malvasia Rei (6%)	Tinto Cão (13%)
	Other whites (2%)	Bastardo (7%)
	Tinta Barroca (12%)	Rufete (7%)
	Tinta Francesa (10%)	Others (3%)
	Tinta Roriz (6%)	
	Tinta da Barca (4%)	
	Other reds (2%)	
Average age of vines	50% – 40< years	25 years
	40% – 14 years	
	10% – 1 year	
Cadastro grade(s)	C, D	C
PDRITM (ha)	5	No
Vineyard layout		
Walled terraces	50%	
Bulldozed terraces	40%	
Vertical planting	10%	
Continuous planting		100%
Average yield of port	145 pipes	45 pipes
Red	57%	100%
White	43%	
Winemaking facilities		None*
Lagares	4 (in use)	
Pumpover tanks	5	
Autovinifiers	4	
Other		
Wine utilization	Part sold to Sandeman: table wine sold under name of quinta	Ruby port
Single quinta port	None	None
Recent vintages		
Visitors	Selected visitors only, by appointment	Trade and wine writers by appointment only
Other information		*Wine vinified at Cockburn's adega at Lamego

Name of Quinta	Quinta de Santo António	Quinta de São Domingos
Full postal address	Vale de Mendiz, 5070 Alijó	5050 Peso da Régua
Concelho (council)	Alijó	Régua
Freguesia (parish)	Vale de Mendiz	Régua
Registered owner	Fonseca-Guimaraens Vinhos, SA	Adriano Ramos-Pinto Vinhos, SA
Year acquired	1979	1915
Total area (ha)	15	3
Altitude (m), min−max	220−330	95−145
Predominant aspect(s)	S	SW
Area of vines (ha)	8	3
Number of vines	30,812	13,500
Vine varieties	Touriga Francesa (26%) Tinta Roriz (26%) Tinta Barroca (18%) Touriga Nacional (7%) Tinta Amarela (4%) Tinto Cão (3%) Others (16%)	*Old plantings* (including replacements and 5% white varieties) (55%) *New plantings* (45%) Touriga Francesa (30%) Tinta Roriz (10%) Tinta Barroca (5%)
Average age of vines	Old plantings − 50 years New plantings − 10 years	New plantings − 20 years Over-all − 30 years
Cadastro grade(s)	A	B
PDRITM (ha)	No	No
Vineyard layout		
Walled terraces	67%	100%
Bulldozed terraces	33%	
Vertical planting		
Continuous planting		
Average yield of port	45 pipes	30 pipes
Red	100%	95%
White		5%
Winemaking facilities	*	
Lagares	3 (last used 1978)	1 (not in regular use)
Pumpover tanks		4 (concrete with ceramic tiles)
Autovinifiers		
Other		
Wine utilization	Fonseca and Guimaraens vintage, 'Bin 27', and aged tawnies	Aged tawny
Single quinta port	None	None*
Recent vintages		
Visitors	Only by letter of introduction	Yes, the quinta has a visitor centre
Other information	*Wine vinified at *Quinta do Cruzeiro*	*A brand sold under the Quinta name has now been discontinued

Name of Quinta	Quinta de São Luíz	Quinta do Seixo
Full postal address	5120 Tabuaço	Valença do Douro, 5120 Tabuaço
Concelho (council)	Tabuaço	Tabuaço
Freguesia (parish)	Adorigo	Valença do Douro
Registered owner	Sociedade Agrícola de Bagaúste	A A Ferreira, SA
Year acquired	1952	1979
Total area (ha)	262	90
Altitude (m), min–max	115–280	80–300
Predominant aspect(s)	E, W	N, SE
Area of vines (ha)	80	75
Number of vines	310,000	260,000
Vine varieties	*Old plantings (58%)*	Touriga Francesa (34%)
	Touriga Francesa (8.7%)	Tinta Roriz (33%)
	Tinta Roriz (5.8%)	Tinta Barroca (23%)
	Tinta Amarela (5.8%)	Touriga Nacional (6%)
	Tinta Carvalha (5.8%)	Others (4%)
	Malvasia Preta (5.8%)	
	Others (26.1%)	
	New plantings (42%)	
	Touriga Francesa (12.6%)	
	Tinta Roriz (8.4%)	
	Tinta Barroca (8.4%)	
	Touriga Nacional (6.3%)	
	Tinto Cão (2.1%)	
	Tinta da Barca (2.1%)	
	Rufete (2.1%)	
Average age of vines	Old plantings – ±50 years	20 years
	New plantings – 4 years	
Cadastro grade(s)	A	A
PDRITM (ha)	10	10
Vineyard layout		
Walled terraces	58%	30%
Bulldozed terraces	32%	15%
Vertical planting	10%	55%
Continuous planting		
Average yield of port	408 pipes	260 pipes*
Red	100%	100%
White		
Winemaking factilities		
Lagares		
Pumpover tanks		38 (stainless steel)
Autovinifiers	25 (concrete)	
Other		
Wine utilization	Single quinta, *colheita* or aged tawny	Vintage and premium quality blends*
Single quinta port	Yes	Yes
Recent vintages	70, 75, 77, 80, 82, 83, 85	83**
Visitors	Trade and journalists by appointment only	No
Other information		*Balance of harvest, together with locally purchased grapes, goes to make a red Douro table wine sold by the name of 'Esteva' **The only single quinta port produced by this property so far

Name of Quinta	Quinta da Senhora da Ribeira	Quinta do Síbio
Full postal address	Seixo de Ansiães, 5140 Carrazeda de Ansiães	Cotas, 5070 Alijó
Concelho (council)	Carrazeda de Ansiães	Alijó
Freguesia (parish)	Seixo de Ansiães	Cotas
Registered owner	Sr António Bernardo F Trige Moutinho	Real Companhia Vinícola do Norte de Portugal
Year acquired	1954	1934
Total area (ha)	25	Approx. 35
Altitude (m), min–max	115–240	90–340
Predominant aspect(s)	S	SSW
Area of vines (ha)	20	15
Number of vines	34,500	22,540
Vine varieties	Mourisco (20%) Tinta Roriz (18%) Touriga Francesa (17%) Tinta Amarela (10%) Touriga Nacional (5%) Tinto Cão (3%) Other reds (27%)	Touriga Francesa (30%) Tinta Francisca (20%) Touriga Nacional (20%) Tinta Amarela (8%) Mourisco Tinto (5%) Tinta Carvalha (5%) Tinta Roriz (3%) Tinta Bairrada (2%) Malvasia Preta (2%) Others (5%)
Average age of vines	80% – 25< years 14% – 4/25 years 6% – 4> years	60± years
Cadastro grade(s)	A	A
PDRITM (ha)	No	No
Vineyard layout		
Walled terraces	92%	100%
Bulldozed terraces	8%	
Vertical planting		
Continuous planting		
Average yield of port	50 pipes	35 pipes
Red	100%	100%
White		
Winemaking facilities		*
Lagares	4 (in use)	1 (not in use)
Pumpover tanks		
Autovinifiers		
Other		
Wine utilization	Sold to Silva & Cosens for Dow's vintage, LBV and aged tawnies	Premium blends
Single quinta port	None	None (but one is planned for the future)**
Recent vintages		
Visitors	No	No
Other information		*Wine vinified at *Quinta das Carvalhas* **Bottles of old vintages (e.g. 1945) still exist. However the *Quinta do Síbio* 1985 vintage port is not exclusively port from the property. A tawny brand is sold in France under the name 'Quinta do Jordão'

Opposite
70
Morning mists give
way to the sun. The
vertical planting of
the Quinta do Seixo is
especially noteworthy.
The white buildings
of the Quinta de Santa
Bárbara, belonging to
the CEVD, can be
seen on the left

Name of Quinta	**Quinta do Sidró**	**Quinta da Soalheira**
Full postal address	5130 São João da Pesqueira	5130 São João da Pesqueira
Concelho (council)	São João da Pesqueira	São João da Pesqueira
Freguesia (parish)	São João da Pesqueira	São João da Pesqueria/Castanheiro do Sul
Registered owner	Real Companhia Velha	Banco Borges & Irmão
Year acquired	1972	1904
Total area (ha)	250	333
Altitude (m), min–max	450–600	200–450
Predominant aspect(s)	E, NE	S
Area of vines (ha)	Approx. 120	40
Number of vines	355,000	110,000
Vine varieties	Tinta Barroca (20%)	Mourisco (25%)
	Tinta Francesa (20%)	Touriga Nacional (15%)
	Tinta Roriz (10%)	Tinto Cão (15%)
	Malvasia Rei (8%)	Tinta Barroca (12%)
	Mourisco Tinto (5%)	Tinta Francesa (10%)
	Pinôt (6%)	Tinta Roriz (8%)
	Tinta Amarela (4%)	Bastardo (5%)
	Tinta Carvalha (4%)	Others (10%)
	Carrego Branco (3%)	
	Gouveio ⎫	
	Malvasia Preta ⎪	
	Rabigato ⎬ (10%)	
	Fernão Pires ⎪	
	Rufete ⎪	
	Códega ⎭	
	Others, red and white (10%)	
Average age of vines	50% – 35 years	Old plantings – 50 years
	50% – 3 years	New plantings – part 15 years, part 6 years and part 3 years
Cadastro grade(s)	D, E, F	A
PDRITM (ha)	10	10
Vineyard layout		
Walled terraces		60%
Bulldozed terraces		40%
Vertical planting	60%	
Continuous planting	40%	
Average yield of port	500 pipes	100 pipes
Red	35%	100%
White	65%	
Winemaking facilities	New *adega* under construction*	
Lagares	6 (not in use)	5 (not in use)
Pumpover tanks		
Autovinifiers		
Other		
Wine utilization	Lower quality blends	Sold to Sociedade dos Vinhos Borges & Irmão
Single quinta port	None**	No*
Recent vintages		
Visitors	Trade, wine writers by appointment only: However, quinta will shortly receive guests on a basis yet to be determined	By appointment only
Other information	*Wine vinified at *Quinta das Carvalhas* **A white table wine is sold under the quinta name	*Tawny ports are sold under the names 'Soalheira' and 'Soalheira Especial'

Opposite
71
The Douro in the
evening, looking
downstream from
Quinta do Porto as
the sun is about to
disappear

Name of Quinta	**Quinta da Terra Feita**	**Quinta do Tua*** (dos Ingleses)
Full postal address	Provenzende, Sabrosa, 5085 Pinhão	Foz-Tua, 5140 Carrazeda de Ansiães
Concelho (council)	Sabrosa	Carrazeda de Ansiães
Freguesia (parish)	Celeirós/Provenzende	Castanheiro do Norte
Registered owner	Taylor, Fladgate & Yeatman Vinhos, SA	Cockburn Smithes & Ca, Lda
Year acquired	1974	1889
Total area (ha)	88	30
Altitude (m), min−max	145−225	150−350
Predominant aspect(s)	S, E	S
Area of vines (ha)	45	25
Number of vines	216,373	80,000
Vine varieties	Touriga Francesa (29%) Tinta Roriz (22%) Tinta Barroca (12%) Touriga Nacional (14%) Tinta Amarela (4%) Tinto Cão (3%) Other reds (16%)	Touriga Nacional, Tinta Roriz, Tinta Barroca, Rufete, Mourisco (70%); Tinto Cão, Tinta da Barca, Touriga Francesa, Malvasia Fina (30%)
Average age of vines	Old plantings − 45 years New plantings − 8 years	Old plantings (5%) − 35 years New plantings − 13 years
Cadastro grade(s)	A	A
PDRITM (ha)	3.5	10
Vineyard layout		
Walled terraces	33%	20%
Bulldozed terraces	59%	80%
Vertical planting	8%	
Continuous planting		
Average yield of port	320 pipes	125 pipes
Red	100%	99%
White		1%
Winemaking factilities		
Lagares	11 (in use)	5 (in occasional use)
Pumpover tanks		7 (mild steel)
Autovinifiers		
Other		Roto-tank
Wine utilization	Vintage, LBV or aged tawnies	Vintage, single quinta, 'Special Reserve' and other premium blends
Single quinta port	Planned for the future	One is to be released in the future
Recent vintages	86 (to be marketed when mature)	87
Visitors	Only by letter of introduction	Trade, wine writers by appointment only
Other information		*Data given include the *Quinta da Chousa* (25 ha, of which 22 ha are planted)

Name of Quinta	**Quinta de Val Coelho*** (Lobazim de Baixo)	**Quinta de Val da Figueira**
Full postal address	Vilarinho da Castanheira, 5140 Carrazeda de Ansiães	Covas do Douro, 5085 Pinhão
Concelho (council)	Carrazeda de Ansiães	Sabrosa
Freguesia (parish)	Vilarinho da Castanheira	Covas do Douro
Registered owner	Cockburn Smithes & Ca, Lda	Sr Alfredo Eugénio Cálem Holzer
Year acquired	c. 1890	1936
Total area (ha)	55	27
Altitude (m), min–max	105–250	80–260
Predominant aspect(s)	S	S, SE
Area of vines (ha)	25	19
Number of vines	80,000	76,761
Vine varieties	Touriga Nacional (predominant) (% *NIS*) Tinta Roriz Tinta Barroca Touriga Francesa Tinto Cão	Tinta Barroca (20.7%) Tinta Roriz (20.7%) Touriga Francesa (16.7%) Touriga Nacional (11.6%) Rufete (10%) Malvasia Preta (8.5%) Tinto Cão (5%) Other reds (6.8%)
Average age of vines	Old plantings (12%) – 30 years New plantings – 2 years	38 years
Cadastro grade(s)	A	A
PDRITM (ha)	14	4
Vineyard layout		
Walled terraces	12%	60%
Bulldozed terraces	80%	33%
Vertical planting	8%	7%
Continuous planting		
Average yield of port	144 pipes**	100 pipes
Red	100%	100%
White		
Winemaking facilities	None***	
Lagares		5
Pumpover tanks		
Autovinifiers		
Other		
Wine utilization	In premium quality ports	Part sold to Cálem, part aged at quinta
Single quinta port	None	Yes – 10 year old tawny
Recent vintages		
Visitors	Trade and wine writers by appointment only	By appointment only
Other information	*Data include *Quinta de Telhada* (50 ha) **Quinta de Telhada* plantings not yet in full production ***Wine, previously vinified at near-by Cadima *adega*, now made at *Quinta do Tua*	

Name of Quinta	**Quinta de Vale de Cavalos***	**Quinta do Vale do Meão**
Full postal address	Numão, 5150 Vila Nova de Foz Côa	5150 Pocinho
Concelho (council)	Vila Nova de Foz Côa	Vila Nova de Foz Côa
Freguesia (parish)	Numão	Vila Nova de Foz Côa
Registered owner	Sociedade Vinícola Terras de Valdigem, Lda	The Olazabal family
Year acquired	1988	1877
Total area (ha)	50	290
Altitude (m), min–max	450–510	105–200
Predominant aspect(s)	E, NE	E
Area of vines (ha)	31	50
Number of vines	134,806	185,000
Vine varieties	Tinta Barroca (35%)	Tinta Roriz (60%)
	Tinta Francisca (15%)	Touriga Francesa (20%)
	Tinta Roriz (15%)	Tinta Barroca (10%)
	Rufete (15%)	Touriga Nacional (5%)
	Other reds and whites (15%)	Tinta Amarela (5%)
Average age of vines	Old plantings – 20/25 years	30% – 40 years
	New plantings – 2/4 years	70% – 2/10 years
Cadastro grade(s)	B, C	B
PDRITM (ha)	No	7
Vineyard layout		
Walled terraces		
Bulldozed terraces	90%	14%
Vertical planting	10%	
Continuous planting		86%
Average yield of port	180 pipes	169 pipes*
Red		100%
White		
Winemaking facilities	None**	
Lagares		7 (last used 1980)
Pumpover tanks		8 (stainless steel)
Autovinifiers		
Other		
Wine utilization	Sold to shippers until 1989, later crops will be retained for blending	Port sold to Ferreira for their premium blends*
Single quinta port	None	None
Recent vintages		
Visitors	No	By appointment with Ferreira's public relations manager
Other information	*Includes *Quinta da Ribeira Teja* **Wine is vinified under contract by a private *adega* at São João da Pesqueira	*The grapes which are not made into port are blended with grapes produced at higher altitudes to make a red Douro table wine which is sold in best years as 'Barca Velha' or as 'Ferreirinha Reserva Especial'

Name of Quinta	**Quinta de Vargellas**	**Quinta do Vau**
Full postal address	Vale de Figueira,	Soutelo do Douro,
	5130 São João da Pesqueira	5130 São João da Pesqueira
Concelho (council)	São João da Pesqueira	São João da Pesqueira
Freguesia (parish)	Vale de Figueira	Soutelo de Douro
Registered owner	Taylor, Fladgate & Yeatman Vinhos, SA	Sandeman & Ca, SA
Year acquired	1893/94	1988
Total area (ha)	101	75
Altitude (m), min–max	110–400	120–225
Predominant aspect(s)	N	WSW, SW
Area of vines (ha)	44.3	56.7
Number of vines	167,205	214,000
Vine varieties	Touriga Francesa (26%)	Tinta Roriz (%NIS)
	Tinta Roriz (23%)	Touriga Francesa
	Touriga Nacional (18%)*	Touriga Nacional
	Tinta Amarela (7%)*	Tinta Barroca
	Tinta Barroca (5%)	Tinto Cão
	Tinto Cão (1%)	
	Other reds (20%)	
Average age of vines	Old plantings (60%) – 75 years	Old plantings (21%) – 30 years
	New plantings (40%) – 4 to 20 years	New plantings – 3 years
Cadastro grade(s)	A	A
PDRITM (ha)	No	No
Vineyard layout		
Walled terraces	51.4%	21%
Bulldozed terraces	44%	75%
Vertical planting	4.1%	4%
Continuous planting	0.5%	
Average yield of port	225 pipes	360 pipes by 1995
Red	100%	
White		
Winemaking facilities		*
Lagares	6 (in use)	
Pumpover tanks	6 (for external produce)	
Autovinifiers		3
Other	2 Vinimatics	
Wine utilization	Vintage, single quinta, LBV or aged tawnies	Vintage, single quinta, LBV and other premium wines
Single quinta port	Yes	Yes
Recent vintages	74, 76, 78, 81, 82, 84, 86, 87, 88	1988
Visitors	Only by letter of introduction	By appointment
Other information	*Future plantings of 32,000 vines will increase the proportions of these varieties	*The adega is being renovated. At present the wine is made in Sandeman's adega at Celeirós

Name of Quinta	**Quinta de Vesúvio**	**Quinta do Zimbro**
Full postal address	Numão,	Ribalonga,
	5155 Cedovim	5145 Foz Tua
Concelho (council)	Vila Nova de Foz Côa	Carrazeda de Ansiães
Freguesia (parish)	Numão	Ribalonga
Registered owner	Sociedade Agrícola da Quinta do	Sr Manuel Maria Menezes Vaz Sampaio
	Vesúvio	Sr Luís Paulo Menezes Melo de Vaz
		Sampaio
Year acquired	1989	1954
Total area (ha)	405	12
Altitude (m), min−max	105−485	110−190
Predominant aspect(s)	NW	S
Area of vines (ha)	85	10
Number of vines	218,360*	42,400
Vine varieties	Tinta Barroca (28%)	Touriga Francesa (50%)
	Touriga Francesa (27%)	Tinta Roriz
	Tinta Roriz (26%)	Periquita
	Tinta Amarela (4%)	Tinta Amarela)
	Touriga Nacional (1%)	Tinta Carvalha } (50%)
	Tinto Cão (1%)	Rufete
	Old mixed reds (13%)	Other reds
Average age of vines	Old plantings − 12/15 years	80% − 25< years
		20% −4/25 years
Cadastro grade(s)	A	A
PDRITM (ha)	10	No
Vineyard layout		
Walled terraces	2.5%	100%
Bulldozed terraces	95%	
Vertical planting		
Continuous planting	2.5%	
Average yield of port	140 pipes	30 pipes
Red	100%	100%
White		
Winemaking facilities		*
Lagares	8 (not in use)**	4 (last used in 1985)
Pumpover tanks		
Autovinifiers		
Other		
Wine utilization	For quinta wine, with balance sold to	Sold to Silva & Cosens for Dow's
	other companies owned by the	vintage, LBV and aged tawnies
	Symingtons	
Single quinta port	Not yet (but 1989 has been bottled	None
	and awaits release)	
Recent vintages		
Visitors	No	No
Other information	*A further 50,000 root stock will be	*Wine vinified at *Quinta do Bomfim*
	grafted in January, 1992	
	**4 combined pump-over and	
	autovinifier cylinders to be ready for	
	1992 vintage	

Notes

Preface

1 Pre-twentieth century names have been rendered, for the most part, in modern Portuguese orthography.

2 In order to sell their own port, producers have to be registered with the Instituto do Vinho do Porto either as *produtores-engarrafadores* (for the home market) or as *produtores-exportadores* (for the export market), and have to submit their port for quality testing by the Instituto to qualify it for the *selo de garantia* – the numbered strip of paper, issued by the Instituto, which goes over the top of all bottles of port authorized for public sale. Some producers sell at their cellar doors, which is illegal but often overlooked by the authorities; some producers, whilst registered, lack distributors at the moment and only sell privately through direct sales. Unfortunately, for reasons of space, it has not been possible to include such producers, or registered producers who do not sell their port under a single quinta label, in this book.

Introduction

1 Rose Macaulay, for example, refers to them as 'pleasant country houses . . . like seignorial manors'. Macaulay, p 248.

2 Statistics kindly supplied by the Casa do Douro.

3 Cordeiro (2). Quinta names proliferate; Cordeiro lists twenty Boa Vistas, fourteen Santo Antónios, etc. There is even a second Quinta do Noval. Quintas, therefore, normally require their location (*freguesia* and *concelho*) as well as their names for unambiguous identification.

4 See Azevedo (3), pp 38–40 and 43–6, and Lencastre, sections IX and XV.

5 *Frade* means 'monk'. This large quinta situated at Folgosa, on the left bank of the Douro, midway between Pinhão and Régua, was owned for over a century, after having been bought at auction in 1841, by the family of Ferreira, Condes da Folgosa. Its fine house, with two castellated towers, stands in an imposing position overlooking the river.

6 Monteiro, p 48.

7 *Ibid*, pp 85–92. This quinta, next to the Quinta das Carvalhas, became at this date the property of the Poço family of Lamego. A descendant of the family, António de Carvalho Rebelo Meneses Teixeira de Sousa e Cirne sold it to the Companhia Vitícola, Vinícola e Agrícola de Ventozelo, founded in 1905, who in 1958 sold, in turn, to the quinta's present owner, the Sociedade Agrícola Edmundo Alves Ferreira. See Azevedo (3), pp 157–8.

8 Monastic leases were occasionally in perpetuity for a peppercorn rent, but were more often designed to provide a limited security of tenure. These extended for a *prazo* (term) of three (sometimes four) lives in the following way: (1) that of the original lessee; (2) generally that of the lessee's surviving spouse or child; (3) with the second lessee (and likewise the third, if there was one) having the right to nominate his succeeding lessee, whose death would terminate the lease. The nomination of a daughter was a frequent way of bestowing a dowry. It was also quite usual for the last lessee to surrender his remaining part of the lease and to negotiate a new lease with his life starting a new cycle, thereby maintaining the tenancy within one family for several generations.

9 Quoted in Santos, pp 143–4, and in Vila Maior (3), pp 17–19.

10 Vila Maior (1), p 75 and p. 179 respectively.

11 Fonseca, I, p 34.

12 This is the Portuguese equivalent of the English word 'factory', used in this context not in the sense of a manufactory of articles, but to indicate an association of 'factors' – i.e. the agents of foreign firms engaged in the export of port (and other articles). Thus, the Factory House in Oporto, which celebrated its bicentenary in 1990, was originally the association of English export factors, and to this day remains the property of the British port shippers.

13 Unfortunately, the documentation giving details of the demarcation on the south bank east of the Cima Corgo has not survived.

14 A M da Fonseca *et al*, p 66.

15 See Fonseca for full details of the three Pombaline demarcations.

16 A M da Fonseca *et al*, p 66.

17 Vizetelly, pp 134–5.

18 Information kindly supplied by Christie's. See also p 111.

19 Ordish, p 170.

20 See p 79.

21 See p 76.

22 see p 107.

23 See pp 34.

24 This arrangement has survived into the present in some areas such as the Terra Quente, but very small producers now tend not to make their own wine at all, selling their grapes either to shippers or to regional co-operatives. The latter now account for 38 per cent of all production.

25 A very satisfactory account can be found in Robertson, Ch 5. See also Fletcher, pp 16 ff. For an account of the staffing of a quinta at the beginning of this century see Monteiro, pp 49 ff. See also pp 152–3.

26 Vizetelly, p 58–9.

27 Cobb, p 23.

28 From an interview with the author. Sadly, Colin Graham died while this book was in preparation.

29 An eccentric figure, he memorably describes his arrival in the Douro: 'I am wearing London clothes with a black coat and striped trousers, and I have a bag and an overcoat, and I carry an umbrella in one hand and a portable type-writer in the other. I have not brought these clothes to be consciously comic . . . but, as I climb down from the high continental-type train I am certainly aware of being a trifle out of the picture. Given my waistcoat, I should probably fit into, say, Cannon Street Station, but here on the Alto Douro I am not so sure . . .' (Gibbons, pp 15–16.) Perhaps he need not have worried. Charles Sellers had pointed out, 40 years previously, that 'in matters sartorial, we English, when travelling abroad have always been peculiar . . . This idea is carried to such an extent – this fancy for extraordinary dress – that once, in Oporto, I recollect seeing a French Zouave officer in uniform who was put down immediately by the populace as an Englishman on a pleasure trip'. (Sellers, pp 15–16.)

30 Gibbons, p 203.

31 *Ibid*, pp 113–14.

32 Amyas Symington, in an interview with the author.

33 Quoted in Cobb, p 16.

34 See Quinta do Bomfim, note 3.

35 Vizetelly provides us with the following account of a lunch at the Quinta do Caedo, which has recently been purchased by Ferreira. '. . . If ever a table really groaned, as tables are often said to do, the one we sat down to might fairly have done so, under the weight of fatted turkeys, ducks, fowls, red-legged partridges, sucking-pigs, and juicy hams, together with cheeses made from sheep's milk, sponge-cakes of incredible dimensions, quince, peach, and pumpkin preserves, olives, apples and huge bunches of luscious purple grapes. At a feast like this, in a remote corner of the Upper Douro, Port wine, as may be supposed, was your only liquor – the traditional cup of cold water was not to be had even if you prayed for it – but it was Port of the grand vintages of 1834 and 1858. Altogether it was hospitality in riot, and prayers and remonstrances at the profuse way in which your plate was constantly being piled up were alike unavailable. Before you had swallowed a few mouthfuls of turkey, or had touched the ribs of sucking-pig with which you had simultaneously been helped, you found a plump partridge in the middle of your plate, and if you only turned your head aside for a moment a slice of ham as thick as an average beefsteak would be placed on the top of it. Fortunately there were a couple of hungry lurchers in the room, and unperceived we shared with them the superfluities which fell to our lot at this over-bounteous banquet.'

36 Cobb, p 24.

37 *Ibid*, p 26.

38 Vila Maior (1), pp 83–4. See also Vila Maior (3), pp 61–2.

39 Many *rogas* consist of teenagers of both sexes, and seeing them dancing together in the *lagares* may suggest several things, but not hard work.

40 Vila Maior (1), p 93.

41 *Gallegos* were itinerant Spanish workers who worked seasonally in the vineyards, and who generally did the heaviest and roughest work, such as levelling terraces and building walls.

42 *Ibid*, pp 92–3.

43 Miguel Torga is the pen name of a solicitor with a practice in Coimbra. This novel is set in an imaginary quinta called Cavadinha which shares only its geographical location with the real Quinta da Cavadinha.

44 As from 4 June, 1989, the minimum wage for whole-time workers (40 hours) was £112.02 per week. Lodging was rated at £7 a week, and food at £5 a day.

45 This does not include travelling time. At the time of my visit to the Quinta do Vau, 15 workers were coming from Mesão Frio six days a week, leaving at 2.30 a.m., starting work at 4.00 a.m. and working without a break until 2.00 p.m., then returning home again. However, as against the figures given here, it was announced as this book was going to press that the wages of quinta workers were due to be increased by some 30 per cent in 1991 – with considerable implications for the economics of port production.

46 *Caldo*, or more usually *caldo verde*, is a hearty soup made from finely chopped cabbage leaves; *sardinha* are sardines; *arroz* is rice; and *bacalhau* is dried salt cod, still the most common of all Portuguese dishes.

47 It is ironic that this is parallel to the situation at the end of last century: 'the cost of hard manual labour has risen considerably of late, owing to the great demand for it on public works, notably the railway to the Spanish frontier in course of construction along the right bank of the Douro' (Vizetelly, p 89.).

48 Further details can be found in Andrew Jefford's 'Trouble on the Terraces' in *Decanter*, Nov 1989.

49 See, for example, p 92.

50 This quinta should not be confused with the quinta of the same name belonging to Poças. See p 42.

51 The Cadastro is a register of vineyards compiled by the Casa do Douro, in which points are allotted for variables which affect the quality of wine made, such as altitude, type of soil, exposure to sun, inclination of land, grape varieties, age of vines, methods of vine cultivation, etc. Vineyards, or more specifically parts of vineyards, are then graded from A to H according to the total points scored. This provides the basis for the *beneficio* – the total amount of wine which may be turned into port by fortifying it – which is allocated to each grower every year. The *beneficio* is a variable number which is determined jointly by the Casa do Douro, the Instituto do Vinho do Porto and the Association of Port Wine Shippers in relation to the current needs of the trade and the state of its markets. In practice all vineyards with an A or B grading are permitted to make their entire authorized production into port. The details of the system are explained in books about the production of port: see, e.g. Fonseca, A M da, *et al*, pp 69–89, and Fletcher, pp 107–14.

52 Where the registration of a quinta name is concerned it is first come, first served. It is not permitted to register the same name twice, even when the quintas are in different *freguesias*. This is forcing some producers to sell single quinta ports either under artificial names – e.g. Quinta da Ervamoira – or brand names – e.g. 'Valriz' (Quinta da Costa) and 'Lamelas' (Quinta das Laranjeiras).

53 Croft, exceptionally, produced a 1970 Quinta da Roêda *as well as* a vintage declaration, and Fonseca, in the same way, a 1977 Quinta do Panascal.

54 Some Portuguese shippers also began to produce single quinta ports about the same time – e.g. Kopke (Barros) with a 1970 Quinta de São Luiz and Messias with a 1976 Quinta do Cachão – but they have not observed the 'vintage' versus 'off-vintage' distinction with the same rigour.

55 Kopke and Feist (both Barros) and Messias, for example, made eight declarations between 1975 – 85.

56 Joanna Simon, 'In and Outs for the Modish Imbiber', in *The Sunday Times*, 30 December 1990.

The Baixo Corgo

1 They are officially defined in terms of the *freguesias*, or parishes, which they contain. For a complete list see Fonseca, A M de *et al*, pp 68–9, or Azevedo (3), pp 62–4.

2 One is Sr Dr Manuel Pedro Martha, whose remarkable Fontão vineyard at Lobrigos has vines reputed to be 120 years old. Dr Martha is hoping to attempt a vintage wine when all the factors next turn out to be propitious. The second is Dr José António da Fonseca Augusto Guedes, owner of the Quinta das Laranjeiras (not to be confused with the property of the same name belonging to Sandeman & Ca, SA) at Rio Bom, Portelo de Cambres, who has made a 1985 vintage port (which I have not tasted). The other two, Sr Miguel Champalimaud and the firm of C da Silva, are considered below.

3 Speaking of the Távora Valley, Rebello da Fonseca, writing at the end of the eighteenth century, says: 'In the whole of the [Douro] region there are no wines more agreeable and delicious for the table; however they lack the body and strength necessary to stand up to being exported without being spoilt'. Quoted in Azevedo (3), p 230.

Quinta de Santa Bárbara

1 This quinta should not be confused with the one of the same name at the mouth of the Rio Torto, which is used as an experimental station by the Centro de Estudos Vitivinícolas do Douro.

Quinta do Monsul

1 A noted civil engineer, viticulturalist and owner of the Quinta do Cachão.
2 The Quinta of the Palace and Tower of Monsul. In the oldest documents Monsul is called *Moçulo*.
3 One of the Coutinho family who held the lease of Monsul was the Grão Magriço, one of the *Doze d'Inglaterra* in *The Luciads* by Camoës.
4 He sold to Dona Elvira Mendes Corea de Magalhães, from whom it passed to Artur Mendes de Magalhães Romalho, a Lamego lawyer.
5 The *paço* (palace) is first mentioned in a lease of 1481, and the *torre* in 1578, which is also the date of the first mention of a *casa dos lagares*.
6 Purchased in 1744, and sometimes known as the Quinta de Salgueiral, this is the oldest continuously owned British property in the Douro. Lacking a vineyard, it is solely a vinification centre. See also p 107.

Quinta de Santa Maria

1 Azevedo (2), p 176.

Quinta de Santa Júlia de Loureiro

1 Not to be confused with the present-day Quinta de Loureiro immediately to the south of the Quinta de Santa Júlia.
2 Paternal grandfather of the present owner of the Quinta da Pacheca.
3 There is a stone marker in the wall of the Pinheiro vineyard, added to the property in 1889, and the area was bounded by the road at Romesal – see Fonseca, III, pp 192–95.
4 A vineyard now incorporated in the quinta. The original house at Romesal has now disappeared.
5 Information communicated by Sr Eduardo da Costa Seixas.

Quinta de Avidagos

1 Cordeiro (1), pp 64–5.

Quinta do Côtto

1 See Azevedo (2), pp 147–9, and (3), pp 324–6, for further details.
2 See p 35.

The Cima Corgo

1 Climate is a major factor in wine production. As one moves eastwards from Oporto conditions become hotter and drier, and by common consent the Cima Corgo, midway between extremes, provides optimum conditions.

	Average annual rainfall		Average annual temperature	
Oporto	1.200 mm	47.5 in	14°C	57°F
Régua	900 mm	39.5 in	14°C	57°F
Pinhão	700 mm	27.5 in	15°C	59°F
Barca d'Alva	400 mm	15.8 in	16.5°C	61°F

Thus, Oporto enjoys an Atlantic climate but that of Barca d'Alva is Mediterranean.

Quinta de Nápoles

1 Leal, XI, pp 1064–5.
2 Fonseca, III, p 56.
3 *Ibid*, p 325.
4 Leal, *op.cit.*, p 1065.
5 From, I believe, the daughter of Ovídio Alpoim, the last member of the Nápoles family to own the quinta.
6 Cordeiro (1), p 64.
7 Information communicated by Jeremy Bull.

Quinta de São Luiz

1 Vila Maior (3), p 133.
2 Fonseca, III, pp 58–9.
3 *Ibid*, p 326.
4 *Ibid*, pp 220–4.
5 Correia (2), p 158.

Quinta do Panascal

1 Vila Maior (3), p 133. Quotation from Rebello da Fonseca.
2 Vila Maior (1), p 241.
3 Taylor and Fonseca are, for practical purposes, one firm.

Quinta do Convento de São Pedro das Águias

1 Leal, IX, p 516.
2 Fonseca, II, pp 154 and 245.
3 Guimarães, p 175.
4 Monteiro, p 60.

Quinta do Seixo

1 Vila Maior (3), p 130.
2 Fonseca, II, p 154.
3 Dionísio, p 192.
4 This firm was established in 1851. According to the commemorative album of the Grémio dos Exportadores de Vinho do Porto, p 164: 'Owing to the liquidation of Baron of Seixo's goods, his chief creditor, Constantino do Vale Cabral, became burdened with a large and famous stock of port wine. Recognizing the unusual qualities of his nephew, Miguel, he sought his help, and so laid the foundation of the house of Miguel de Sousa Guedes, which had its origin in 1851. Little by little, the business increased and the Firm acquired properties in the Upper Douro, amongst which the Quinta das Carvalhas . . .' This appears to imply that the quinta was not sequestrated with the Barão de Seixo's other property but was acquired later. All the same, it is odd that, given that such was the origin of the firm, it had later dealings with the Barão de Seixo. See also next note.
5 Visconde Vilarinho de São Romão, p 536. São Romão's account, which presents Sousa Guedes as yet another shipper who shrewdly took advantage of cheap, *phyllox-era*-ruined quintas, appears to suggest that he acquired the Quinta do Seixo shortly after Carvalhas: 'Sr Miguel de Sousa Guedes, struck by the ruin into which some of the most renowned quintas in our region had fallen . . . decided to become a farmer in the region, to which end he acquired the famous Quinta da Pedra Caldeira. Recognizing . . . the profits which he would be able to reap, he decided greatly to increase his vineyards, and thus acquired, in a few years, the quintas of Carvalhas, Aguillar, Seixo, etc.'
6 Vizetelly, p 49.
7 Monteiro, p 97.

Quinta das Carvalhas

1 Its only competitor for size is the neighbouring Quinta do Ventozelo, founded in 1569, also said to cover 600 ha.

2 Fonseca, III, p 62.
3 Vila Maior (1), p 241.
4 Vila Maior (3), p 123.
5 Vizetelly, p 78.
6 Monteiro, p 96.
7 See Quinta do Seixo, note no 4.
8 A fascinating table of vintage production since 1880 to the present day is painted just inside the *armazém*.
9 Monteiro, pp 96–7.

Quinta Dona Matilde

1 This is not the only quinta to have been renamed in honour of a lady. See also the Quinta de Santa Júlia de Loureiro.
2 See Fonseca, II, pp 60-1. A second, neighbouring quinta with the same name was not included in the *feitoria* until 1761: see Fonseca, III, pp 165 and 305.
3 The mountain behind the quinta.
4 Leal, VII, p 122.

Quinta dos Murças

1 This quinta, at the eastern extreme of the Baixo Corgo on the left bank of the Douro, has belonged to the Delaforce family since 1931. Marked on Forrester's map as the Quinta da Foz Mil Lobos, the house is of much earlier construction and a stone dated 1753 is to be found in the *adega*. See Azevedo (3), pp 299–300 for details of previous ownership.
2 See Fonseca, III, p 178.
3 Vila Maior (3), p 135. See also Sellers, p 103.
4 See, however, p 151.

Quinta da Costa

1 'In the Douro, as I have already said at times, the almost complete lack of good public roads . . . is general, though not, because of that, excusable. Given these steep slopes, covered in all parts by rich vineyards and without a single means of earthly communication, such as civilized men must have, it appears that the proprietors and workers in this region must have wings like birds to take them from one place to another . . . In view of what still goes on today, at a period in which we all lack roads and yet, it seems, understand the advantages of convenient and regular road systems, one cannot admire the indifference and lack of supervision of the municipal administration in allowing the growth of important estates in the Douro without earmarking the least space between them to construct roads which could give quick and easy communication between villages, between properties, and between them and the river.' Thus wrote Vila Maior in 1868. Vila Maior (1), p 227.
2 See Fonseca, II, pp 96–7, and III, p 176.
3 'Valriz' has been chosen as the name under which the wines of the Quinta da Costa *prédio* are sold only because the name Quinta da Costa has already been registered as an approved *marque* by another quinta owner.

Quinta da Costa de Baixo

1 Fonseca, II, p 97. Another marker, this time of the 1761 demarcation, which is not recorded in Fonseca's book, has been used as part of the lintel of a small derelict house just above the railway line.
2 See Fonseca, III, p 178.

Quinta do Crasto

1 Fonseca, II, p 98.
2 His plan had been to re-erect on the quinta a beautiful seventeenth century house, complete with chapel, which he had purchased in Beira, but the village where the house stood rebelled against the idea, and in the end only the chapel was moved – not to Crasto, but to another property which the family owns in the Minho.
3 *Pasteleira* means 'pastry cook'. *Sobreira* means 'cork tree' (several of which, of course, grow there).
4 See Fonseca, III, p 35; also p 311. The quinta has had a sex-change: in the eighteenth century it was *o pasteleiro*!

Quinta da Água Alta

1 Fonseca, I, pp 167-8; II, pp 98-9 and 176; III, pp 34, 229, 311–12.
2 See photograph in Fonseca, A M *et al*, p 40.
3 On 7 September 1987.
4 Other properties include the Quintas da Manuela and do Fojo.

Quinta Nova

1 Fonseca, II, pp 99-100. There is a puzzle about the quinta in the 1757 demarcation, where it is apparently mentioned twice: once as belonging to João Lopes de Carvalho 'of the city of Oporto', and once as belonging to the successors of João Francisco Teixeira. See Fonseca, II, p 167 (especially footnote 8) and p 169. Possibly this is a mistake or there were two adjacent Quintas Novas.

Quinta do Infantado

1 See p 35.

Quinta da Boa Vista

1 Fonseca, I, pp 183–4; III, p 36.
2 Sellers, p 143.
3 Information communicated by Sr José Bras, who had worked for the firm for more than fifty years when he retired in 1975. There is also a tradition that Boa Vista was actually planted by Joseph Forrester – according to André Simon, quoted by Bradford, p 91. – though I have completely failed to unearth any proof of this contention.
4 Vizetelly, p 38.
5 Sellers, p 103.
6 *Ibid*, p 145.
7 Cordeiro (2), p 202.
8 Sandeman and Martini Rossi each had a 50 per cent share. When Sandeman was itself acquired by Seagram, its share in Offley-Forrester was sold to Martini Rossi.
9 I am indebted to Sr Bras for the information contained in the previous two paragraphs.
10 Ujo produced no wine at all in 1878 and 1879. See Cockburn (1), p 24.
11 15 September 1988 – compare Howkins, p. 42. The local normal average date is five days later.

Quinta do Porto

1 This episode is told in somewhat greater detail in Paiva, pp 25–32.
2 Data from the Ferreira *Arquivo Histórico*.

Quinta de Val da Figueira

1 Fonseca, III, p 36. It is also curious insofar as the petition claims that the quinta was included for white wine in the 1758 *feitoria* demarcation, when the demarcation boundary, the Ribeiro do Sagrado, clearly excluded the bank on which Val da Figueira stands.
2 See also Soavedra, pp 198–9.

Quinta de la Rosa

1 Gaudy Old Style.

2 One of two: the other is on the opposite bank of the Douro. Bateiras was a rapid at the mouth of the Rio Torto.
3 Feuerheerd Brothers had been founded in 1805 by his great-grandfather.
4 This quinta, not to be confused with the now-demolished Quinta Amarela in Pinhão, belonged for many generations to the Cunha family, who had the ferry concession for the Bateiras rapids. It was purchased in 1916.
5 The original table and wine-cooler, which had been purchased by the Feuerheerds, were returned to the ship when it became a national monument.
6 Cobb, p 25.
7 *Ibid*, p 26.
8 See page 92.
9 Cobb, p 26.

Quinta da Foz

1 Fonseca, II, p 102.
2 Fonseca, III, pp 275–8.
3 See p 137.
4 The Quintas da Carvalheira, dos Hortos and do Monte Bravo.

Quinta da Eira Velha

1 See Introduction note 8.
2 51 x 119 m.
3 21 *almudes* = 1 pipe.
4 Fonseca, III p 39.
5 Croft-Cooke, p 133.
6 See Anon (1).
7 See Santos, pp 93 and 110.
8 See p 149.

Quinta da Casa Nova

1 These are the Quinta do Junco and the Quinta da Soalheira.
2 Fonseca, II, p 103. The mistake of thinking the marker indicated inclusion within the *feitoria*, made by Monteiro, p 192, is repeated in Sousa, p 213.
3 Fonseca, III, pp 38 and 230. Oddly enough, the quinta's being 'difficult to cultivate and with few profits' is given as a reason for inclusion.
4 Monteiro, p 192.

Quinta do Junco

1 Monteiro, p 47.
2 See also p 89.

Quinta da Cavadinha

1 Azevedo (3), p 240.
2 See Fonseca, II, p 109: III, p 181; also p 39.
3 See p 89.
4 See p 139.
5 A similar question arises over the Graham's vintage, for which the new production from the Quinta dos Malvedos will be increasingly used. See p 117.

Quinta da Terra Feita

1 Fonseca, II, pp 159 and 177; III p 181.

Quinta Casal de Celeirós

1 Vizetelly, p 67: Visconde Vilarinho de São Romão, p 431.
2 Visconde Vilarinho de São Romão, p 432.
3 Vizetelly, p 67.
4 Ibid.
5 Visconde Vilarinho de São Romão, p 434.
6 See p 64.

7 Vizetelly, p. 70.
8 Vizetelly, p 66.
9 Sellers, p 102.
10 See Azevedo (2), p. 234.
11 Azevedo (3), p 242.

Quinta do Estanho

1 Fonseca, III, p 316.

Quinta de Santo António

1 See Fonseca, II, especially p 117, footnote 5, where the quinta is referred to as 'de Santo António or da Patuleia'.
2 This little quinta, with just under 3 ha of broad and narrow terraces, which has belonged to the Pinto Gouveia family for three generations, has been rented by Sandeman since 1980. Its production goes towards Sandeman's declared vintages, or to LBV and other premium ports.

Quinta do Noval

1 Vila Maior (1), p 215: Monteiro, p 103, says 'a widow of S Christovão do Douro', and other authors follow him, but I do not know on what authority.
2 Vila Maior (1), p 219. Only 11 times in 50 years did it exceed 100 pipes, and only once after 1825. Its lowest was 44 pipes in 1830, though after 1825 it was 8 times less than 60 pipes. See Vila Maior (1), p 237.
3 Vila Maior (1), p 216.
4 *Ibid*, p 227.
5 At this time the only public road from Pinhão to Alijó led via Casal de Loivos, Vilarinho de Cotas and across the sierra to Faváios. See Fonseca, II, p 223, note 2. Rebello Valente was apparently deterred from installing roads within the quinta itself because the planned new public road (the one which presently exists) would bisect the quinta, and he wished its position to be settled prior to putting in his own roads. Vila Maior (1), p 229.
6 Vila Maior (1), p 219. He still held this view 7 years later – see Vila Maior (3), p 128.
7 The date is uncertain, the quinta archives having perished in a fire on 20 October 1981.
8 Monteiro, p 105.
9 *Ibid*, p 106.
10 *Ibid*.
11 Robertson, p 79.

Quinta do Bomfim

1 Vila Maior (1), p 204.
2 Many quintas adjacent to the developing railway took advantage of this to acquire a loading facility or even a special siding.
3 The Zimbro (latterly Bomfim) visitors' book covers the period from 1889 until after the Second World War in a single volume. The subsequent 45 years has required 6 further volumes.

Quinta da Roêda

1 In the eighteenth century, however, another Quinta da Roêda existed on the opposite bank of the Douro. See Fonseca, II, p 155.
2 Vizetelly, p 77.
3 Vila Maior (1), p 210.
4 Fladgate was created Barão da Roêda for his unrelenting efforts to combat *oïdium* and *phylloxera*, and is one of only three British men in the port trade to have been honoured with such a title. The others were William Glas-Sandeman, created Barão de Sandeman in 1883, and, of course, Joseph Forrester, the Barão de Forrester. On the latter, see p 76.

5 Vizetelly, p 77.
6 Vila Maior (3), p 121.
7 Sellers, p 133.
8 Vila Maior (1), p 206-7.
9 Vila Maior gives a very full description of the quinta buildings as they were in the middle of last century, remarking that the grouping of the buildings according to their function was 'certainly a novelty in the Douro'. See Vila Maior (1), pp 208–10.
10 Croft have a bottle of 1891 Quinta da Roêda in their wine museum. Robertson, p 140, therefore appears to be wrong in implying that Croft did not ship a single Quinta da Roêda until the 1967 vintage.

Quinta do Síbio

1 Vila Maior, (1), p 201. The Quinta de Dona Rosa, which is next door to Síbio, is now called the Quinta de Roncão de Magalhães and belongs to the heirs of Francisco de Sousa Magalhães, who was Dona Rosa's great-grandson and died in 1971. See also Azevedo (3), p 200. Azevedo confuses the Quinta de Dona Rosa (Roncão de Magalhães) with yet another Quinta de Roncão which is further down-stream, on the right bank of the Ribeira de Póvoa, adjoining the Quinta da Roêda. This quinta belonged to Robertson Brothers & Co, Ltd, (now part of Sandeman) from 1893 until 1952, when it was purchased by Sr Edmundo Alves Ferreira, the owner of the Quinta do Ventozelo. It is now known as the Quinta de Roncão da Cima. Another Quinta de Roncão also exists, further upstream, on the right bank of the Ribeira de Póvoa, known locally as 'Roncãe': a Portuguese pun – 'Ron-bitch' to distinguish it from 'Ron-dog'! To compound this potential for confusion, Vizetelly visited a Quinta de Roncão in 1877 'belonging to Senhor Souza, our host at Celleirós, with its long adega, flanked on one side by a cyprus tree, and on the other by a lofty cedar'. This appears not to be any of the quintas de Roncão so far mentioned, and I have to confess that, despite considerable effort, I have been unable to identify it.
2 Very confusingly. Just as there are now several quintas de Roncão (such as the Quinta de Roncão de Serôdio, situated between Síbio (Jordão) and Roncão de Magalhães, which was formerly called Síbio – see Correia (1), p 98 – but which appears in Forrester's map as the Quinta do Serôdio), so there are also some other Síbios in the area, including a Síbio do Roncão! – see Correia (2), p 164.
3 See also p 114.
4 Vila Maior (1), p 199. She evidently married a Ferreira da Silva – see Vila Maior (3), p 119. However, in both editions of Cordeiro it is said that Síbio belonged in 1865 to Sr João António Mariz da Veiga e Castro. This must, I think, be a mistake.
5 Ibid.

Quinta da Romaneira

1 Vila Maior (3), p 119.
2 Information supplied by Christie's.
3 Vizetelly, p 74.
4 Vila Maior (1), p 198.
5 According to Fonseca, II, p 241, footnote 2, around about 1920, when the quinta belonged to Albino de Sousa Rebelo, its armazéms were attacked and destroyed by people from Ervedosa, Casais and Pinhão.
6 Monteiro, p 43.
7 See p 17.
8 The port of the Quinta da Roêda, immediately adjacent to the Costa de Roncão, is also said to have a smell of esteva – most evident, apparently, in port just over a year old.

Quinta Casal de Granja

1 Monteiro, p 46. According to a topographical survey made in 1943, it comprised 41 different sizable properties and 11 small vineyards.

Quinta dos Malvedos

1 Fonseca, III, p 231: see also p 89 and p 318.
2 Vila Maior (1), p 192.
3 Ibid.
4 It still contributes to the vintage blend.
5 According to Cordeiro, at this time it must have been 'the major producer of grapefruit in the north of the country, with an average annual production of 8,000 fruit. It [had] an appreciable production of the extremely celebrated oranges of S Mamede de Tua, as well as of lemons . . . becoming, through this, one of the most famous quintas in this field in the Douro'. – Cordeiro (2), p 100.
6 See page 92.
7 Fletcher, p 75.

Quinta do Tua

1 Fonseca, II, p 202.
2 Information from Ferreira's Arquivo Histórico.
3 According to Monteiro, p 29, it was the Viscondessa de São Jorge to whom the quinta originally belonged.
4 Vila Maior (3), p 109.
5 Monteiro, p 30.
6 For the information in the two previous paragraphs I am indebted to Sr Malheiro, who started to work at Tua when he was 8, and who has been there for more than 50 years.
7 Fletcher, p 12.
8 Bradford, p 143.

Quinta do Zimbro

1 Sellers, p 176.
2 See p 105.

Quinta do Sidrô

1 Vizetelly, p 82.
2 Azevedo (2), p 319.
3 Vizetelly, p 83.
4 Cabral, p 148.
5 In 1988 the Real Companhia Velha purchased the Quinta da Ferradoza, on the north bank of the Douro immediately east of the Cachão de Valeira. It had previously belonged to the Banco Borges & Irmão (see Sousa. pp 211–2), but lost most of its vineyards with the damming of the river, and now has only 3 ha of vines. Sr da Silva Reis has it in mind, however, to develop its potential for leisure activities, particularly by making a private marina, as a complement to Sidrô.
6 Vila Maior says of Sidrô that, although 'worthy of consideration, it is situated outside the port region of the Douro through its high situation close to São João da Pesqueira'. (1), p 155.

Quinta dos Aciprestes

1 Dionisio, p 195.
2 Not to be confused with the quinta of the same name which belonged to Barão de Forrester, as does Azevedo – see (3), p 150.
3 A vineyard with the same name had already been purchased in the 1860s. Two other independently owned quintas of the same name still exist in the region.
4 Fonseca, II, pp 241–2.
5 Vila Maior (1), pp 163-73. Other information has been obtained from the Ferreira Arquivo Histórico.
6 Cordeiro (2), p 34.

Quinta do Vau

1 See Fonseca, Vol II, p 241.

Quinta do Roriz

1 Vila Maior (3), p 114.
2 Dr Pedro van Zeller has a photograph of the shooting-box.
3 Fonseca, I, pp 75–7.
4 *Ibid*, p 62.
5 Fonseca, II, p 165 and p 244.
6 Fonseca, III, pp 64–5, p 93, and pp 327–8.
7 *Ibid*, p 232.
8 *Ibid*, pp 249–52.
9 *Ibid*, p 65, note (1) and p 93, note (7).
10 Vila Maior (3), p 179.
11 Bradford, p 39.
12 Vila Maior (3), p 179.
13 Fletcher, p 76.
14 See p 19.
15 Vila Maior gives the date as 1768 – (1), p 184 – but 1764 is the date painted over the *adega* door, and one presumes that it has been faithfully copied from one repainting to the next.
16 Vila Maior (1), p 179. See also p 17.
17 *Ibid*, p 178.
18 *Ibid*, p 180.
19 *Ibid*, p 176.
20 Information communicated by Dr Pedro van Zeller. 21 *almudes* = 1 pipe.
21 Sellers, p 100.
22 The house shown in the lithograph illustrating Vila Maior (3), facing p 60, according to Dr Pedro van Zeller, never existed, and the building shown to the left is part of other *armazéms* which have disappeared with new planting.
23 Claire Bergqvist, quoted in Cobb, p 16.
24 Information supplied by Christie's Wine Department. Three of these bottles have subsequently been sold by International Wine Auctions (London) between 1987 and 1990.
25 This was just over a month after the first recorded sale of a single quinta port on 25 and 26 June. Other sales followed. 2 April 1875: 11 dozen and six bottles of 'Kopke Roriz Port 1854', bottled by Cathcart & Co, Leith, at from 63 to 64 shillings (£3.15 to £3.20) a dozen. 4 May 1889: 29 dozen and two bottles of 'Kopke & Co. Roriz Port 1863, bottled 1865 by Parker of Hull', at 86 shillings (£4.30). 30 April 1897: 11 dozen and 5 bottles of 'Kopke Roriz 1873, bottled 1876', at 86 to 90 shillings (£4.30 to £4.50). 8 December 1899: 9 dozen and 5 bottles of 'Kopke Roriz 1847, bottled Butchinson & Greenwell, Durham, in April 1856'. Bought in at 165 to 175 shillings (£8.25 to £8.75), the reserve having been 180 shillings (£9.00). Information kindly supplied by Christie's Wine Department.
26 Fletcher, p 74.

The Rio Torto Valley

1 The Quinta de Alempassa, situated on the north bank some way up the river, belongs to Dr António Figureido and produces on average more than 100 pipes a year. Frequently purchased by Graham, it is also shipped to England as a late bottled single quinta port by Eldridge Pope & Co., and sold as The Chairman's Late Bottled Port.

Quinta da Soalheira

1 See p 128.
2 Vizetelly, pp 80–1.

3 Sousa, p 65. See also p 89.
4 Vizetelly, p 81.

Quinta das Lages

1 A photograph of the petition is kept at the quinta.
2 Vila Maior, (1), p 241.
3 Information communicated by Sr Paulo Fernando Duarte, the quinta manager.

Quinta do Retiro Nova

1 Sarzedinho, the neighbouring village, now has electricity but (1989) has yet to get water and drainage.

Quinta do Bom Retiro

1 See França.
2 As early as 1887 a *rapido* service from Paris to Lisbon had been instituted – see Cockburn (1), pp 36–7 – and the completion of the line from Oporto to Barca d'Alva in December of the same year connected Oporto with the intercontinental network.
3 In 1925, closely followed by the Quinta de la Rosa. For some reason swimming pools in quintas were considered to be improperly sybaritic, to be cunningly disguised or discreetly hidden in improbable corners, and they are still strongly disapproved of by one senior member of the trade.
4 Azevedo (3), p 254. See also Fonseca *et al*, p 59.
5 Monteiro, p 53.
6 But see p 68. See, also, the Quinta da Ervamoira, which is the first quinta to be totally planted vertically.
7 Touriga Nacional, Touriga Francesa, Tinta Barroca, Tinta Roriz and Tinto Cão.
8 Azevedo (3), p 222.
9 Information supplied by Christie's, London.

Douro Superior

1 The Quinta do Silho, which until 1990 belonged to the Banco Borges & Irmão, is situated at Barca d'Alva. Founded in 1820 by Miguel António Ferreira, it was producing around 100 pipes by the middle of the century and became the most easterly quinta of any repute. Nowadays it specializes in producing high quality olives and its wine production is only around 18 pipes a year.
2 Vila Maior (1), p 102.

Quinta do Cachão

1 Vila Maior (1), p 96.
2 *Ibid* (1), p 96; (3), p 101.
3 Cordeiro (1), p 18.
4 See p 45.
5 Visconde Vilarinho de São Romão, pp 540–1. São Romão also gives a plan of the quinta at this time.
6 The Quinta do Cachão is now sometimes known as the Quinta Velha de Cachão, but last century it was, for obvious reasons, known as the Quinta Nova. When acquired from Gonzalez Byass, the Quinta do Rei was called the Quinta Nova. The quinta also incorporates the Quinta do Vale de Agodinho.

Quinta de Vargellas

1 See Introduction, note 1.
2 In Ferreira's *Arquivo Histórico*, from which all the information concerning the Ferreiras' involvement in the Vargelas quintas has been taken.
3 Vila Maior (3), p 101.
4 Vila Maior (1), p. 96.
5 Vila Maior (3), p 101.

6 The production figures are:

1838	103 pipes	1867	34 pipes
1839	81 pipes	1868	24 pipes
1840	85 pipes	1869	43 pipes
1841	126 pipes	1870	unrecorded
1842	91 pipes	1871	unrecorded
1843	102½ pipes	1872	36 pipes
1844	[a]83 pipes	1873	53 pipes
1845	[b]82 pipes	1874	36 pipes
1846	85 pipes	1875	21 pipes
1847	[c]97½ pipes	1876	38 pipes
1848	[d]124 pipes	1877	41 pipes
1849	97 pipes	1878	[f]24 pipes
1850	82 pipes	1879	41 pipes
1851	72 pipes	1880	45 pipes
1852	90 pipes	1881	25 pipes
1853	76 pipes	1882	unrecorded
1854	69 pipes	1883	unrecorded
1855	[e]35 pipes	1884	unrecorded
1856	13 pipes	1885	unrecorded
1857	unrecorded	1886	3 pipes
1858	unrecorded	1887	2 pipes
1859	unrecorded	1888	3 pipes
1860	unrecorded	1889	5 pipes
1861	60 pipes	1890	unrecorded
1862	unrecorded	1891	1 pipe
1863	unrecorded	1892	2 pipes
1864	unrecorded	1893	zero
1865	unrecorded	1894	[g]16 almudes
1866	63 pipes	1895	16 almudes

[a]69 red, 14 white
[b]60 red, 22 white and ordinary
[c]plus 8 of spirit
[d]plus 11 of spirit
[e]including spirit
[f]start of phylloxera
[g]21 almudes = 1 pipe

7 Azevedo (3), p 222.
8 The information concerning this quinta is derived from a short typescript history in the possession of Taylor. It should be noted that the details do not at all times correspond with the data derived from the Ferreira archive.
9 A distinguished Portuguese family: see also Quinta do Vesúvio.
10 Ignácio van Zeller, one of the three partners in the firm - with João Pereira Viana de Lima and António Bernardo Brito e Cunha – is an ancestor of the present owners of Quinta do Noval and the Quinta do Roriz.
11 See p 19.
12 Sellers, p 133, my italics.
13 See p 64 for the story about Skeffington and Sousa Guedes.
14 Azevedo (3), pp. 138–9
15 Monteiro, p 15.
16 A 1947 Quinta de Vargellas was, however, shipped to the USA. See Fletcher, p 49.

Quinta do Vesúvio

1 Sellers, p 96.
2 Vila Maior (3), p 92.
3 The name was changed to Vesúvio on 23 November 1830.
4 For further details of the quinta's early history see Monteiro, pp 69–70.
5 Vila Maior wrongly gives the date as 1820.
6 Azevedo (3), p 118.
7 Vila Maior (3), p 95.
8 Ibid, p 96.

9 The production of Vesúvio, as recorded in the Ferreira Arquivo Histórico, is as follows:

1838	561 pipes	1868	unrecorded
1839	512 pipes	1869	254 pipes
1840	444 pipes	1870	181 pipes
1841	451 pipes	1871	233 pipes
1842	553 pipes	1872	167 pipes
1843	530 pipes	1873	295 pipes
1844	445 pipes	1874	179 pipes
1845	421 pipes	1875	105 pipes
1846	456 pipes	1876	201 pipes
1847	[a]596 pipes	1877	256 pipes
1848	[b]548 pipes	1878	132 pipes
1849	414 pipes	1879	221 pipes
1850	unrecorded	1880	204 pipes
1851	unrecorded	1881	220 pipes
1852	unrecorded	1882	unrecorded
1853	313 pipes	1883	unrecorded
1854	278 pipes	1884	unrecorded
1855	169 pipes	1885	unrecorded
1856	69 pipes	1886	112 pipes
1857	unrecorded	1887	106 pipes
1858	unrecorded	1888	93 pipes
1859	186 pipes	1889	109 pipes
1860	unrecorded	1890	unrecorded
1861	280½ pipes	1891	20 pipes
1862	unrecorded	1892	54 pipes
1863	260 pipes	1893	41 pipes
1864	139 pipes	1894	41 pipes
1865	280 pipes	1895	90 pipes
1866	319 pipes	1896	106 pipes
1867	214 pipes	1897	unrecorded

[a]indicates without the addition of spirit.
[b]Phylloxera was found at the neighbouring Quinta do Arnozelo, on the other side of the Rio Teja, in 1879, but had not then reached Vesúvio.

10 Vila Maior (3), p 92. According to a footnote, a conto of réis was worth about £222 in 1876.
11 Sellers, p 97.
12 There were over 15 red varieties – Alvarilhão, Bastardo, Cornifesto, Donzelinho, Malvasia Preta, Mourisco Preto, Moscatel Roxo, Nevoeira, Sousão, Tinta Amarela, Tinta Francisca, Tinta Vigaria, Tinto Cão, and Tourigas of various kinds. See Vila Maior (1), p 80.
13 Vila Maior (1), p 85, and also Vila Maior (3), pp 97-8.
14 Reproduced in Guimarães, opposite p 184.
15 Some idea of their size may be gained from the fact that during the visit of the President of the Portuguese Republic to the Douro in July 1988, a lunch was held for 250 people sitting at tables in the lagares. This repeated a similar lunch held in 1896 for a congress of journalists.
16 It is less than 3 m smaller than the biggest in the Douro, at the Quinta do Vale do Meão.
17 Quoted in Guimarães, p 184.
18 Azevedo (3), p 118.
19 Vila Maior (1), p 73.
20 The one in use was designed for Portuguese workers: the sheep shelters were originally built for Gallegos. See p 30.
21 Ibid, p 94.

Quinta da Ervamoira

1 The irrigation of port vines is at present against the law, although 'experimental' irrigation is in evidence in several other Douro quintas.
2 See Introduction, notes 47 and 52.

Quinta da Leda

1 These belong to Sr Eduardo da Costa Seixas, the proprietor of the Quinta de Santa Júlia de Loureiro.

Quinta do Vale do Meão

1 The information in this and the previous paragraph has been gleaned from Ferreira's *Arquivo Histórico*.
2 Cabral, p 108. However, much of what Cabral says is not supported by documents in the Ferreira archive and his narrative and figures should be treated with caution. In fact, the cost may well have been greater. The Barca Velha *armazém* alone cost 8,633,000 *réis*.
3 Sellers, p 95.

Quinta de Val Coelho

1 It appears as such on an Instituto Geográfico e Cadastral map published in 1962.
2 Vila Maior (3), p 91.
3 Cordeiro (2), p 94.
4 Monteiro, p 14.
5 Cobb, p 80.
6 Bradford, p 95.

Quinta da Senhora da Ribeira

1 An earlier portrait is given by Monteiro, pp 78–9.
2 See also Cobb, p 40.
3 See p 105.

Quinta dos Canais

1 Vila Maior (1), p 97.
2 Monteiro, p 15.
3 Cobb, p 40.
4 See Bradford, p 54, and Howkins, p 103.
5 Monteiro, p 16.

Appendix III

1 Sellers, p 13.
2 Cockburn, p 9.
3 Perfeito, p 21.

Select bibliography

Of the vast literature I have included here only those books to which
I refer, or which have a specific bearing on port or on the quintas of
the Douro. *References in the text are cited under the author's name,
with the addition of a number when more than one work by that
author has been listed. The only exception to this is 'Fonseca', which,
with the volume number, refers to A M da Fonseca's book on the
Pombaline demarcations. Page numbers in all cases refer to the latest
edition cited.*

Almeida e Brito, F d'	*O Paço do Monsul.* Reprinted from the review *A Vinha Portugueza,* November 1916.
Alvarenga, Kol d'	*O Douro em Brasas.* Companhia Portuguesa Editora, Lda., Porto, n.d.
Anon	(1) *The Story of Hunt, Roope & Company, London & Oporto, Newman Hunt & Company, London, and Newman & Company, Newfoundland 1395–1951.* Hunt, Roope & Co Ltd. Privately printed and published. 1961.
	(2) *Grémio dos Exportadores de Vinho do Porto.* Album commemorating its definitive establishment in the Palace of the Commercial Association of Oporto. Porto, 1947 [actually 1949]. 1969, 2nd ed. 1988.
Azevedo, Correia de	(1) *Património Artístico da Região Duriense.* n.p. [Vila do Conde], n.d. [1972].
	(2) *Brasões e Casas Brasonadas do Douro.* Gráfica de Lamigo, Lamigo, 1974.
	(3) *O Douro Maravilhoso.* n.p., n.d. [1976]. With a general section in English and French.
Barreto, António	*Um Retrato do Douro.* Vista Alegre, Portugal, 1st ed. May, 1984.
Bradford, Sarah	*The Story of Port.* Christie's Wine Publications, London, 1978. First published as *The Englishman's Wine,* Macmillan, London, 1969.
Bolitho, Hector	*The Wine of the Douro.* Sidgwick and Jackson, London, 1956.
Cabral, Affonso de Valle Coelho Pereira	*A Região Vinhateira do Alto Douro desde Barca d'Alva até ao Cachão de Valleira.* Imprensa Nacional, Lisboa, 1895.
Cockburn, Ernest H	(1) *Port Wine and Oporto.* Wine and Spirit Publications Ltd., n.d.
	(2) *Lecture on Port Wine.* n.p. [London], n.d. [?1935]
Cobb, Gerald	*Oporto Older and Newer.* Privately printed, n.p. [Chichester] n.d. [1966].
Cordeiro, J. Alcino	(1) *Quintas do Douro.* Imprensa do Douro, Régua, 1941.
	(2) *Quintas do Douro.* 2nd ed., Centro Gráfico, V. N. de Famalicão, 1960.
Croft-Cooke, Rupert	*Port.* Putnam, London, 1957.
Ciclo de Conferéncias	*O Vinho na História Portuguesa – Séculos XIII–XIX.* Fundação Eng António de Almeida, Porto, 1983.
Dionísio, Sant'Anna	*Alto Douro Ignoto.* Lello & Irmão, Lisboa, 1973.

Fletcher, Wyndham	*Port – An Introduction to its History and Delights.* Sotheby Publications, London, 1978, rep. 1981.
Fonseca, Álvaro Moreira da	*As Demarcações Pombalinas no Douro Vinhateiro.* 3 Vol. Instituto do Vinho do Porto, Porto, 1949–1951.
Fonseca, Álvaro Moreira da and others	*Port Wine. Notes on its History, Production and Technology.* Instituto do Vinho do Porto, Porto, 1982. 3rd ed., 1987.
Fonseca, Francisco Pereira Rebello da	*Descrição economica do Territorio que vulgarmente se chama Alto-Douro.* In *Memorias Economicas da Academia Real das Sciencias de Lisboa para adiantamento da agricultura,* etc. Vol. III, pp. 36–72. Officina da Mesma Academia, Lisboa, 1791.
França, José-Augusto	*Ramos-Pinto 1880–1980.* Empresa do Bolhão, Lda., Porto, 2nd ed., 1987.
Gibbons, John	*I Gathered No Moss.* Robert Hale, Ltd., London, 1939. *Não Criei Musgo.* Portuguese translation of the above. Edição da Câmara Municipal de Carrazeda de Ansiães, 1984.
Guimarães, Gonçalves:	*Um Português em Londres* *Cartas de J M Virginiano.* With English translation. A A Ferreira SA. *Arquivo Histórico,* Porto, 1988.
Howkins, Ben	*Rich, Rare and Red – A Guide to Port.* Wm Heinemann, London, 1982. Rev. ed. Christopher Helm, London, and The Wine Appreciation Guild, San Francisco, 1987.
Jefford, Andrew	*Port – An Essential Guide to the Classic Drink.* Exeter Books, New York, 1988.
Leal, Augusto de Pinho	*Portugal Antigo e Moderno. Diccionario . . . de Todas as Cidades, Villas e Freguezias de Portugal.* 12 vol. & Supp. Tavares, Cardoso & Irmão, Lisboa, 1886.
Lecouty, Chantal	*Le Porto.* Éditions Robert Laffont, SA, Paris, 1989.
Lencastre, José de	*A Vitivinicultura Através de Alguns Documentos Medievais de Arquivos Portugueses.* Instituto do Vinho do Porto, Porto, 1953.
Macaulay, Rose	*They Went to Portugal.* Jonathan Cape, London, 1946. Repr. Penguin Books, Harmondsworth, 1985 and 1988.
Monteiro, Manuel	*O Douro.* Emilio Biel & Co, Porto, 1911.
Oliveira, Âguedo de	*O Vinho do Porto nos Tempos Clássicos.* Livraria Portugália, Lisboa, 1941.
Ordish, George	*The Great Wine Blight,* 1st ed., J M Dent, London, 1972; 2nd ed., Sidgwick and Jackson, London, 1987.
Paiva, Maria Adelaide da Silva	*D. Antónia Adelaide Ferreira.* Conferência Realizada na Exposição Histórica do Vinho do Porto. Salão Silva Pôrto, 11 de Novembro, 1931. Depósito: Livraria Sá da Costa, Lisboa, n.d. [1931]
Read, Jan	*The Wines of Portugal.* London, Faber and Faber, 1982.
Robertson, George	*Port.* Faber and Faber, London and Boston, 1978, Repr. 1982.
Santos, Júlio Eduardo dos	*O Vinho do Porto.* Typografia Universal, Lisboa 1916.
Schneider, Susan	*O Marquês de Pombal e O Vinho do Porto.* A Regra do Jogo Edicões, Lda., Lisboa, 1980.
Sellers, Charles	*Oporto, Old and New.* Herbert E Harper, London, 1899.
Soavedra, José Pinto da Cunha	*Provezende Antigo e Moderno.* Lisboa, 1935.

Sousa, Fernando de — *Banco Borges & Irmão 1884–1984*. Published privately, Porto, 1984.

Suckling, James — *Vintage Port*. Wine Spectator Press, San Francisco, 1990.

Tait, Geoffrey Murat — *Port – from the Vine to the Glass*. Harper & Co, London, 1936.

Valente, Vasco —
(1) *Notas Genealogicos, Vol I: Van Zeller*. Typographia Luzitania, Porto, 1916.
(2) *Van Zeller: Descendencia de Arnaldo João van Zeller*. Gráf da Pax, Braga, 1932.

Valente-Perfeito, J C — *O Vinho do Porto*. [Lecture given to Section V of the first Congresso Nacional de Turismo]. Cartaz de Portugal, Lisboa, 1936.

Visconde de Vila Maior —
(1) *Preliminares na Ampelographia e Oenologia do Paiz Vinhateiro do Douro*. 1 vol in 4 *fasciculos*. Imprensa Nacional, Lisboa, 1865–1869.
(2) *Ampelographia e Oenologia do Paiz Vinhateiro do Douro*. Typografia Academica, Lisboa, n.d.
(3) *O Douro Illustrado*. Album do Rio Douro e Paiz Vinhateiro. Livraria Universal de Magalhães e Moniz, Porto, 1876. With parallel French and English texts: the English title being: *The Illustrated Douro*. An Album of the River Douro and Adjacent Wine Country.

Visconde Vilarinho de São Romão — *Viticultura e Vinicultura Traz os Montes – Alto Douro Central*. Imprensa Nacional, Lisboa, 1896.

Vizetelly, Henry —
(1) *Facts about Port and Madeira*. Ward, Lock & Co., London, 1880: Scribner & Welford, New York, 1880.
(2) *No País do Vinho do Porto*. Tradução de Mário Bernardes Pereira [of Part II of the above]. Instituto do Vinho do Porto, Porto, 1947.

Manuscript sources

Note: Many quintas possess diaries, journals and visitors' books, and some shippers have letter and accounts books from which valuable material can be gleaned, but these have not been listed here. Indications of such sources are given in the text where appropriate.

Almada, Canelas P — *Levamento Topográfico – Casa Grande Granja Alijó*, 1943. In the possession of the Real Companhia Velha.

Ferreira, A A, SA — *Arquivo Histórico*. A large and rich collection of papers relating to Dona Antónia and other members of the family in possession of the firm.

Newman, Sir Ralph, Bart. — *The Story of the Quinta Eira Velha, 1382 – 1959*. In possession of the proprietors of Quinta da Eira Velha.

Brito E Cunha, João — *A Quinta de Vargelas*, 1978.
The First Owner of Vargellas 'Quinta', a partial translation of the above. In possession of Messrs. Taylor, Fladgate and Yeatman.

Valente, Vasco — *Casa do Paço e Torre do Monsul*. Unpublished Vol III of *Ensaios Genealôgicos*. 1932(?). In possession of Sr Eng° Gonçalo Cabral.

Novels

Chantal, Suzanne — *Ervamoira*. Oliver Orban, Paris, 1982.

Diniz, Júlio — *Uma Família Inglesa*. Oporto, 1868 and various editions. Biblioteca Ulisseia de Autores Portugueses, No 20. Printer Portuguesa Lda, n.p., n.d. [1988].

Gidley, Charles — *The River Running By*. André Deutsch, London, 1981.

Torga, Miguel — *Vindima*. Coimbra, 1945. 4th revised ed, Coimbra, 1971.
Grape Harvest. English translation of the above, n.p. [Coimbra], 1989.

Index

Note: Page numbers in bold type under quinta names denote main descriptive sections

garden, 25, 48, 51, 62, 69, 82, 88, 106, 117, 125, 137, 138
house, 16, 21, 22–3, 26
housekeeper, 26, 153
kitchen, 24, 65, 70, 71, 78, 80, 101, 113, 122, 133, 135, 139, 164
laboratory, 24, 53, 69, 103
management of, 22, 25, 29, 31, 32, 78, 114, 151
organization of, 25
origin of word, 15
owner, 23, 25, 26, 29
price of, 141
privations of life in, 26, 27, 28, 122, 161
refectório, 24, 73, 78, 101, 113, 133, 149
visitors' books, 28, 104, 105, 123, 124, 160, 161, 162
visits to, 175–6, 178
workers, 22, 23, 25–6, 27, 29–32, 134, 153, 163
— accommodation of, 24, 30–1, 78, 125
Quintas:
Abade, 111
Abrahão, 101
Aciprestes, 116, 120, **126–7**, 179, 220
Água Alta, 60, **72–3**, 166, 179, 218
Alegria, 60
Alempassa, 221
Alvarelhão, 43
Amarela nas Bateiras, 82
Amêda, **115–6**, 180
Aradas, 101
Atayde, 121, **159**, 166, 180
Avaleira, 63
Avidagos, **51–2**, 67, 168, 181, 217
Bairral, 111, 113
Baratas, 66
Barca:
(1) 111, 113
(2) 167
Barreira, 126, 127
Barroca, 70
Bartol, 163, 164
Bateiras, 82
Beatas, 108
Boa Vista:
(1) 19, 20, 22, 32, 37, 73, **75–8**, 166, 181, 218
(2) 126, 127, 167
Bom Dia, 72, 73
Bomfim, 21, 27, 37, **104–6**, 108, 123, 124, 148, 162, 168, 182, 219
Bom Retiro, 16, 19, 47, 108, 134, **136–8**, 139, 167, 182, 221
Bom Retiro Pequeno, 92, 136, 137, **139**, 183

Bons Ares, 154, 156, 174
Brito, 146
Cachão, 24, **143–4**, 150, 167, 183, 221
Cachucha, 73, 76, 77
Cadima, 161
Caêdo, 166, 184, 216
Campo Redondo, 68
Canada, 159
Canadas, 101, 102, 103, 167
Canais, 148, **162–5**, 166, 184, 223
Capela, 68
Carrapata, 111, 113
Carvalhal:
(1) **115**, 167, 185
(2) 126
Carvalhas, 19, 64, **65–7**, 86, 104, 110, 117, 125, 127, 133, 134, 167, 185, 217
Carvalheira, 219
Carvalheiro, 111, 113
Carvalho:
(1) 72
(2) 164
Carvoeira, 68
Casa de Capela, 115, 116
Casa das Covas, 17
Casa Nova, 88, **89–90**, 112, 116, 187, 219
Casal de Celeirós, **94–6**, 186, 219
Casal de Granja, 110, 111, **114–5**, 127, 167, 186, 220
Casal da Moreira, 17
Cascalheira, 66
Castelo de Borges, 56
Cavadinha, 37, 84, **91–2**, 93, 101, 118, 168, 187, 216, 219
Cedavim, 136
Chousa, 120–1, 122
Comparado, 165
Condessa, 70
Confradeiro, 95
Convento de São Pedro das Águias, 16, **62–3**, 167, 188, 217
Côrte, 37, 61, 137, **139–40**, 186, 188
Corval, **104**, 167, 189
Corvos, 96
Costa, **69–70**, 189, 218
Costa de Baixo, **70–1**, 190, 218
Costa da Cima, 70
Côtto, 13, 17, 35, 39, **52–4**, 190, 217
Covadas, 66
Crasto, 35, 39, 60, **71–2**, 191, 218
Cruz, 70
Cruz de Ventolzelo, 66
Cruzeiro, 61, 93, **97–8**, 166, 191
Deveza, 65

Dom Pedro, 57
Dona Clara, 111
Dona Esménia, 111
Dona Matilde, **67–8**, 166, 192, 218
Dona Rosa, 110
Eira Velha, 17, **85–9**, 192, 219
Enxodreiro, 67, 68
Ervamoira, **154–6**, 167, 193, 222
Escravelheira, 111
Espinhal da Cima, 72, 73
Espinheiro, 76
Esporão, 111
Estanho, **96**, 193, 219
Ferradoza, 112, 167, 220
Figueiras, 151
Fojo:
(1) 70
(2) 179
Fonte do Mouro, 111
Fonte Santa, 57
Forneiras, 163
Foz, 21, 65, 82, **84–5**, 88, 166, 174, 176, 194, 219
Foz Ceira, 70
Foz do Temilobos, 68
Frades, 16, 56, 68, 215
Galeira, 60
Galgas, 66
Golegã, 144
Hortos, 112, 219
Igreja, 16
Infantado, 35, 39, **74–5**, 194, 218
Ingleses:
(1) 120
(2) 160
Jordão, 110
Junco, 89, **90–1**, 101, 112, 133, 166, 195, 219
Laceira, 70
Lagares, 97
Lages, 117, 133, **134–5**, 195, 221
Lamas, 70
Lameirão, 91
Lameiro do Rego, 82, 83
Lamelas, 82, 83
Lapa, 136
Laranjeiras:
(1) **158**, 168, 196
(2) 216
Leda, **156–7**, 166, 196, 222
Liceiras, 111, 113
Lobata, 60
Lobazim de Baixo, 160
Lobazim da Cima, 160
Loureiro, 50
Malhadal Novo, 111, 113
Malhadal Velho, 111, 113
Malheiros, 111
Malvedos, 21, 27, 92,

106, 111, 114, **116–20**, 126, 167, 197, 220
Manuela, 17, 179
Marco, 101
Massas, 17
Mateus, 13
Melo, 70
Merouço, 111, 116
Mesquita, 60
Mileu da Cima, 126, 167
Monsul, 16, **45–7**, 197, 217
Monte Bravo, 219
Monte Meão, 20, 157
Monte Redondo, 63, 167
Monteiras, 66
Mosteirô, 16
Murças, 34, 67, **68–9**, 138, 198, 218
Muro, 90
Nápoles, 17, **56–7**, 167, 198, 217
Negrilhos, 126, 167
Nova:
(1) 72, **73–4**, 167, 199, 218
(2) 135
(3) 151
Noval, 19, 21, 24, 37, 38, 39, 51, 67, 91, **98–103**, 108, 167, 199, 219
Obra Nova, 101
Orgueiras, 101
Pacheca, 17, **43–4**, 46, 200
Paço, 63, 167
Panascal, 17, **61–2**, 166, 200, 217
Passadouro, 97, 168
Pasteleira, 72
Pedra Caldeira, 217
Pego, 76
Pena Chão, 43
Penedo Marçal, 111
Pescoça, 161
Pimentel, 50
Plombeira, 66
Porto, 22, **78–80**, 82, 83, 166, 201, 218
Pulga, 111, 113
Quartas, 43, **49**, 167, 201
Reguengo, 157
Rei, 144, 167
Reis, 111
Reitor, 72
Retiro Novo, **135–6**, 168, 202, 221
Renova, 91
Ribeira Teja, 150
Rodo, 17
Roêda, 19, 20, 21, 24, 37, 65, 66, 104, 105, **106–9**, 110, 134, 140, 148, 166, 202, 219–20
Romaneira, 17, 19, 20, 24, 35, 39, 91, 109, **110–14**, 127, 203, 220
Roncão, 19, 220